MURDER AND PENAL POLICY

WITHDRAWN

2 3 APR 2023

Murder and Penal Policy

Barry Mitchell

Barrister-at-Law,
Senior Lecturer in Law, Coventry Polytechnic

Palgrave Macmillan

ISBN 978-0-333-49639-8   ISBN 978-1-349-20745-9 (eBook)
DOI 10.1007/978-1-349-20745-9

First published in the United States of America in 1990

Library of Congress Cataloging-in-Publication Data
Mitchell, Barry, 1952–
Murder and Penal Policy/Barry Mitchell.
    p.   cm.
Includes bibliographical references.
ISBN 978-0-312-03994-3
1. Murder–England.   2. Life imprisonment–England.   I. Title.
HV6535.G42E545 1990
365'.941–dc20   89–39640
                                                          CIP

Contents

List of Abbreviations

CLRC   Criminal Law Revision Committee
CRC   Control Review Committee
DPMS   Directorate of the Prison Medical Service
LCJ   Lord Chief Justice
LRC   Local Review Committee
PRES   Pre-Release Employment Scheme
RAG   Research and Advisory Group
YCC   Youth Custody Centre (known as a Young Offender Institution by virtue of the Criminal Justice Act 1988)
YP   Young Prisoners (or Young Offenders)

List of Tables

Table of Cases

Table of Statutes

Acknowledgements

In pursuing the research which forms the basis of this book and in preparing the manuscript in which the material is presented I have required and received tremendous support from many people, and it is only right and proper that I formally acknowledge the debt that I owe them.

My work was funded by a research grant from the Home Office: £7000 was allocated and in the event about £4500 was expended, mainly in travelling costs. A number of civil servants in the Home Office facilitated the study, especially John Ditchfield and Roy Walmsley of the Research and Planning Unit, and Dennis Brown and Lawrie Scudder of the Life-Sentence Section of the Prison Department. I spent a lot of time visiting prisons up and down the country, talking to staff and life-sentence prisoners, and I should very much like to record my thanks to them. Inevitably, my presence interrupted the work of the staff, but they were always extremely helpful and co-operative. The participation of the lifers was purely voluntary, and although it may be argued that their conversations with me gave them a brief respite from their usual routine and an opportunity to air their views, it must also be said that they had all previously been interviewed 'ad nauseam' and some of them clearly found it very difficult reliving their sentence and the offence.

Before undertaking this research, I had managed to avoid/evade instruments of modern technology such as computers and word-processors, but in order to collate and present my results I had to acquire a few very basic skills in this area. In this respect, I am extremely grateful to Ann Davies of the Computer Services Centre at Coventry Polytechnic for her guidance and patience. As for the preparation of the manuscript, parts containing confidential information were produced by myself on my own computer, but a good deal of painstaking typing was done by Mrs Pauline Brennan, the Legal Studies Departmental Senior Clerk at the Polytechnic, who spent many hours trying to decipher my hand-written drafts.

Finally, of course, I should like to thank my wife Helen for her constant support and encouragement which gave me the impetus and motivation to complete the study and to write this book.

Introduction

Like many people, I had long been fascinated by the thought of one person taking the life of another. It seemed that, with the possible exception of treason, this was the worst offence that could be committed, the 'ultimate' crime. It was, to say the least, extremely difficult to comprehend the sort of circumstances that would be necessary for me to carry out such a contemptible act. The notion of the sanctity of life had always been so powerful that I assumed that those who killed another human being must be very 'different' from me. But it was as a criminal lawyer that I became professionally involved and engrossed in the study of homicide. The law on this subject, as it applies in England and Wales, has been shown by the courts to be unclear so that, for example, the boundary between murder and manslaughter is uncertain. Only rarely have I found myself in agreement with judicial pronouncements, and I have almost invariably regarded the legal definition of murder as being too wide.

Hence I set about finding out what murder is like, what sorts of situations are legally interpreted as murder, and I was both amazed and horrified to discover that very little work has been done in this area. In a society which purports to be seriously concerned about levels of violence, one would have expected to find a considerable amount of information about unlawful killings. Thus the research that I have done is intended very much as an initial investigation; it is certainly not intended as definitive in any way. This book, which is based on my research and a few of my own ideas, seeks to provide information and thereby provoke thought and debate. Obviously, I would have liked to have been able to analyse cases of manslaughter as well as murder, but it was impracticable for me to do so. I fully accept, however, that a comparative examination of the two crimes should be undertaken.

Having looked at the sorts of cases that result in a conviction for murder, it was a simple logical progression to turn to the question of how the penal system deals with convicted murderers. Here I have not sought to examine the merits and demerits of capital punishment, and I have touched only very briefly on the correctness of requiring judges to sentence murderers to life imprisonment, as opposed to giving them some form of discretion. Nor have I considered whether life imprisonment should inevitably mean that the offender will spend the rest of his/her natural life in custody. Instead I have based this part of my work very largely on the assumption that the current policy of mandatory life sentences for murder will continue, so that most people who are convicted of murder will be released on life licence. More specifically, I have focussed my attention on the time that life-sentence prisoners ('lifers') spend in custody after the trial judge has passed sentence on the defendant. I have not investigated what happens when lifers are released into the community. Rather I have examined the way in which the Prison Department's policy, which presumes that lifers will spend the early part of their sentence in 'closed' (that is, Category A and B establishments), and then be moved to 'semi-open' and 'open' prisons (in Category C and D establishments) in later stages, operates in practice.

Naturally, I hope the book will be of value to those who are professionally involved with homicide and the criminal justice system – lawyers, criminologists, prison staff, Home Office civil servants, probation officers and political scientists. But the issues at stake here are too important to be left solely to small groups of individuals, and I also hope that the book will be interesting to the layman. Some reference to what might be seen as technical terms is inescapable, but I have tried to present the information and ideas without pre-supposing any specialist knowledge or expertise.

The first four chapters, which comprise the first part of the book, deal with the nature of murder and how it should be defined. Chapter 1 sets out the current law relating to murder, rehearses some of the more influential proposals for its reform and includes my own personal views on the subject. The second chapter explains my investigation of the factual nature of murder, relating the results of my research in a largely statistical form. It also discusses earlier studies on homicide in England and Wales, identifying points of comparison and contrast, to determine the extent to which murder changes with the passing of the years and its similarity (or otherwise) to what has been learned about manslaughter. In an attempt to broaden the presentation of the study, chapter 3 provides a series of brief accounts of a majority of the murder cases I examined; (summaries of the other cases are given in chapter 2). Obviously, these accounts are subjective, and they tend to reflect the court's interpretation of what happened. Chapter 4 contains my conclusions and some suggestions as to how I think the law might be adjusted in the future.

The second part of the book is concerned with the response of the criminal justice system and the management of life-sentence prisoners. A description of the Prison Department's policy for 'looking after' lifers is given in the fifth chapter, along with a résumé of some of the main criticisms and proposed reforms that have hitherto been put forward. In chapter 6 I describe the nature of the fieldwork and the sources of my information. A predominantly numerical analysis of the results of this fieldwork is set out in chapter 7, supplemented in the following chapter by a series of précised accounts of my interviews with a sample of lifers. The ninth chapter summarises a number of discussions I had with various staff who have worked in prisons with lifers. They offered their opinions on the efficiency and efficacy of the current policy and made some suggestions for future improvements. The final chapter sets out what I regard as the implications of this part of the study and what is necessary for any progress to be made.

The subject of murder and how society should respond to those convicted of such serious crimes is clearly one which is likely to arouse emotions, but questions such as the legal definition of the offence and the way in which the penal system manages life-sentence prisoners must be addressed with a rational and objective mind. We must determine what sort of situations ought to be capable of falling within the description of 'murder' so that judicial decisions will (almost invariably) coincide with the prevailing social view. The fact that there are relatively few convictions for murder each year does not in any way reduce this necessity. Similarly, the modest size of the lifer population should not diminish our resolve to ensure that life-sentence prisoners are treated in the most appropriate manner. That the number of such prisoners is steadily increasing reinforces the need to adopt a sensible and practical mangement policy. Given that most lifers will be released on licence, it is vital that the period spent in custody is used constructively to maximise the chances of successful re-establishment in the community, as well as meeting the requirements of retribution and deterrence.

Finally, it must be stressed that the views expressed in this book are mine alone, and should not be attributed to the Home Office, unless expressly stated otherwise.

Part I

A Legal and Sociological Examination of Murder

1 The Law: Present and Future

Since one of the primary aims of my research has been to determine whether the criminal law should be reformed, it is appropriate to look at the definition of murder, the legal limits of the offence and how it differs from manslaughter. This requires a detailed examination of the law relating to murder and an outline of the scope of manslaughter. It is also necessary to review some of the major criticisms that have been made of existing law and proposals for legal reform.

The word 'homicide' refers to the killing of a human being, whether the killing is lawful or unlawful, but there is no crime of homicide. At common law, unlawful homicide comprises the two offences of murder and manslaughter. Other types of unlawful homicide have been created by Act of Parliament, such as manslaughter by reason of diminished responsibility or a suicide pact, infanticide, and causing death by reckless driving. There is only one definition of murder, whereas there are a number of different ways of defining manslaughter. The essential distinguishing features between murder and manslaughter are the element of fault and the presence of mitigating circumstances. In murder, death must have been caused 'with malice aforethought', whereas in some forms of manslaughter this element is absent. In other types of manslaughter, the defendant may well have killed 'with malice aforethought' but there was also some extraneous or mitigating circumstance which justifies a manslaughter conviction instead.

The classic definition of murder, and that which is generally accepted both academically and in practice, is that of Sir Edward Coke:

> Murder is when a man of sound memory, and of the age of discretion, unlawfully killeth within any county of the realm any reasonable creature in rerum natura under the King's peace, with malice aforethought, either expressed by the party or implied by law, so as the party wounded, or hurt, etc. die of the wound or hurt, etc. within a year and a day after the same.[1]

Manslaughter, on the other hand, is either 'voluntary' or 'involuntary'. It is voluntary where the offender (i) was provoked to kill; or

3

(ii) was suffering from such abnormality of mind that his mental responsibility for his behaviour was substantially impaired, so that he might plead 'diminished responsibility'; or (iii) killed in pursuance of a suicide pact. In the majority of cases of provocation and suicide pacts, the killer acts with malice aforethought so that the offence may be regarded very much as one of 'mitigated murder'. The person who kills with diminished responsibility may also act with malice afore-thought, though this is less likely than in other instances of voluntary manslaughter. Conversely, where there is no malice aforethought, and no mitigating circumstances, the offence is one of involuntary manslaughter. Here, the state of mind of the offender must fall within one of two possibilities. Either the killing must have been committed recklessly, or the fatal act (which was unlawful and dangerous) must have been committed intentionally. In each case, a manslaughter verdict is justified on the ground that the offender lacked sufficient foresight or awareness of the consequences of his actions for a conviction for murder.

In essence, in both murder and manslaughter, the prosecution must show that one person has unlawfully caused the death of another, and death must have occurred within a year and a day of the commission of the fatal act.[2] In practice, arguably two of the most controversial aspects of the law have centred on causation and the meaning of 'malice aforethought'.

CAUSATION

Since all human beings are mortal, it follows that killing a person is only an acceleration of what would otherwise be the natural process of death. For the purposes of murder or manslaughter, it is irrelevant that the victim may already be suffering from a terminal illness or may be under sentence of death. It is part of the task of the prosecution to show that life has been foreshortened.

In cases where there is only one possible cause of death, there will usually be no difficulty in deciding whether or not the accused is criminally responsible. However, there are instances where there is more than one possible cause – the deceased may have been attacked more than once, or a badly-injured victim may be given inappropriate medical treatment and subsequently die. In such situations it appears that the law has changed recently, arguably in a manner which assists the prosecution to obtain a conviction. Consider first the case of

R v Jordan[3] in which the accused stabbed his victim in the abdomen. Whilst in hospital, the victim was given terramycin in order to prevent infection, but tragically he was allergic to the drug, a fact of which the doctor was unaware. A pathologist called by the prosecution at the trial testified that death was caused by broncho-pneumonia following the injury to the abdomen. Yet the Court of Criminal Appeal admitted fresh evidence from two doctors to the effect that in their opinion death was caused not by the stab wound but by administration of terramycin and by the intravenous introduction of large quantities of liquid. Quashing the conviction, Hallett J concluded:

> ... two separate and independent features of treatment were, in the opinion of the doctors, palpably wrong and these produced the symptoms discovered at the post-mortem examination which were the direct and immediate cause of death, namely, the pneumonia resulting from the condition of oedema which was found. We feel no uncertainty at all that ... the jury would have felt precluded from saying that they were satisfied that death was caused by the stab wound. (pp. 157, 158)

Jordan's case is often contrasted with that of R v Smith.[4] The latter case arose out of a fight between soldiers from different regiments, during which the accused stabbed his victim twice with a bayonet. One of the victim's friends tried to carry him to a medical reception station, but during the course of doing so he twice tripped and dropped him! At the medical reception station the medical officer, who was endeavouring to deal with a number of other cases at the same time, failed to realise that one of the stab wounds had pierced the lung and caused a haemorrhage. The medical treatment that the soldier received was later described at the trial as 'thoroughly bad and might well have affected his chances of recovery.' In dismissing Smith's appeal against conviction for murder, Lord Parker CJ remarked:

> The court is satisfied that Jordan was a very particular case depending on its exact facts. It incidentally arose in the Court of Criminal Appeal on the grant of an application to call further evidence, and, leave having been obtained, two well-known medical experts gave evidence that in their opinion death had been caused, not by the stabbing, but by the introduction of terramycin after the deceased had shown that he was intolerant to it and by the intravenous introduction of abnormal quantities of liquid. It also

appears that, at the time when that was done, the stab wound, which had penetrated the intestine in two places, had mainly healed. In those circumstances the court felt bound to quash the conviction because they could not say that a reasonable jury, properly directed, would not have been able, on that evidence, to say that there had been a break in the chain of causation; the court could uphold the conviction in that case only if they were satisfied that no reasonable jury could have come to that conclusion. (pp. 198, 199)

Thus, it appears that Jordan's is to be regarded as a rather unique case, such that its importance and authoritativeness should not be overestimated (although more recently the Court of Appeal in R v Blaue[5] thought that Jordan was 'probably rightly decided on its facts').

The significance of Smith's case, however, is to be found slightly earlier in the judgement of Lord Parker C J where he stated:

It seems to the court that, if at the time of death the original wound is still *an operating cause and a substantial cause*, then the death can properly be said to be the result of the wound, albeit that some other cause of death is also operating. Only if it can be said that the original wounding is merely the setting in which another cause operates can it be said that the death does not result from the wound. Putting it in another way, only if the second cause is so overwhelming as to make the original wound merely part of the history can it be said that the death does not flow from the wound. (p. 198)

Although it may be argued that there are at least apparent contradictions in the cases of Jordan and Smith, it is submitted that they can both be regarded simply as illustrations of the application of what was the 'substantial and operating cause' principle. In Jordan the stab wound was not such a cause; in Smith it was.

A similar approach was adopted in R v Hennigan[6] where the accused's conviction for causing death by dangerous driving[7] was upheld on appeal. As to the meaning of 'substantial cause', Lord Parker C J approved the words of the trial judge:

'Substantial' means that it is not a remote cause of the death, but it is an appreciable cause of the death. It is rather like this: in a collision between two motor-cars there may be both drivers each 50 per cent to blame, and each would be a substantial cause of the collision. If, on the other hand, you get a situation where you can say that one of the drivers was four-fifths to blame and the other was one-fifth, you can say: 'I don't regard one-fifth as being a substantial cause of the accident, if it is as low as that, then the fellow who really caused the accident was the one who was four-fifths to blame.' It is hard to define, but it means the real cause as opposed to being a minimal cause. (at p. 264)

In the light of more recent discussions, however, it appears that the concept of 'substantial and operating cause' has been watered down. In R v Cato[8] the appellant had injected the deceased, his friend, with a mixture of heroin and water several times during the night. The deceased had himself prepared the strength of the mixture of each 'fix'. The following day he was found dead, and the appellant was later convicted of manslaughter and of administering a noxious thing contrary to Section 23 Offences Against the Person Act 1861. In dismissing his appeal against conviction for manslaughter Lord Widgery C J took the view that:

Of course, behind this whole question of the sufficiency of evidence of causation is the fact that it was not necessary for the prosecution to prove that the heroin was the only cause. *As a matter of law, it was sufficient if the prosecution could establish that it was a cause, provided it was a cause outside the de minimis range, and effectively bearing on the acceleration of the moment of the victim's death.* When one has that in mind, it is, we think, really possible to say that if the jury had been directed to look for heroin as a cause, not de minimis but a cause of substance, and they came back with a verdict of not guilty, the verdict could really be described as a perverse one. The whole background of the evidence was the other way and there certainly was ample evidence, given a proper direction, on which a charge of manslaughter could be supported. (p. 265)

Most recently, in R v Malcherek, R v Steel,[9] cases involving the switching off of a life-support machine, the Lord Chief Justice, Lord Lane, remarked '... it need hardly be added that it [that is, the original wound or injury] need not be substantial to render the assailant guilty' (p. 428). Thus, the present position seems to be that it would be misleading to direct a jury that the accused's conduct must be a substantial cause of the victim's death. Rather, the law requires that the accused's conduct must not be so minimal as to be ignored under 'de minimis' principle, though it must still be a 'sine qua non' of death.

INTERVENING ACT OR EVENT

Cases such as Jordan and Smith raise the problem of proving causation where there has been some sort of intervening act or event. An accused person is not responsible for the death of another where that other dies as a result of some subsequent act or event which would have caused death even if the accused had not inflicted any injury in the first place. This was illustrated in the case of R v White [10] in which the defendant administered a potentially fatal dose of poison to his mother. The mother duly died, but the evidence was that death was due to heart failure precipitated by fright or some other external cause. The defendant could not be guilty of the full offence of murder, although the Court of Criminal Appeal upheld his conviction for attempted murder.

At the same time, it should be appreciated that the fact that there is an intervening act or event may not necessarily break the chain of causation. There are, perhaps, three distinguishable situations in which the general principle shown in White's case would not absolve a person from liability for murder (or manslaughter).

Firstly, although an intervening act or event may occur, the original injury inflicted by the defendant may nonetheless be re-garded as 'an operating cause' of death. For example, in People v Lewis [11] the victim received a fatal gunshot wound, but then cut his own throat and died a few minutes later. The defendant was convicted of manslaughter on the basis that the original gunshot wound which he inflicted was an operating cause of death. Both the gunshot wound and the cutting of the throat were potentially fatal. Much more recently, the English courts have had to deal with the situation where a badly injured person is placed on a life-support machine which is subsequently switched off. Does the patient die from switching off the machine or from the original injury? This question was considered in two cases which were materially similar and heard at the same time.

In R v Malcherek a husband stabbed his wife nine times with a kitchen knife. She was taken to hospital and connected to a life-support machine, but after carrying out various tests for brain death the doctors disconnected the machine and pronounced her dead. In R v Steel, the accused hit a woman on the head with a 50-pound stone, fracturing her skull and causing severe brain damage. On arrival at hospital she was immediately placed on a ventilator but, again, after tests the doctors concluded that her brain had ceased to function and switched off the machine. Both Malcherek and Steel were convicted at the Crown Court of murder. Both appealed against conviction on the basis that the jury ought to have been directed to consider whether the death of each of their victims was in fact caused by switching off the life-support machines rather than the original injuries which they had inflicted. Upholding their convictions, however, the Court of Appeal concluded that in each case the defendant's conduct was still a continuing or operating cause of death, and that whether or not the doctors' actions were also a cause was immaterial (for they were not on trial!).[12]

The second type of situation where the causal chain may not be broken by an intervening act or event arises when the victim dies as a result of an act or event which would not have occurred but for the defendant's conduct and which is a natural consequence of that conduct. In this instance, though, it should be noted that any original injury inflicted by the defendant will *not* be an 'operating cause' in the sense described above. A recent and very tragic illustration was provided in the case of R v Pagett[13] in which the defendant, in order to resist (lawful) arrest, held a pregnant girl in front of him as a shield and shot at armed policemen. The police instinctively fired back, and the girl was shot and killed. The Court of Appeal held that Pagett had caused her death and his conviction for manslaughter was upheld.[14] The principle in Pagett applies where the intervening act is probable and reasonable, as well as being an instinctive or involuntary thing to do. Robert Goff L J confirmed that:

> ... the accused's act need not be the sole cause, or even the main cause, of the victim's death, it being enough that his act contributed significantly to that result.[15] (p. 288)

On the question of causation and the intervention of third parties, his Lordship referred to the treatise by Professors Hart and Honore, 'Causation in the Law'.[16] If the third party's intervention takes the form of voluntary conduct then it will usually relieve the accused of criminal responsibility. Conversely, the intervention may be involuntary in the sense that it was not 'free, deliberate and informed'. The learned authors offer a list of illustrations of such involuntary intervention, two of which were particularly germane to Pagett's case:

(i) Where the victim performs a reasonable though not strictly necessary act of self-preservation, and that act is itself caused by the accused's act. For example, the victim may attempt to escape from the accused's threatened violence and in so doing injures himself and dies from the injuries.[17]

(ii) Where the victim acts in performance of a legal duty. Although there appears to be no relevant English authority, Robert Goff L J accepted this proposition as being legally sound. He drew a parallel here with 'rescue' cases in the civil law of negligence, where the defendant may be liable to a third party who is injured whilst going to the rescue of one who has been put in danger by the defendant's negligence. Thus argues his Lordship:

> Where ... a police officer in the execution of his duty acts to prevent a crime, or to apprehend a person suspected of a crime, the case is surely a fortiori. (at p. 290)

In other words, the police officer's actions do not interrupt the chain of causation.

The third and final exception to the general rule on causation arises as a consequence of the principle that, in criminal law as in civil law, the defendant must take his victim as he finds him. This relates to the victim's mind as well as his body. Thus, if the accused causes the victim to do, or to omit to do something, which causes the victim's death, the accused may be held responsible even though the victim's intervening conduct was not foreseeable. A clear example of this arose in R v Blaue (supra) where the defendant stabbed a young girl, thereby piercing her lung. She was advised by a doctor that she would die unless she had a blood transfusion. But she refused the transfusion because it conflicted with her religious beliefs as a Jehovah's Witness, and died the following day from bleeding caused by the original stab wound. In dimissing Blaue's appeal against conviction for manslaughter, Lawton L J said:

> It has long been the policy of the law that those who use violence on other people must take their victims as they find them. This in our judgement means the whole man, not just the physical man. It does not lie in the mouth of the assailant to say that his victim's

religious beliefs which inhibited him from accepting certain kinds of treatment were unreasonable. The question for decision is what caused her death. The answer is the stab wound. The fact that the victim refused to stop this end coming about did not break the causal connection between the act and death. (p. 450)

The one limitation to the principle upon which the decision in Blaue was based is that the intervening act or omission must be committed or caused by the victim.

PAIN-RELIEVING DRUGS

One situation which has presented the courts with a problem which has yet to be solved entirely satisfactorily is that of the prescription and administration of pain-relieving drugs by the medical profession. Arguably one of the leading cases on this point is that of R v Adams,[18] one of the most infamous in modern criminal history. The charge of murder arose out of the death in November 1950 of an 81-year-old lady, Mrs Morrell, who had been a patient of Dr Adams since 1948. The prosecution evidence was that the accused had prescribed and administered such large quantities of drugs (particularly heroin and morphia) that he must have known that the result would be to kill his patient. Moreover, it was contended that Mrs Morrell was not suffering from such severe pain or restlessness as to justify such lethal doses.

The difficulty of this case lies in the interpretation of the judgement of the then Devlin J. Initially, he directed the jury that doctors have no special defence in law when giving pain-relieving drugs which also shorten the life of the patient. 'If life were cut short by weeks or months it was just as much murder as if it were cut short by years', he commented. But later on he seemed to contradict himself, saying:

But that does not mean that a doctor aiding the sick or dying has to calculate in minutes or hours, or perhaps in days or weeks, the effect on a patient's life of the medicines which he administers. If the first purpose of medicine – the restoration of health – can no longer be achieved, there is still much for the doctor to do, and he is entitled to do all that is proper and necessary to relieve pain and suffering even if the measures he takes may incidentally shorten life.

Clearly, Devlin J's remarks are very difficult to assess. A doctor who administers pain-relieving drugs to a dying patient knowing that they will shorten the life of that patient must surely be said to intend to accelerate the process of death. Yet Devlin J began by stating that doctors do not enjoy an immunity from the rigours of this area of the criminal law. It may be that Adams' case should be regarded as an example of the principle which existed at the time (that is, the mid-1950s) that the accused could only be guilty of murder if his act was the substantial cause of the victim's death. It may be argued that if death is close at hand then the doctor could relieve pain because to do so would only shorten life to a small degree. The terminal illness remained the substantial cause of death.

MALICE AFORETHOUGHT

The phrase 'malice aforethought' is potentially very misleading. It is not to be interpreted according to its ordinary popular meaning, but as a technical legal term. To incur liability for murder there need be no malice in the sense of spite or ill-will. Thus, in cases of mercy-killing, as where a parent kills a suffering child out of compassion, there may well be sufficient malice aforethought. Moreover, the degree of forethought that is required may be measured in mere seconds or fractions of a second; no premeditation is necessary.

It is generally regarded that the prosecution must prove an intention to kill or to cause grievous bodily harm.[19] In DPP v Smith[20] the House of Lords laid down a largely objective approach. The defendant was guilty of murder if he intended to do something to another person (the so-called 'aimed at' rule) knowing of circumstances which, whether he realised it or not, rendered the act likely to cause death or really serious bodily injury. Although the earlier part of this interpretation is subjective, the latter element is clearly objective. There need be no actual foresight by the defendant of death or grievous bodily harm. He was deemed, in effect, to have intended what the reasonable man would have foreseen as the natural and probably consequences of his act. Subsequently, the Law Commission were very critical of this objective requirement and made proposals that led to the passing of section 8 of the Criminal Justice Act 1967[21] which prescribes a wholly subjective approach. The court is solely concerned with the state of mind of the accused, and not with that of any hypothetical individual.

In the majority of cases it will be sufficient for the trial judge to direct the jury simply to consider whether they are satisfied that the accused intended to kill or do grievous bodily harm. Exceptionally, however, the facts may be such that it will be necessary for the judge to explain what, in this context, is meant by the concept of 'intention'. This extended form of direction should only have to be given very rarely. If it is not needed, there is a danger, as was pointed out by Lawton L J in R v Beer,[22] that the jury may be confused. Lord Lane C J, in delivering the leading judgment in the Court of Appeal in R v Hancock and Shankland,[23] indicated that the extended direction was appropriate in 'cases in which the defendant's motive or purpose was not primarily to kill or injure . . .'

It is quite evident that the courts have experienced some difficulty in describing the precise nature of the intention in malice aforethought. More specifically, there has been much confusion about the relationship between what a person intends and what he foresees as being the consequences of his actions. 'Intention' and 'foresight' are not synonymous, but the jury may infer the accused's intentions from the conclusions they reach as to his foresight. It may be helpful to consider carefully the four cases of Hyam v DPP,[24] R v Moloney,[25] R v Hancock and Shankland,[26] and R v Nedrick.[27]

In Hyam the appellant was the discarded, or partly discarded, lover of a man named Jones. She became suspicious of his relationship with another woman, Mrs Booth. The appellant went to the house of Mrs Booth, poured petrol through the letter-box and also pushed newspaper through it. Then she lit the paper, setting fire to the building, and left without raising the alarm. Mrs Booth and her son managed to escape through a window, but her two daughters died from asphyxia caused by fumes from the fire. Whilst admitting that she realised that what she had done was very dangerous, Hyam maintained that she merely intended to frighten Mrs Booth into leaving the neighbourhood, and that she did not intend to kill anyone or cause them serious bodily harm. Nevertheless, she was convicted of murder and appealed against conviction largely on the ground that the trial judge had misdirected the jury on the mental element. The jury had been directed by Ackner J in the following terms:

> The prosecution must prove, beyond all reasonable doubt, that the accused intended to (kill or) do serious bodily harm to Mrs Booth,

Hyam's case. Firstly, Lord Bridge could not accept that the so-called 'aimed at' rule, referred to above, was a legal requirement. What of the terrorist who plants a bomb in a public place in the expectation that a bomb-disposal expert will attempt to defuse it? The bomb explodes and the expert is killed, yet it cannot properly be argued that the bomb was 'aimed at' him.

The other uncertainty concerned the definition of the degree of probability where some risk of death or really serious personal injury is foreseen. Lord Bridge was not happy with Lord Hailsham's L C statement in Hyam, that the prosecution had to show 'the intention to expose a potential victim ... to a serious risk that ... grievous bodily harm from [the accused's] act'. The danger he felt was that the mental element in murder might be confused with that in causing death by reckless driving[29] and 'motor' manslaughter.[30] In R v Lawrence (Stephen)[31] Lord Diplock held that a person is guilty of reckless driving if he creates 'an obvious and serious risk of causing physical injury to some other person' and 'having recognised that there was some risk involved had nonetheless gone on to take it'. The unacceptable implication of this, according to Lord Bridge, is that it might be argued that a motorist overtaking in a narrow country lane in the face of an oncoming cyclist, who knowingly takes a serious risk of hitting the cyclist may be guilty of murder.

After Hyam's case there was considerable debate as to the precise degree of probability with which the defendant must have foreseen that death or really serious personal injury would occur in order to be guilty of murder. Lord Bridge commented:

> ... it is impossible to define degrees of probability in any of the infinite variety of situations arising in human affairs, in precise or scientific terms.

In this respect his Lordship approved the observations made by Lord Reid in Southern Portland Cement Ltd v Cooper,[32] that:

> Chance probability or likelihood is always a matter of degree. It is rarely capable of precise assessment.

Lord Bridge argued – no doubt bearing in mind the so-called 'objective' test in DPP v Smith and the provisions of section 8 Criminal Justice Act 1967 – that a jury could determine a defendant's intention by making appropriate inferences. In particular, the jury ought to be able to infer that an accused intended the 'natural' consequence of his actions. The word 'natural', he said, 'conveys the idea that in the ordinary course of events a certain act will lead to a certain consequence unless something unexpected supervenes to prevent it'. It should be stressed that the inference is one which the jury *may* make; it is not automatic. But the effect will be that if the prosecution establishes that death or grievous bodily harm was a natural consequence of the accused's act, the burden will then be upon the defence to provide some other evidence or explanation.

It is clear that Lord Bridge based his argument on the judgment of Lord Goddard C J in R v Steane[33]:

> No doubt, if the prosecution prove an act, the natural consequence of which would be a certain result and no evidence or explanation is given, then a jury may, on a proper direction, find that the prisoner is guilty of doing the act with the intent alleged, but if on the totality of the evidence there is room for more than one view as to the intent of the prisoner, the jury should be directed that it is for the prosecution to prove the intent to the jury's satisfaction, and, if on a review of the whole evidence, they either think that the intent did not exist or they are left in doubt as to the intent, the prisoner is entitled to be acquitted.

It appears, therefore that the 'broad' intent illustrated in Hyam's case, where foresight of death or grievous bodily harm as being (highly) probable suffices, was abolished by Moloney.

In his commentary on the decision in Moloney, Professor J. C. Smith argued that there is a theoretical doubt, at least, about the effect of the law as stated by Lord Bridge.[34] He referred to his Lordship's remarks concerning the terrorist who plants a bomb in a public place, and the learned commentator found it less than wholly convincing that the likelihood that the bomb disposal expert will be killed or seriously injured is overwhelming. Surely the terrorist will be aware that bombs have been defused without any injury being incurred, and, although there may be a risk of harm, it is far from certain or perhaps even likely, that harm will be caused. Professor Smith did, though, suggest one way in which the example of the terrorist can be reconciled with the apparent abolition of the broad intent. It would be necessary for the terrorist to want the bomb to explode at the time the expert is trying to defuse it. The only possible problem with such an interpretation is that it strongly implies that the bomb is aimed at the expert and yet, ironically, Lord Bridge was using the example to indicate that the 'aimed at' rule should not be part of the law! In response to Professor Smith's comments, it may be suggested that when he plants the bomb the terrorist intends to kill or seriously injure anyone who happens to be within its range when it explodes. It is not aimed at anyone in particular. But whether or not the terrorist is guilty of murder will depend on the degree of certainty with which he thought his actions would kill or gravely harm somebody.

In those comparatively few cases in which it is appropriate to direct the jury as to the meaning of intent by reference to the accused's foresight of the consequences of his act, Lord Bridge suggested that the judge should invite them to consider two questions:

(i) Was death or really serious injury a natural consequence of the defendant's voluntary act?; and

(ii) Did the defendant foresee the consequence as being a natural consequence of his act?

Only if both questions are answered in the affirmative may the jury properly infer that the defendant intended the consequence. At the risk of using expression of which some (senior) members of the judiciary disapprove, it might be said that the first question is a largely objective one, and the second largely subjective.

The guidelines set down by Lord Bridge were then adopted by the trial judge, Mann J, in directing the jury in R v Hancock and Shankland. There the two defendants, who were miners on strike, pushed a block of concrete and a concrete post from the Rhymney Bridge over the Heads of the Valley Road in South Wales. The concrete block hit the windscreen of a taxi which was travelling along the road, and the driver was killed. The defendants' case was that they did not intend to kill or harm anyone, for they thought that the block and post were positioned over the middle of the three lanes in the road when the taxi was travelling in the nearside lane. Their intention was simply to block the road and to frighten the passenger in the taxi who was also a miner and who continued to go to work during the strike. After they had been considering their verdict for more than five hours, the jury returned with a note indicating that they were having difficulties 'because of lack of knowledge, particularly with regard to intent and foreseeable consequences'. The trial judge gave them a further direction in almost the same terms as those which he had originally used.

The Court of Appeal quashed the convictions for murder and substituted convictions for manslaughter, holding that the Moloney guidelines were defective and potentially misleading. It was accepted that where, as in Hancock and Shankland, the defendant's primary purpose or motive was not to kill or injure, the jury should be given an extended direction on the meaning of intent. But Lord Lane C J maintained that Lord Bridge (in Moloney) had been wrong to deliberately omit any reference to the probability of the consequences of the defendant's act. This criticism was shared by the House of Lords, where Lord Scarman remarked:

> In a murder case where it is necessary to direct a jury on the issue of intent by reference to foresight of consequences, the probability of death or serious injury resulting from the act done may be critically important. Its importance will depend on the degree of probability: if the likelihood that death or serious injury will result is high, the probability of that result may . . . be seen as overwhelming evidence of the existence of the intent to kill or injure. Failure to explain the relevance of probability may, therefore, mislead a jury into thinking that it is of little or no importance and into concentrating exclusively on the causal link between the act and its consequence. (p. 364)

Lord Scarman then went on to suggest how the jury should be directed. They should be told that:

> . . . the greater the probability of a consequence the more likely it is that the consequence was foreseen and that if that consequence was foreseen the greater the probability is that that consequence was also intended.

It may be argued that Hancock and Shankland has effectively resurrected the broad intent adopted in Hyam and overruled the approach recommended in Moloney. The Court of Appeal in Hancock and Shankland said that it might be a sufficient step towards establishing intention that the defendant knew that it was 'highly likely' that his act would cause the appropriate consequence. The decision of the House of Lords does not appear to resolve the conflict between the statements of the Court of Appeal and those of Lord Bridge in Moloney.

There is, moreover, as Professor J. C. Smith points out in his commentary on the House of Lords' decision in Hancock and Shankland,[35] a further uncertainty in the law. Referring to Lord Bridge's speech in Moloney, Lord Scarman stated that the defendant's awareness or foresight is not to be equated with intention but is to be regarded as evidence of intention.

Foresight does not necessarily imply the existence of intention, though it may be a fact from which, when considered with all the other evidence, a jury may think it right to infer the necessary intent. (p. 363)

What is particularly worrying is that there is no indication as to how a judge should direct a jury who have concluded that the defendant did not want to kill or do grievous bodily harm but did think it was highly likely that his act would have one of those consequences. What else is necessary to lead the jury to make the inference that the defendant had the required intent? It appears that the jury are left to decide for themselves whether the defendant ought to be convicted of murder. This specific meaning of 'intention' remains undefined.

That the nature of the foresight necessary to establish malice aforethought remains uncertain was shown most recently in the Court of Appeal's decision in R v Nedrick. In a case where the facts bore a striking resemblence to those in Hyam, the defendant allegedly poured paraffin through the letter box and on to the front door of a house, and set it alight. The house was burnt down and a 12-year-old boy died of asphyxiation and burns. Nedrick, who gave no warning of his action, denied intending to kill anyone: he said he had only wanted to frighten the boy's mother. In substituting a verdict of manslaughter for one of murder, the Court confirmed that where a person commits a manifestly dangerous act, resulting in the death of another, and the primary purpose or motive was not to harm anyone, the jury should have the nature of the necessary intent explained to them in some depth. In delivering the leading judgment Lord Lane made two significant statements. At one time he said that the jury must be satisfied the accused 'recognised that death or serious harm would be virtually certain (barring some unforeseen intervention) to result from his voluntary act'. A little later, he said the defendant must have realised that death or serious harm was 'inevitable'. The use of the word 'inevitable',[36] together with the notion of 'barring some unforeseen intervention', strongly suggests that the case supports the view adopted by Lord Bridge in Moloney. No-one can be absolutely sure of the consequences of his or her actions, but he/she may be 'virtually certain'. At the time of doing an act, a consequence may be foreseen as inevitable, though there will always be a theoretical possibility (albeit an extremely remote one) that the consequence will not come about.

However, as Professor Smith remarks in his commentary,[37] 'virtual certainty' requires a greater degree of foresight than 'high probability', so that Nedrick differs from Hancock and Shankland and Hyam. This is particularly unfortunate for it could be argued that since Hancock and Shankland was decided in a higher court (viz. the House of Lords, as opposed to the Court of Appeal), the ruling in Nedrick is wrong. Ironically, on the face of it at least, the appeals in Hancock and Shankland were simply to 'clarify' the law as laid down in Moloney, rather than to modify it. The apparent confusion in the law may tragically have been brought about simply because the Moloney guidelines merely referred to the idea of 'natural consequences' without offering any explanation of it. Had such an explanation been included, it may well have been that the jury in Hancock and Shankland would not have been confused and the debate would have ended in 1985.

THE YEAR AND A DAY RULE

In murder and manslaughter, the victim must die within a year and a day of the infliction of the injury by which death is alleged to have been caused.[38] This requirement was originally evolved because of the difficulty in proving that a defendant's act had caused death where there was a lengthy lapse of time between the two. However, advances in medical science have effectively rendered these difficulties obsolete so that the cause of death can be diagnosed even though it occurred a substantial time later. The obvious and unfortunate implication is that where the victim dies more than a year and a day after the defendant's act there can be no liability for murder or manslaughter even though the defendant caused death. Suppose a man, badly injured as the result of a criminal assault, is placed on a life-support machine, and the machine is switched off a year and two days later, the doctors having declared him clinically dead. The absurd implication is that by keeping the victim on the machine for a sufficient length of time, doctors can effectively prevent the assailant from being guilty of unlawful homicide. The only possible justification for retaining the 'year-and-a-day' rule now is that it would be unacceptable to keep a person waiting indefinitely at the risk of being prosecuted for murder or manslaughter.

'VOLUNTARY' MANSLAUGHTER

Provocation

Provocation may consist of what is said, or what is done, or both.[39] A defendant who seeks to rely on provocation must satisfy the court on a number of points. Firstly, he must show that at the time he committed the fatal act he had lost his self-control.[40] It should be emphasised that the mere fact that a person has been provoked is insufficient to avoid conviction for murder. The court must be satisfied that the defendant was still affected by the provocation when he carried out the lethal act. Thus, if there is a time lapse between the provocation and the killing, so that the defendant had 'cooled off', his plea will fail.

Secondly, the jury must be satisfied that the 'reasonable person' of the same age and sex as the defendant, and possessing other characteristics of the defendant which are relevant to the provocation, would also have lost his self-control.[41] So, if a black defendant has been racially provoked, the question is whether a reasonable black man, of the same age and sex as the accused, would have lost his self-control. The court's attention will also be focussed on the reasonableness of the defendant's action in relation to the nature of the provocation. If it is felt that the defendant has gone beyond what was reasonable in the circumstances, his plea of provocation will not automatically fail, but the chances of it succeeding will invariably have been reduced.[42] In the vast majority of cases the provocation will have come from the victim, though this is not required by law.[43]

Diminished Responsibility

This concept was introduced by the Homicide Act 1957, and it applies where the balance of the defendant's mind was disturbed at the time he committed the fatal act. Section 2(1) of the Act states:

> Where a person kills or is a party to the killing of another, he shall not be convicted of murder if he was suffering from such abnormality of mind (whether arising from a condition of arrested or retarded development of mind or any inherent causes or induced by disease or injury) as substantially impaired his mental responsibility for his acts and omissions in doing or being a party to the killing.

In R v Byrne[44] the then Lord Chief Justice, Lord Parker, sought to explain the phrase 'abnormality of mind' which lies at the heart of a plea under section 2(1):

> 'Abnormality of mind' . . . means a state of mind so different from that of ordinary human beings that the reasonable man would term it abnormal. It appears to us to be wide enough to cover the mind's activities in all its aspects, not only the perception of physical acts and matters and the ability to form a rational judgment whether an act is right or wrong, but also the ability to exercise will power to control physical acts in accordance with that rational judgment.

Thus, the fact that the accused's ability to exercise self-control was seriously impaired would be very pertinent to the question whether he was suffering from diminished responsibility.

The abnormality of mind must arise from one of the specified causes – that is, from a condition of arrested or retarded development of mind or any inherent causes or be induced by disease or injury. It was recently held that alcoholism can form the basis of a diminished responsibility plea if it either results in injury to the brain causing gross impairment of judgment and emotional responses, or the drinking has become involuntary in that the accused was unable to resist the impulse to drink.[45]

In addition, the abnormality of mind must have impaired the accused's mental responsibility 'substantially' and this, of course is a question of degree. For example, if the abnormality was due to a specified cause which affected the accused's self-control, there would be a 'substantial' impairment where there was an *inability* to exercise self-control, but where there was *difficulty* in exercising self-control the situation is less clear. The question would then be decided by the degree of difficulty. In any event, the difficulty which the accused had in controlling his behaviour must be substantially greater than would have been felt by an ordinary individual, without any mental abnormality.

Where it appears that the accused was suffering from an abnormality of mind due to two or more causes, one of which is intoxication (or some cause not specified in section 2(1) of the Act), the jury should be directed to ignore the effects of the intoxication (or other cause) and consider the effects of the other admissible cause(s).[46]

Suicide Pacts

If one person intentionally kills another, the crime is generally one of murder even if the deceased wished to be killed. The one exception to this is where the killing is in pursuance of a suicide pact.[47] Such a pact is an agreement between two or more persons whose settled and common object is the death of all of them, whether or not each is to take his own life. Any survivor of a suicide pact is liable to be convicted of manslaughter.

'INVOLUNTARY' MANSLAUGHTER

In these cases the defendant has unlawfully killed another human being without malice aforethought. But the prosecution must still satisfy the court that he killed either by committing a reckless act (or omission to act), or by committing an act which was unlawful and dangerous. The latter type of crime is sometimes called 'constructive manslaughter'. Although the law recognises a distinction between these two types of involuntary manslaughter, the prosecution may allege that a single incident falls within both of them.

Killing by a Reckless Act or Omission[48]

This type of involuntary manslaughter frequently applies where the defendant lacked sufficient foresight of the consequences of what he did to be said to have acted with malice aforethought. Put simply, he has killed recklessly, rather than intentionally. Problems arise, however, in trying to define the nature of the recklessness which the law requires. Until recently, a person was guilty of this type of manslaughter if either he knowingly took the risk of killing or causing some bodily harm to another,[49] or he was grossly negligent as to whether he might bring about one of these consequences. In the latter instance the prosecution must show that:

> ... the negligence of the accused went beyond a mere matter of compensation between subjects and showed such disregard for the life and safety of others as to amount to a crime against the state and conduct deserving of punishment.[50]

One of the distinguishing features of gross negligence manslaughter was that the accused did not have to be aware of the risk he was taking. As the result of a series of cases[51] in the last few years, however, the principles outlined in the preceding paragraph have been amended. The law currently appears to be that a person is guilty of this type of manslaughter if, by his behaviour, he has created an obvious and serious risk of causing unlawful physical injury to another, and either he has not given any thought to the possibility of there being any such risk or, having recognised that there was such a risk, has nonetheless gone on to take it. The risk which he has created must have been one which would have been obvious to the ordinary, prudent person, though the defendant may not have been aware of it himself. Moreover, in considering whether the ordinary, prudent individual would have known of the risk, no account will be taken of any special characteristics of the defendant (for example, the fact that he had the mental age of a child seems to be irrelevant). It may be that there is a third way in which this type of involuntary manslaughter may arise – that is, a person intentionally commits an act (or omits to act when he was under a duty to act), and he is grossly negligent whether he kills or seriously injures anyone.

Killing by an Intentional Act which is Unlawful and Dangerous (Constructive Manslaughter)

According to the Lord Chief Justice, Lord Lane, in R v Goodfellow, the jury must consider four questions to determine liability for this variety of manslaughter: (i) Was the defendant's act intentional? (ii) Was it unlawful? (iii) Was it an act which any reasonable person would realise was bound to subject some other human being to the risk of physical harm, albeit not necessarily serious harm? (iv) Was that act the cause of death? It seems that the defendant need only intend to do the act; he need not know or believe that it is unlawful and dangerous.[52]

An act can never be criminally unlawful in itself. There must be something about the act, its circumstances and/or consequences which render it unlawful. Thus, if a child unexpectedly dies having been chastised by one of its parents, there is no unlawful act (and therefore no manslaughter) provided the parent used no more than reasonable force. But if the force is unreasonable, the parent has committed an unlawful act and may be convicted of manslaughter. The third question which the jury must ask themselves is one which essentially poses an objective test – would all reasonable and sober people recognise that the defendant's act exposed some other person to the risk of harm, albeit not serious harm? This test is to be applied on the basis of what was known to the defendant.[53] In addition, the 'harm' which has been risked by the defendant's act must be of a physical nature.

POSSIBLE CHANGES IN THE LAW

From time to time it has been suggested that the law should be amended so as to abolish the distinction between murder and manslaughter, and substitute a single offence of 'unlawful homicide'. The trial judge would then be given the freedom to reflect the gravity of the particular offence in the sentence he imposes, with a maximum possible penalty of life imprisonment. A number of reasons may be advanced for this proposed change in the law. Firstly, capital punishment no longer applies to murder, so that offenders convicted of manslaughter may receive the same sentence as convicted murderers. Secondly, there is a view which is shared by many people who work in the criminal justice system that the decisions which the courts make do not always precisely reflect the legal distinctions between murder and manslaughter. In other words, whether a defendant is convicted of one offence or the other is not a matter of strict legal judgment but is more likely to represent the court's personal view of the nature of the case. Thirdly, it may be argued that the current law relating to the mental element in murder (malice aforethought) is in such a confused and lamentable state that juries may well be hard-pressed to appreciate the exact legal boundary between murder and involuntary manslaughter. A single crime of unlawful homicide would thus be simpler for the trial judge to explain and easier for the jury to comprehend.

However, in its Working Paper on Offences Against The Person, published in September 1976, the Criminal Law Revision Committee (CLRC) invited comments on the proposal to amend the law in this way.[54] Only the Law Commission responded favourably to the proposal: the public generally favoured the retention of murder as a separate crime. In its Fourteenth Report on Offences Against The Person, in 1980 the CLRC[55] stated:

> If we were to propose the abolition of the separate crime of murder and its incorporation in a wider offence of unlawful homicide,

many people would certainly find it hard to appreciate that the proposal was not meant to weaken the law and would be likely to think that the law no longer regarded the intentional taking of another's life as being especially grave. We recommend that murder should continue to be a separate crime. (para 15)

Apart from the apparent views of the general public, the other main objections to changing the law are that an offence of unlawful homicide would be unacceptably wide, and that the trial judge would have too much responsibility in assessing the gravity of the particular crime.

The CLRC (1980) felt that a principal reason for preserving murder as a separate offence is the stigma which it attracts, and it was argued that the legal definition should ensure, as far as it is possible to do so, that those convicted of murder deserve this stigma (para 19). The inescapable difficulty here is that of identifying an appropriate formula or set of words which would mean that only the most serious cases result in a murder conviction. The CLRC (1980) put the position bluntly:

It is . . . not practicable to provide in the definition of an offence for the wide variety of motives which may induce men to act. It is equally impracticable to take into account other surrounding circumstances which may make the killing more or less serious. The most that a definition can achieve is that the generality of cases falling within the definition of the graver offence will be more serious than the generality of cases falling within the definition of the less grave offence. (para 19)

Notwithstanding this difficulty, the Committee stated that it is the mental element which primarily distinguishes the gravest from the less grave homicides. At the time the CLRC produced their recommendations, the leading authority on malice aforethought was the case of Hyam. It was acknowledged that, in addition to a person's intention with respect to the consequences of his act, his motive is a very significant factor. Here, of course, is a prime example of the impossible task of drafting a perfect definition that will encompass all cases, but only those cases, which should be treated as murder. The CLRC recommended that a person should be guilty of murder if he (a) with an intent to kill, causes death; or (b) causes death by an unlawful act intended to cause serious injury and known to him to involve a risk of causing death (para 31). In (a), the phrase 'intent to kill' means that the defendant knows that his actions will result in death, as described by the House of Lords in R v Moloney. No-one can ever be absolutely certain that a particular result will occur, but knowledge in this context means knowing what will happen in the ordinary course of events (see para 25). The alternative case, set out in (b), was designed to cover those cases where, for example, the offender shoots at a pursuer when escaping from a robbery which he has committed. His intention may be only to disable the pursuer, but he appreciates that there was a risk of mortally wounding his victim and, because of this appreciation, he should be regarded as a murderer.

Aware of the strength of public feeling about terrorism, the CLRC recognised that their proposals would nevertheless not bring certain terrorist killings within the realms of murder. Those who plant bombs to damage property and cause fear, but not intending to take life (where the bomb is timed to explode when it is unlikely that people will be around) should be guilty of manslaughter. This is because such terrorists do not think it probable that their actions will kill or seriously injure anyone. At the same time, they must appreciate there is a risk that someone might be killed and that it is unreasonable for them to take the risk. Factors such as these can be taken into account when passing sentence, and the CLRC envisaged that this type of manslaughter would result either in a life sentence or a long determinate sentence. In the event that Parliament should consider such cases as meriting a mandatory life sentence, the CLRC recommended:

> that it should be murder if a person causes death by an unlawful act intended to cause fear (of death or serious injury) and known to the defendant to involve a risk of causing death. (paras 27 and 30)

As has been illustrated, the law as to the precise nature of the intention in malice aforethought is far from clear, but the courts have – so far at least – not been influenced by the opinion expressed by the CLRC. In the Fourteenth Report, it was argued that to require anything less than foresight of the certainty of death or grievous bodily harm would create an unacceptable level of consistency in the law. Thus:

> A person who does an act knowing that serious bodily harm is a probable, even a highly probable, result, may, if serious bodily harm in fact results, be guilty of maliciously inflicting such harm,

contrary to section 20 of the Offences Against The Person Act 1861, but he is not guilty of the graver offence of causing grievous bodily harm with intent, contrary to section 18 of that Act: Belfon (1976) 63 Cr App R 59. Yet if the victim dies, on the Hyam test he is guilty of murder. His blameworthiness is the same whether the victim lives or dies; yet if the victim lives, he is liable only for a lesser offence against the person. We are of opinion that a death so caused should not be murder. (para 20)

Criticism has also been expressed of the fact that a person may be convicted of murder even though he did not intend to kill anyone. In general the criminal law does not hold liable a person who causes a result in circumstances when it is forbidden unless he intended to do so or was at least reckless whether he did so. The CLRC felt that since they were attempting to restrict murder to the worst examples of unlawful homicide, 'it would be remarkable if we incorporated into it a fault element less than that which is to be required in crimes generally' (para 21).[56] Nonetheless, in 1981 the House of Lords confirmed, in R v Cunningham,[57] that a person who kills intending to do grievous bodily harm may still be guilty of murder.

Support for the approach of the CLRC was provided recently in an article by Robert Goff, a Lord of Appeal in Ordinary.[58] As well as endorsing the view that the decision in Cunningham is inconsistent with the notion that murder should be confined to the most serious unlawful killings, he makes the point that sometimes the defendant positively intends that the victim should not die. For example, terrorists may punish traitors by 'knee-capping' them – shooting them in the knee – intending that the traitor should survive, maimed, 'pour encourager les autres'. If the traitor in fact dies, the terrorist may be convicted of murder. This may be regarded by many as a perfectly proper and desirable outcome, but Goff goes on to describe a case of 'glassing' – ramming a piece of jagged glass into a victim's face – which resulted in a conviction for manslaughter. Intending to 'glass' his victim, a young man, who had had too much to drink, struck his victim not in the face but in the side of his neck, severing the jugular vein. The jury acquitted the young man of murder even though it was obvious that he intended to cause serious bodily harm. Goff's explanation was that it could never have crossed the defendant's mind that he might kill his victim and, indeed, he had been horrified to discover that his victim had died.

As for the alternative state of mind for murder, proposed by the

CLRC (that the defendant kills by an unlawful act intended to cause serious injury and known to him to carry a risk of killing), Goff raises two objections. Firstly, he says it is too narrow because it is limited to cases where there is an intention to cause serious injury. It is the knowledge of the risk that death might result which renders the defendant a murderer, so if only a slight injury is intended, or even no injury at all, the offence should still be murder. Thus, Goff suggests that a man who launches a missile in the vicinity of another, not intending harm but realising there is a risk that it may kill the other man, should be treated as a murderer. Yet surely this ought to be seen as a clear case of involuntary manslaughter, of killing recklessly – death is a possibility, but no more than that. The situation is very different from one in which the offender believes that he will cause death and so it merits less condemnation.

Secondly, the CLRC's proposal is objected to on the ground that it is too wide. What if a person recognises there is a risk of killing, but discounts it as unrealistic? Or what if he hopes to avoid it? Goff fears that the CLRC's proposal would unjustifiably classify such a person as a murderer. Yet it may be argued that a risk can be real or unreal, but not both. Either a person believes there is a risk, (albeit a very minor one), or he believes there is no risk. The risk of killing may be only minimal, the likelihood of causing death may be very small, but there is still a perceived risk. Presumably, therefore, whether the escaping robber who shoots at and kills his pursuer is guilty of murder or manslaughter depends on his estimation of the risk. Indeed, the CLRC pointed out that if the risk is thought to be merely a slight one, for example, where thieves cut railway signalling cable and cause a derailment with much loss of life, the offence should be manslaughter and not murder (para 23). The justification for treating the escaping robber as a murderer is that there is very little difference between that and an intentional killing. The CLRC appear to have anticipated Goff's objections by stating:

> To classify this particular type of risk-taking as murder does not involve the danger of escalation to cases of recklessness in general, since it is tied specifically to circumstances in which the defendant intended to inflict serious injury. (para 28)

Homicides that occur during a robbery or in the furtherance of some other gain are clearly regarded as very serious offences, and those who commit them can expect to be dealt with accordingly. The robber who kills in order to complete his robbery will surely find it difficult to persuade a court of law that, although he knew there was a risk of causing death, he hoped that such a consequence would not ensue and he should therefore be treated as a manslaughterer. Only if he can show that he thought that death was no more than a possibility will he be able to satisfy the court that what he did was quite different from an intentional killing and thus not to be treated as murder.

As for the CLRC's additional recommendation to meet public fears about terrorism, Goff objects that it would lead to the

> startling consequence that if a terrorist, not intending to cause fear of death or serious injury, but realising that his action involves a risk of causing death, blows up a national monument in order to publicise his cause and thereby kills the night watchman, then that cannot be murder. (p. 50)

Admittedly, the wording of the CLRC's proposal is a little ambiguous, but surely the point is that the terrorist's liability depends on his perception of the consequences of planting the bomb. If his objective is essentially to make some sort of 'political statement' and alarm and outrage the public in general, and he believes there is no more than a remote chance that someone might be badly injured or killed, then he ought to be convicted of manslaughter. The gravity of his apparent indifference to the possibility of causing personal harm can be reflected in the court's sentence. Obviously, a court would want to hear evidence as to the number of people in the vicinity at the time when the bomb was due to explode. The more likely he foresees death or serious injury, the more likely it is that he should be convicted of murder, but the difficulty is to determine at what precise point his liability changes from manslaughter to murder. It is painfully and patently clear that the courts have not found this an easy task, and it may be that the matter will ultimately have to be resolved by Parliament.

Goff argues that there are cases in which there was no intention to kill or seriously injure, but which lawyers feel ought to be regarded as murder. Yet he cites as an illustration the situation posed by Professor Glanville Williams, of a man who sends an insured parcel on an aeroplane and includes in it a time-bomb. The man's purpose is to destroy the parcel and collect the insurance. He knows that the plane will also be destroyed and he says he does not care less whether the people on board live or die. With respect to Robert Goff, this man might well be convicted of murder on the basis that he intended to kill, for he knows that people on the plane will inevitably die.

Nevertheless, let us continue to examine Goff's suggestions. He seeks to identify a mental element which goes beyond intention but falls short of recklessness 'in the sense of conscious and unreasonable risk-taking' (p. 52). Drawing on Scots law, he focusses attention on what has been described as 'wicked recklessness' which leads him to propose that if an accused did not care whether the victim lived or died – he was indifferent to death – he should be guilty of murder. Goff stresses that the accused need not consciously appreciate the risk of killing, where 'a man acts in the heat of the moment, as when he lashes out with a knife in the heat of a fight; or when a man acts in panic, or in blind rage' (p. 55). But again, it may be countered that although the individual does not 'consciously appreciate' the risk, he may have experienced what Birch has described as a 'flash of awareness', or of the possibility that he might kill.[59] In other words, at the time of acting he simply did not bring to the forefront of his mind the relevant knowledge and information, he did not think things through. In any event, whether or not wicked recklessness involves the conscious appreciation of the risk of killing, the broader and more crucial question is whether the concept of indifference to death should suffice for murder (as an alternative to an intention to kill). With the possible exception of the escaping robber who kills his pursuer, the CLRC clearly disagreed with Goff's suggestion.

Finally, Goff claims that, in their quest to embrace those cases which they feel *ought* to come within the definition of murder, lawyers have effectively expanded the idea of intention beyond its natural meaning. He proposes that instead of asking juries to consider whether the defendant *intended* to kill or seriously injure, judges should direct them to consider whether he *meant* to do so. According to the Shorter Oxford English Dictionary, to 'mean' is to 'have in mind as a purpose', and yet Goff rejects purpose as a synonym for intention because a man may have more than one purpose, as where A kills B in order to get B's money. A's immediate purpose is to kill B, but he also has an ulterior purpose, to get his money. For our present purposes, Goff used the word 'mean' in the sense of immediate purpose.

Glanville Williams' hypothetical situation of the man who puts an insured parcel, containing a time-bomb, on a plane is referred to in order to illustrate apparent deficiencies in the concept of intention, which states that a person's intention may be inferred from his foresight. In the example, the man clearly means to destroy the parcel, but did he mean to kill the people on board the plane? Goff answers in the negative, for if the man saw them descending safely by parachute he may have been delighted. Yet he agrees with Glanville Williams that if people were killed by the bomb, the offence should be murder. (This, of course, leads Goff to justify wicked recklessness as a valid alternative state of mind). But the case could be determined by examining the extent to which the man foresaw death (or serious injury). The fact that he would have been delighted if the people parachuted to their safety does not prevent him from foreseeing their death when he secreted the bomb on the plane. It may be that he would have preferred them to survive, but that does not automatically show that he did not intend to kill them.

One of the main problems with Goff's proposal to substitute 'mean' for 'intend' is that, without further explanation at least, it is likely to lead to confusion in the juries' minds. They might, for example, confuse 'mean' with 'want' or 'desire'. Moreover, the question is essentially whether the notions of 'immediate purpose' and 'indifference to death' are the appropriate ways of determining the mental element in murder. There is a very real danger that if indifference to death is accepted as a species of malice aforethought, it may become very difficult to differentiate between murder and involuntary manslaughter where a person has killed recklessly. Indeed, Goff is forced to admit that indifference and 'not caring less' are examples of recklessness, albeit serious ones. Is it right to leave it to juries to decide whether the recklessness in a particular case is sufficiently wicked to warrant a conviction for murder? Surely to do so would be a recipe for inconsistency and contradiction, and some cases which could not be regarded as instances of the worst type of unlawful killing would almost certainly result, quite unjustifiably, in a murder conviction.

Not infrequently, people have expressed the view that the most serious crimes are those that are premeditated. Whilst it is easy to see why such views are held, it has long been felt to be impractical to treat premeditation as the way to identifying the worst cases. As Hollis illustrates, one of the most striking examples of a premeditated murder is a mercy killing, yet no one would seriously argue that such an offender deserves a mandatory life sentence.[60] Moreover, even if mercy killing was regarded as an exception, there is the problem of determining how long a time is necessary to constitute premeditation. The Gowers Commission[61] was informed that in Belgium, for example, evidence was needed of an intention to kill two or three hours before the fatal act was committed. But in other countries, such as the USA and in the UK, no real forethought is required.

It may be preferable to concentrate on the degree to which a person has shown a readiness or preparedness to kill. No pre-planning as such is necessary; the prosecution would not have to show that the defendant had carefully thought how he was going to commit the offence. Instead, the court would be concerned with evidence which indicated that the defendant had, before carrying out the fatal act, decided that he would or might kill in appropriate circumstances. He may not have consciously thought that he might kill, but he may still have been subconsciously aware of the possibility.[62] A killer may, indeed, hope that he will not kill, but if he recognises the possibility that he might and is ready to do so, he deserves whole-hearted condemnation for his action. The robber who kills so as to escape may be acting on the spur of the moment. It may be that he had genuinely taken the gun with him solely to frighten and thereby facilitate the theft, and had fired it purely in a moment of panic. Of course, it may well be extremely difficult for the defence to satisfy a court that this was the situation, but we are concerned with a matter of principle – how to define the crime of murder – and not with evidential problems of trying to influence a jury. This robber should be treated quite differently from the one who, before setting out, had decided that he was prepared to use the gun if he felt the occasion required him to do so. In this sense, the concept of 'indifference to death' is quite apposite, but our attention should focus on what happened *before* the fatal act is committed, and not simply at the time it is committed.

MERCY KILLING

Although it has been stated that a mercy killing is a prime example of a premeditated offence, and it theoretically falls within the definition of murder, the reality is that the majority of mercy killers are convicted of manslaughter. This is because, as the CLRC (1980) acknowledged:

> No one connected with the case wants to see the defendant convicted of murder. The result is that legal and medical consciences are strained to bring about a verdict of manslaughter by reason of diminished responsibility. (para 115)

Thus, a legal fiction is perpetrated – in view of the immense strain and trauma, the defendant is regarded as having been temporarily unbalanced and so not fully responsible for his actions. It is accepted that his condition does not strictly fall within the ambit of section 2(1) of the 1957 Homicide Act, but the interests of justice dictate that his liability be reduced so as to reflect the invidious circumstances surrounding the offence.

In their 1976 Working Paper, the CLRC had suggested that there should be a separate crime, punishable with a maximum of two years' imprisonment, where a person who, from compassion, unlawfully kills another who is or is believed by him to be:

(i) permanently subject to great bodily pain or suffering, or
(ii) permanently helpless from bodily or mental incapacity, or
(iii) subject to rapid and incurable bodily or mental degeneration.

However, in the Fourteenth Report four years later, the CLRC withdrew the suggestion because most of the comments they received were against it, and because they were persuaded that such fundamental ethical considerations were involved that, as lawyers, they were not sufficiently qualified or experienced to deal with it (para 115). It was argued that the 1976 suggestion would have increased suffering (rather than prevented it), because the potential victim would be less protected by the law since the crux of the proposed new offence was the defendant's assessment of the victim's condition. In particular, the defendant may be quite unaware of the potential benefits which medical science might achieve for the sufferer. Furthermore, the CLRC agreed with the Gowers Commission that there would be immense difficulties in drafting an appropriate definition. In the meantime, notwithstanding these objections and difficulties, it seems that the courts can and do identify cases of compassionate killing although, of course, we cannot be certain just how many deserving cases actually result in convictions for manslaughter rather than murder.

SENTENCING KILLERS

If murder and manslaughter are to remain separate offences, it may be argued that the sentencing laws should reflect the distinction between them. The members of the CLRC were evenly divided on the issue of the retention or abolition of the mandatory life sentence for murder. Amongst the arguments in favour of its retention were retribution and the opportunity to express public revulsion at the offence.

If murder is to be retained as a special form of culpable homicide so that it stands out as a particularly serious offence, then it should attract a unique penalty which demonstrates that society will not tolerate such grave criminal conduct. (para 44)

Whilst the logic behind this statement may be sound, there is some evidence to suggest, albeit rather tentatively, that the position should be examined more carefully. The punishment for murder in New South Wales used to be the mandatory sentence of penal servitude for life. But in 1982 the mandatory nature of the penalty was abolished, and yet this has not caused a public outcry nor has it precipitated any erosion of public confidence in the criminal justice system.[63] It is reported that in practice about one in five convicted murderers avoid penal servitude for life.

A life sentence need not be imposed if 'it appears to the judge that the person's culpability for the crime is significantly diminished by mitigating circumstances, whether disclosed by the evidence in the trial or otherwise'. The judge must begin by treating the life sentence as the most appropriate penalty for murder, and he must be satisfied there is sufficient mitigation to significantly reduce the offender's liability. It is only right to emphasise that in manslaughter cases the judge has an unfettered discretion to impose any sentence up to and including life. In addition, the New South Wales Court of Criminal Appeal has revealed a further distinction between murder and manslaughter.[64] In murder cases, the judge is required to identify two categories of mitigation. The first comprises factors which directly affect culpability, and these must (i) be present when the crime is committed, and (ii) have affected either the defendant's conduct or his state of mind such that his blameworthiness would have been significantly greater had the mitigating factor not been present and operating when the offence was committed. The second category consists of the remaining factors which do not relate to the defendant's culpability at the time of the crime but are traditionally taken into account when passing sentence. The trial judge must be satisfied that the first group of factors exists before considering the latter type. In manslaughter cases, on the other hand, there is no need to differentiate between different categories of mitigation.

To an extent, therefore, it is the case that in New South Wales murderers and manslaughterers may be punished in the same manner, although penal servitude for life remains the usual penalty for murder. Those members of the CLRC who rejected the mandatory life sentence did so partly because they felt that such a penalty could not reflect the varying degrees of heinousness which follow the diverse nature of murder. They denied that it can provide the appropriate retribution, for retribution must be proportionate to the gravity of the crime and this can only be achieved by a fixed term of years (para 55). Furthermore, they claimed that there was no evidence of the unique value of the life sentence (para 58). Life sentences would be retained only for the most outrageous offences and the most dangerous offenders.

Like the New South Wales Parliament, these members of the CLRC did not want to abandon the distinction between murder and manslaughter. It appears, therefore, that if they remain separate offences, it need not necessarily be on the basis that murder should carry a mandatory life penalty whereas manslaughter should attract only a maximum of life imprisonment. Life imprisonment (or the equivalent) should be the maximum penalty for both offences, and the trial judge can reflect the gravity of the case by the way in which he exercises his sentencing discretion. Preserving the distinction between the crimes allows the stigma of murder to be maintained and recognises the variations that exist between one unlawful killing and another.

NOTES

1. 3 Inst 47.
2. This requirement is discussed later in the chapter.
3. (1956) 40 Cr App Rep 152.
4. [1959] 2 All E R 193.
5. [1975] 3 All E R 446.
6. (1971) 55 Cr App Rep 262.
7. This offence has since been abolished and replaced by that of causing death by reckless driving under section 1 Road Traffic Act 1972.
8. [1976] 1 All E R 260.
9. [1981] 2 All E R 422.
10. [1910] 2 K B 124.
11. 124 Cal 551 (1899) Sup Ct of California.
12. It remains to be decided by the courts whether a person on a life-support machine is still alive, or whether the machine is simply 'ventilating a corpse'.
13. (1983) 76 Cr App R 279.
14. The police officer who fired the shot which actually killed the girl most

directly caused her death. But so far as he was concerned the result was one of accidental death since his shooting was a reasonable act of defence.

15. His Lordship might be criticised for using such a vague and ambiguous phrase as 'contributed significantly'. However, it should be said that he was talking of the way in which a jury should be directed, and was not stating a principle of law.

16. H. L. A. Hart and A. M. Honore, *Causation in the Law*, (Oxford: Oxford University Press, 1959).

17. See R v Pitts (1842) C & M 284.

18. [1957] Crim L R 365.

19. See R v Vickers [1957] 2 Q B 664.

20. [1961] A C 290.

21. Section 8. Criminal Justice Act 1967 provides:

    'A court or jury, in determining whether a person has committed an offence:
    (a) shall not be bound in law to infer that he intended or foresaw a result of his actions by reason only of it being a natural and probable consequence of those actions; but
    (b) shall decide whether he did intend or foresee that result by reference to all the evidence drawing such inferences from the evidence as appear proper in the circumstances.'.

22. (1976) 63 Cr App R 222 at 225.

23. [1985] 3 W L R 1014 at 1019.

24. [1974] 2 All E R 41.

25. [1985] 2 W L R 648.

26. The House of Lords' decision is to be found in [1986] 2 W L R 357.

27. [1986] 1 W L R 1025.

28. S. Mitchell (ed.), Archbold, *Criminal Pleading Evidence and Practice*, 40th edition (1979) para 1441a, p. 948.

29. Section 1 Road Traffic Act 1972.

30. The expression 'motor' manslaughter refers to the crime of involuntary manslaughter where the defendant has killed someone by driving a vehicle in a reckless or grossly negligent manner.

31. [1982] A C 510 at 525 and 527.

32. [1974] A C 623 at 640.

33. [1947] K B 997 at 1004.

34. [1985] Crim L R 378 at 381, 382.

35. [1986] Crim L R 400 at 402, 403.

36. Defined in the Oxford English Dictionary as, 'that cannot be avoided; not admitting of escape or evasion; unavoidable'.

37. [1986] Crim L R 742 at 743.

38. See R v Dyson [1908] 2 K B 454.

39. Section 3 Homicide Act 1957.

40. See R v Duffy [1949] 1 All E R 932n.

41. See DPP v Camplin [1978] 1 All E R 1236.

42. See R v Brown [1972] 2 Q B 229.

43. See R v Davies [1975] 1 Q B 691.

44. [1960] 3 All E R 1 at 4.
45. See R v Tandy [1988] Crim L R 308.
46. See R v Gittens [1984] Q B 698.
47. Section 4 Homicide Act 1957.
48. A person can only be guilty of manslaughter by failing to do something if he was under a legal duty to take positive action – see R v Stone and Dobinson [1977] Q B 354.
49. See Gray v Barr [1971] 2 All E R 949 at 961.
50. See R v Bateman (1925) 19 Cr App Rep 8 at 11.
51. See R v Seymour (1983) 77 Cr App R 215, Kong Cheuk Kwan v R (1985) 82 Cr App R 18, and R v Goodfellow (1986) 83 Cr App R 23.
52. See DPP v Newbury and Jones [1977] A C 500.
53. See R v Dawson (1985) 81 Cr App R 150.
54. Criminal Law Revision Committee. Working Paper on Offences Against The Person (1976) London: HMSO.
55. Criminal Law Revision Committee. Fourteenth Report Offences Against The Person (1980) London: HMSO Cmnd 7844.
56. In his dissenting speech in Hyam's case, Lord Diplock claimed that the proposition that an intent to do serious bodily harm sufficed to establish malice aforethought had effectively been abolished by section 1 Homicide Act 1957.
57. [1982] A C 566.
58. Robert Goff. The Mental Element in the Crime of Murder (1988) 104 L Q R 30–59.
59. D. J. Birch. 'The Foresight Saga: The Biggest Mistake of All?' [1988] Crim L R 4–18.
60. Christopher Hollis. The Homicide Act (1964) London: Victor Gollancz, at p. 31.
61. Report of the Royal Commission on Capital Punishment 1949–1953 (1953) London: HMSO Cmnd 8932.
62. Thus, the motorist who overtakes the car in front of him without being able to see if anything is coming in the opposite direction, does not mechanically think to himself, 'Oh, I am taking a risk', but he is still cognisant of the danger he is creating.
63. Stanley Meng Heong Yeo. 'Sentencing Murderers: A New South Wales Innovation'. [1987] Crim L R 23–27.
64. See R v Burke [1983] 2 NSW L R 93, approved in R v Bell [1985] 2 NSW L R 466.

2 An Examination of Murder

THE BACKGROUND

The gravity of murder and the consequences of being convicted and formally labelled a murderer might suggest that a good deal is known about the subject. In the United Kingdom relatively little research has been undertaken in this area, despite the concern that has been expressed in the media about levels of violence in our society. Instead, various assumptions have been made about the nature of murder and moral judgments have been offered about what should be done with those found guilty of the offence.

The only regular information available comes in the Criminal Statistics produced annually by the Home Office, which includes a chapter on homicide. These provide some statistics and a limited amount of detail about the numbers of offences recorded as murder or manslaughter, the methods and surrounding circumstances of the killings, the nature of the relationship between offender and victim, and a few personal characteristics of the parties involved. Before I carried out my investigation, there were really only two studies which shed any light on the contemporary nature of homicide – viz. Evelyn Gibson's analysis of cases between 1967 and 1971,[1] and Morris and Blom-Cooper's examination of people indicted for murder from 1957 to 1977.[2]

Not surprisingly, attention has tended to be focussed on both murder and manslaughter, for at times it seems difficult to identify clear distinctions between the crimes. Perhaps courts reach verdicts which are based on their moral assessment of the facts, and do not always strictly accord with the legal definitions of the offences. But my study was confined to murder cases, and there were three principal reasons for this. Firstly, murder is a unique crime insofar as it carries a mandatory sentence of life imprisonment, or the equivalent thereof.[3] Secondly, and this is the main justification for the mandatory sanction, it is generally accepted that the offence of murder should be retained for what are regarded as the very worst examples of unlawful killing. Thirdly, I had to take account of some inescapable logistical considerations – the research was carried out by me alone, on a part-time basis, and I simply did not have sufficient time to investigate manslaughter cases as well.

One of my principal objectives was to discover what sort of cases are judged by the courts to amount to murder. Opinions may differ about whether a particular set of facts deserves to be treated as one of the worst types of homicide and thus merits the label 'murder'. As a lawyer I was keen to identify the range of situations which are currently categorised as such by the criminal justice system. There may be some cases which do not deserve to result in a murder conviction, so that the law may require redefinition. Moreover, it often seems to be assumed that murder is predominantly a 'domestic' offence – a rather vague expression, but one which implies that a man of previously good character who is not a 'criminal' in the real sense, has killed a member of his family because of some acute domestic difficulties. Indeed, commencing on statistics relating to murder cases during a 20-year period ending in 1905, Sir John Macdonell concluded:

> I am inclined to think that this crime is not generally the crime of the so-called criminal classes, but is in most cases rather an incident in miserable lives in which disputes, quarrels, angry words and blows are common. The short history of a large number of the cases which have been examined might be summed up thus:– Domestic quarrels and brawls; much previous ill-treatment; drinking, fighting, blows; a long course of brutality and continued absence of self-restraint. This crime is generally the last of a series of acts of violence.[4]

Is this true today, or does the nature of murder change as the years pass by? Other forms of murder, such as where an offender kills in the course of committing robbery or in the pursuance of some other form of gain, are usually regarded as more serious in that they pose a greater threat to the public at large. It is important to know whether the number of these crimes is changing and, if so, in what way.

My research was based on a largely random sample of 250 cases of people convicted of murder between 1978 and 1982 inclusively. This represents roughly one in three of the total number of recorded convictions during those years. In each year 50 cases were examined, consisting of 41 adult males,[5] two adult females and seven young persons (YPs),[6] so that the sample was generally reflective of the situation overall. Permission was granted to me to collect information from files kept in the Life Sentence Section (P2 Division) of the Prison

Department at the Home Office. Much of my data was taken from a document called the 'Confidental Memorandum'[7] (sometimes known as the 'Home Office Summary'), and which provides a succinct but comprehensive account of the offence, its investigation and the court hearing.

For each of the 250 cases, details were gathered on the following matters:–

(i) The defendant's sex, age, occupation and marital status; previous convictions for criminal offences and the sentences imposed; the charges against the defendant; the defendant's plea (to murder), and the sentence passed (that is, whether a minimum period of imprisonment was recommended or not);

(ii) The victim's sex, age, occupation and marital status;

(iii) The nature of the relationship, if any, between the defendant and victim;

(iv) The method by which the victim was killed;

(v) The circumstances surrounding the offence, including any apparent motive for it;

(vi) When the offence was committed – that is, at what time of day the fatal act was carried out;

(vii) Where the offence – the fatal act – was executed;

(viii) Whether there were any co-defendants and, if so, whether they were charged with the same murder as the defendant or with other offences;

(ix) How the defendant was apprehended – whether he gave himself up, either by surrendering himself to the police or as a result of the police being informed by a friend or relative; or whether he was arrested by the police.

THE RESULTS

Arguably the single most glaring feature of the study was the discovery that categorisation of murder was possible only at a superficial level. General patterns could sometimes be seen when matching one factor against another, such as the apparent motive for the offence and the making of a recommendation of a minimum period of imprisonment. But it was impossible confidently to detect any significance when three or more factors were cross-tabulated. Occasionally, this was simply because the figures were too small to provide reliable data.

The Offenders

(i) Their Sex

Earlier research indicated that the great majority of murders are committed by men. Whilst admitting that since 1971 numerically the role of women had altered in that they had a greater involvement than previously, Morris and Blom-Cooper (1979) found that proportionately the increase was only slight. From 1957 to 1970 between 6 per cent and 16 per cent of those indicted for murder were female, whereas from 1971 to 1977 the figures varied between 11 per cent and 16 per cent. (It is worth noting that at the same time the number of women convicted of or cautioned for indictable offences rose from just under 51 000 in 1969 to 98 500 in 1977, an increase of 93.9 per cent). One of the YPs in my study, convicted in 1982, was female so that there were 11 females in the total sample of 250 (that is, 4.4 per cent). This is more than twice the proportion shown in Gibson's (1975) research where only ten out of the 496 'normal' murders,[8] 2.0 per cent, were committed by women, though the figures are so small that it would be dangerous to attach great significance to them.

That so few convicted murderers were female obviously makes it difficult to draw any confident conclusions about the characteristics of the cases, but the following observations may be made. Seven of the female defendants were married, whereas just over half (51.5 per cent) the male offenders were single, though there was no statistical significance between the defendant's sex and marital status. But the converse was true of the relationship between sex and previous convictions. Six female offenders had no criminal record at all and none had been convicted of any prior crimes of personal violence. In contrast, for less than a fifth of their male counterparts the murder was their first conviction and nearly 45 per cent of them had already been found guilty of offences against the person. Moreover, none of the female defendants had previously received custodial sentences.

More than a third of the male offenders were charged with other offences in addition to murder, yet only one female was in this situation. All female defendants pleaded not guilty, and they all received life sentences with no minimum periods of imprisonment being recommended by the trial judge.

None of the victims of the female offenders were over 70 years of age. Six of the 11 women killed someone between 30 and 49. None of their victims were professional people, though in eight instances they were in some form of non-professional employment. All victims of female murderers were married or single; there were no divorcees or widows/widowers.

Four killed their spouse or cohabitant, and only one woman killed a total stranger. None of them killed by shooting. Four females committed the crime during a quarrel, and three as an act of jealousy or revenge. None killed for financial gain and (not surprisingly), none in the course of a gang fight. Six of them executed the fatal act between 6 p.m. and midnight; and none of them gave themselves up.

(ii) Their Age
One of the apparent characteristics of those who commit homicide is that they are often relatively young. Morris and Blom-Cooper (1979) reported that 40 per cent of those indicted for murder between 1957 and 1977 were 15 to 24 years old, and about two-thirds were between 15 and 34. Gibson's (1975) survey suggested that male murderers were getting younger. Between 1957 and 1971 those under 21 increased from 14.7 per cent to 31.8 per cent, the lowest proportion being 10.5 per cent in 1961, and the highest was 40.5 per cent in 1969. The middle group, aged at least 21 but less than 40, gradually decreased from 61.8 per cent in 1957 to 54.1 per cent in 1971. Male murderers aged 40 or more 'were a relatively small proportion that fluctuates but shows no trend' (p. 27).

The ages of those convicted of murder in my study are shown in Table 2.1. As already stated, 35 defendants aged under 18 at the time of the offence were deliberately selected to ensure that the proportion of such cases in the sample mirrored the total numbers of murders nationally. Of these 35, 20 were aged 17, 13 were 16-years-old, one was 15 and the other was 14 years of age. The fact that more

TABLE 2.1   *Age of Defendants Convicted of Murder* (as at date of offence)

	No.	Relative Frequency	Cumulative Frequency
10 to 17	35	14.0%	14.0%
18 to 29	119	47.6%	61.6%
30 to 39	59	23.6%	85.2%
40 to 49	26	10.4%	95.6%
50 to 59	9	3.6%	99.2%
60 or more	2	0.8%	100.0%
Totals	250	100.0%	

than 71 per cent of the defendants in the sample were between 18 and 40 years old generally confirms the results of previous studies. During the period 1978 to 1982 there were, of course, slight fluctuations in the defendants' ages, but these were not statistically significant.

Gibson (1975) noted that, with the exception of those who committed infanticide (that is, where natural mothers kill their babies, who are under 12 months old, and the balance of their minds is disturbed because of the effects of childbirth), 'the women were in general older than the male offenders' (p. 31). Although it is very dangerous to make confident statements on the basis of small numbers, my survey of murder, as shown in Table 2.2, seems to support this pattern.

TABLE 2.2 *Age of Defendants According to Their Sex*

	Males	Females
10 to 17	34 (14.2%)	1 (9.1%)
18 to 29	117 (49.0%)	2 (18.2%)
30 to 39	52 (21.7%)	7 (63.6%)
40 to 49	25 (10.5%)	1 (9.1%)
50 to 59	9 (3.8%)	0
60 or more	2 (0.8%)	0
Totals	239 (100.0%)	11 (100.0%)

Almost a third of those under 18 (that is, YPs), had previously been convicted of a crime of personal violence, though for more than two-thirds this was their first custodial sentence. Similar prior convictions had been recorded against nearly half the defendants aged 18 to 29 and nearly two-thirds of those between 40 and 49. Older offenders were less likely to have such a background: neither of those aged 60 or more did.

Defendants of 18 to 29 years and 50 to 59 years were more likely than other age-groups to plead guilty, though the figures overall were not statistically significant. None of those aged 50 or more were given a minimum recommendation of imprisonment. Indeed, such a recommendation was made in respect of only two offenders aged 40 or over, the longest being 17 years. (Minimum periods of imprisonment can only be recommended where the defendant is at least 21 years old).[9]

Defendants under 40 killed relatively more male victims than females (133 and 80 respectively). Conversely, those aged 40 or more murdered more females (23) than males (14). The six victims under five years were killed by defendants who were no more than 29-years-old. The victims of most YPs were either under 30 or over 50: only three YPs killed 'middle-aged' victims.

There appears to be some statistical significance between the murderer's age and the relationship between the parties involved ($X^2 = 0.0262$). None of the YPs killed close relatives. Thirty of the 35 killed friends or strangers (in almost equal numbers). Three of the four children murdered by parents were victims of 18-to 29-year-olds, as was the one parent killed by his son. Most spouses or cohabitants were killed by those betwen 30 and 50, and the great majority of strangers were murdered by someone under 40 years of age.

Although overall a sharp instrument was the most popular method of causing death, it was particularly favoured by YPs and offenders aged 40 to 49. Strangulation was used by all age-groups, but less so by YPs. Most of those who hit or kicked their victims to death were between 18 and 29 years old. Not surprisingly, all gang fights involved offenders under 30. Almost half the YPs killed in the furtherance of theft or gain, and fewer than average during a quarrel. Conversely, a larger than average number of offenders between 40 and 49 killed in a fit of temper, and none of the murderers in this age-group were motivated by financial gain.

Defendants aged at least 40 were particularly likely to carry out the fatal act between 6 p.m. and midnight, and in the victim's home. Predictably, perhaps, most offences in the street were perpetrated by young offenders (namely, those under 30 years). Finally, five of the 11 defendants aged at least 50 gave themselves up to the police ($X^2 = 0.0384$). As the killers got older there was a steady increase in the likelihood that they would take such a course of action.

(iii) Their Occupation

It appears that those who are convicted of murder are unlikely to be people pursuing professional careers.[10] Only four defendants in my study belonged to this group. The majority of murderers either had a non-professional occupation, of whom there were 119 (47.6 per cent), or were unemployed at the time of the offence, of whom there were 114 (45.6 per cent). The remaining 13 cases consisted of four housewives or mothers and nine pupils/students.

It was interesting, though not unexpected, to find that in 1981 and 1982 the proportion of unemployed murderers increased.[11] There appears to be some significance in the relationship between the offender's occupation and his previous criminal record ($X^2 = 0.0017$), though in some cases the figures were very small. Three of the four professional defendants had no prior convictions, and likewise six of the 13 housewives/mothers. Those with a record of crimes of personal violence were more likely to be unemployed when they murdered than in a non-professional occupation. Similarly, occupation seems to be related to previous experience of custody ($X^2 = 0.0002$), though again caution is needed because of the smallness of some of the figures. None of the professional offenders had previously been deprived of their liberty, but most (32 out of 44) of those who had served custodial sentences of at least 12 months were out of work at the time of the offence.

Three of the four victims of professional defendants were female, whereas 12 of the housewives and students killed males. None of the professional offenders used a sharp instrument – two strangled their victims, one used a blunt instrument and the other used poison. Shooting was more common amongst defendants in non-professional jobs, whereas hitting and kicking was more prevalent amongst the unemployed. The defendant's occupation and his apparent motive also seemed to be significantly related ($X^2 = 0.0076$). Not surprisingly, unemployed offenders were more likely to kill for financial gain than other groups.

(iv) Their Marital Status

Of the 250 cases I examined, 90 defendants were married (though possibly separated from their spouses), 126 were single and the remaining 34 were divorcees. There appeared to be no real significance in the relationship between marital status and previous convictions, yet single and divorced offenders were proportionately more likely to have a prior record of crimes of personal violence. Of greater significance, (p<0.01), is the fact that married defendants tended not to have had any earlier experience of custody, whereas divorcees were relatively over-represented in this respect. Moreover, divorcees were more likely to have served longer periods in detention – 14 of the 28 who had been given sentences of at least two years were divorced – and yet married defendants were under-represented in this respect.

A disproportionately large number of the victims of single offenders were male ($X^2 = 0.0387$). Married and divorced defendants killed equal numbers of male and female victims, and they were more likely to kill people aged between 30 and 49 than other age-groups. A high number of elderly victims (aged 70 or more) were killed by single defendants (15 out of 24). Predictably, perhaps, the marital status of killers seems to be significantly related to the marital status of the deceased ($X^2 = 0.0005$). More than half the married offenders killed married victims, which was no doubt explained by the fact that nearly a third of married offenders killed their spouse or cohabitant. Exactly half the single offenders killed single victims, and a large proportion of the murders of complete strangers were committed by single defendants.

The two heaviest sentences in the sample (minimum recommendations of at least 30 years), were both imposed on single defendants. Such defendants were much more likely to kill for financial gain, and seven of the eight gang fight murders were by young unmarried men. Married offenders usually killed in a fit of temper. Two-thirds of the shootings were by single defendants, whereas strangulation tended to be the method adopted by married or divorced killers.

(v) Their Previous Convictions
Apart from age and sex, the only other characteristic of unlawful killers which has previously been researched is their prior criminal record. Of the male offenders convicted of 'normal' murder between 1967 and 1971, Gibson (1975) found that 36.3 per cent had no previous convictions at all, 33.2 per cent had been convicted of offences against property only, and 30.5 per cent had convictions for sexual offences and/or crimes of personal violence. The corresponding figures for my survey were 19.6 per cent (49 cases), 29.2 per cent (73 cases), and 44.8 per cent (112 cases). One of the murderers in my sample, convicted in 1980, had a previous conviction for unlawful killing, and this is in keeping with the figures for homicide generally. Only two people convicted of homicide in 1986 had a previous similar conviction, and from 1976 to 1986 inclusive 0.7 per cent of murderers and manslaughterers had such a criminal record.[12] Again, although the figures are not statistically significant, there were annual fluctuations in the nature of offenders' prior convictions. In 1980 60 per cent of defendants had a previous record of personal violence, whereas in the other four years the proportion only varied from 40–42 per cent. Those with no convictions at all fluctuated from 12 per cent in 1980 to 26 per cent in 1981, and those convicted of property crimes varied from 22 per cent in 1980 and 1981 to 36 per cent in 1978.

Predictably, those with a prior record of personal violence were much more likely to have had earlier experience of imprisonment. Where the offender had such previous convictions there were proportionately more male than female victims. Defendants with no criminal record seemed to kill relatively few victims aged 50 or older, but were more likely to kill housewives and mothers. More of their victims were married than was the case in other groups. Offenders who had already been violent killed fewer relatives and lovers, and seemed in particular to kill more strangers. On the one hand, those with convictions for crimes excluding personal violence favoured the use of blunt instruments and strangulation, whereas those with a record of offences against the person preferred sharp instruments. All those who killed in a gang feud had already been acquainted with the penal system, and six of them had committed crimes of violence. Interestingly, eight of the 54 who murdered for theft or gain were first offenders, a proportion only just below that for the sample as a whole.

(vi) Their Previous Experience of Imprisonment
As well as the 49 murderers who had no previous convictions, 95 (another 38 per cent), had never received a custodial sentence of any sort. Thus, for nearly 58 per cent of the sample the life sentence for murder was their first taste of imprisonment. Indeed, I found that very few defendants had had any prior experience of long-term detention. Only seven had previously been sentenced to a term of at least five years imprisonment, and only two of those had been given ten years or more. In other words, the vast majority of murderers in this study began their indeterminate sentence either with no prior experience of custody or without having served a lengthy sentence. There was no statistical significance in the annual figures, although the proportion of those who had previously received a custodial sentence varied from 32 per cent in 1981 to 58 per cent in 1980.

Offenders who had already served custodial sentences killed more male victims. Most young victims (that is, less than 16 years old), were killed by people with no such prior experience. Similarly, murderers who had never formerly lost their liberty killed proportionately more married victims. In more than three-quarters of the cases where there was a close family relationship between the parties (that is, parents, children, spouses or cohabitants), the life sentence was the first custodial sentence for the offender.

The Charges against the Defendants

The very nature of a murder case may indicate the likely number and variety of charges that will be brought against the defendant. If the case is one of so-called 'domestic' murder, then a single count in the indictment may be expected, whereas if the killing occurred in the course of a robbery or burglary, additional charges reflecting the nature of the incident may be brought. Of the cases I examined, 167 defendants (66.8 per cent) faced a single count of murder. Sixty were indicted for murder and offences of non-fatal personal violence, and a further 14 were accused of property crimes as well as murder.

Nine defendants, however, were charged with more than one murder. Such cases are, it seems, quite rare and it is interesting to look at the sort of circumstances that surrounded them. In most instances the murders were committed in one incident, though this was not always true.

Case 77 The defendant, an epileptic, had been dismissed from his job for stealing from his employers. This theft had been reported by a workmate. Two days later he went to his workmate's house and killed his workmate's wife and two young children – he slashed their throats and then set fire to the house.

Case 120 A man and two co-accused had planned to kidnap a woman and then blackmail her wealthy husband. But they went to the wrong location, raped two women there and shot them to prevent the victims from identifying them.

Case 146 On two separate occasions – that is, in the early hours of two consecutive mornings – a teenager killed two middle-aged men in the course of robbing them in the street. The victims were hit and kicked, mainly about the head, and struck with a brick.

Case 154 The defendant's late father had invested money in and helped to run a company. Before his death, the father had borrowed money from the company, which had been formed by the two victims in the case. One of the victims had been anxious that the loan should be repaid and visited the defendant's mother, as a result of which she was very upset. The defendant became depressed by this and, after a bout of drinking, shot his victims.

Case 155 The defendant was separated from his wife but they had been attempting a reconciliation. They quarrelled and he killed her (for which he was convicted of manslaughter). But this had been witnessed by his mother-in-law, and so he killed her as well to prevent her from identifying him.

Case 165 The facts of this case occurred some years before the trial. The defendant was a soldier who had been instructed to gather information about terrorist activities. He and his co-defendant, another soldier, had an argument with two men who were suspected of recruiting terrorists and, as a result, the two suspects were stabbed to death.

Case 205 A man suspected that his wife was being unfaithful and that she was having a lesbian relationship with their daughter. These factors, together with other domestic problems, created tension and pressures on the defendant which he was unable to withstand and he strangled both of them.

Case 234 The defendant, with the help of his co-accused, killed his wife and three daughters. The marriage proved unsuccessful and the defendant sought an 'escape route'. His wife was strangled and the house was set on fire.

Case 237 The defendant and his co-accused were Hells Angels, and their victims were members of rival groups. The first victim was killed because he had allegedly raped the defendant's girlfriend. The second was thought to have brought Hells Angels into disrepute, and the third had pestered the defendant for drugs and when refused had become very abusive.

It is worth noting that six of these nine defendants pleaded guilty, a proportion very much against the general pattern of the sample. Both 30-year minimum recommendations were made against defendants charged with more than one murder, and both 25-year recommendations concerned offenders who were indicted on counts alleging non-fatal personal violence as well as murder (see pages 53 to 56). Also, those accused of two or more murders were more likely to have had no previous experience of a custodial sentence.

The numbers of those accused of more than one murder, or with murder plus crimes against property, were small, but in both cases female victims were relatively more common than males. The converse was true of those charged with just murder or murder and other offences against the person. In addition, in the sample overall roughly twice as many cases involved the killing of a friend or acquaintance as a complete stranger, but where the accused was charged with crimes of violence as well as murder, the opposite was true. Almost half of this latter group of cases were committed in the furtherance of gain, and exactly half of the cases where a property crime was also charged bore this motive. On the other hand, where the offence was executed in a fit of rage, a single count of murder was most likely.

The Defendant's Plea (to murder)

194 of the 250 defendants (77.6 per cent), pleaded not guilty to murder. This is not surprising since a conviction for murder carries an automatic life sentence and the offender must forever bear the label 'murderer' and the social stigma which that embraces. A plea of guilty, insofar as it prevents any undue delay to the court, minimises costs and reflects a readiness to accept responsibility, may be regarded as a mitigating factor. Yet a smaller proportion of not guilty pleas resulted in minimum recommendations of imprisonment being made, though the figures were not statistically significant. Moreover, the defendant's previous experience of the criminal justice system seemed to have no bearing on the way in which he pleaded.

The relationship between plea and the victim's age appeared to be important ($X^2 = 0.0317$), though some of the figures were rather small. In all six cases where the victim was under five-years-old, and in eight of the ten cases where the victim was between five and 15, a 'not guilty' plea was entered. Where the deceased was aged 70 or more there was a disproportionately high number of admissions of guilt.

It was not surprising to find statistical significance in the relationship between plea and both the occupation and marital status of the victim ($X^2 = 0.0373$ and 0.0166 respectively). A high number of guilty pleas were entered in respect of offences against children, parents/housewives and old-aged pensioners, and in almost half of the crimes against widows and widowers culpability was admitted. (Again, however, the figures are small so that they should be treated cautiously.)

In all cases of gang fights and where there was no apparent motive, a 'not guilty' plea was entered. Conversely, where the motive was one of gain a guilty plea was more common than in the sample as a whole.

Confessions and Incriminating Admissions

Notwithstanding the fact that more than three-quarters of the offenders in the sample denied liability for murder, the great majority of defendants were alleged by the prosecution to have confessed to the charge or to have made incriminating admissions, either verbally and/or in writing; 158 of the 194 who pleaded not guilty (81.4 per cent) had apparently admitted responsibility for causing the victim's death. In some cases they admitted killing with malice aforethought but sought to rely on provocation, diminished responsibility or self-defence. In others they denied malice aforethought and usually offered a plea of guilty to involuntary manslaughter.

Sentence

The Murder (Abolition of Death Penalty) Act 1965 suspended the death penalty for murder for an experimental period of five years, and the penalty was finally abolished in 1969. The trial judge is now required by law to impose a sentence of life imprisonment, or the equivalent thereof, on all persons convicted of murder. He does, however, have the discretion to recommend to the Home Secretary (who is ultimately responsible for determining if and when a life sentence prisoner is to be released on licence), that the offender should serve a minimum number of years in detention. It was originally intended that this discretionary power might be used by judges across the full range of murder cases, including those where it was felt that release was appropriate sooner than might normally be expected, as well as in the more serious cases. In practice, however, it seems that judges only exercise this power in what they consider to be the more heinous offences. In October 1983 Mr Leon Brittan, the then Home Secretary, said that in certain types of murder – namely the killing of police or prison officers, terrorist murders, sexual or sadistic murders of children, and murders with firearms in the course of armed robbery – the offender would normally have to serve at least 20 years in prison. Shortly afterwards he added that there might well be other cases which would merit even longer sentences. This policy was said to apply to all convicted murderers, including those under 18 years of age at the time of the offence.

Of the 250 offenders in my study, 223 (89.2 per cent) received a life sentence with no minimum recommendation. Two were recommended to serve at least ten but less than 15 years, and 14 were given recommendations of at least 15 but less than 20 years. These sentences are obviously severe but those cases where there is a recommendation of 20 years or more are especially significant, not simply because of the nature of the offence, but also because of the management implications for those who have to look after them whilst they are in custody. Seven offenders were recommended to serve at least 20 years, two received recommendations of at least 25 years, and two more were recommended a minimum of 30 years.

the defendant, who declined to give his name and refused to plead to the charges against him (of murder and kidnapping).

Case 231 The two co-defendants were each recommended to serve at least 25 years in prison for their part in the murder. All three defendants were described as 'winos', and their victim was a middle-aged man who was acquainted with one of the co-defendants. He was said to be an alcoholic and it seems that he was killed because he was known by the defendants to have indecently assaulted young girls (for which he had been convicted). The killing was particularly brutal – the deceased was struck over the head with a machete and put into a bath of very hot water. Then, whilst he was still alive, his body was dismembered with an electric carving-knife, saw and machete. The defendants gave various accounts of what had happened, including that it was an accident and that they could not recall the events because of their intoxication, and they also sought to blame each other.

The lengthiest sentences, 30-year recommendations, were made in the following cases:

Case 120 In the case mentioned above on page 50, a man and his two co-accused each pleaded guilty to a double murder. They planned to kidnap a woman and blackmail her husband, who was believed to be a wealthy man. But they went to the wrong place. Two housewives were raped and then shot so that they could not identify their assailants.

Case 237 This case was also discussed earlier on page 51. Two Hells Angels committed three murders of members of rival groups. The first victim, who had allegedly raped the defendant's girlfriend, was bludgeoned with a spade. The second, thought to have brought Hells Angels into disrepute, was struck with an iron bar, and the third who had pestered and abused the defendant was shot in the neck.

During the period 1978 to 1982 gradually more minimum recommendations were made, although the figures are not statistically significant. The results are set out in Table 2.3. No minimum recommendations were made either where the victim was under five or at least seventy-years-old. Similarly, where there was a close family relationship (parents, children, spouses or cohabitants) between the parties, it was very rare for the trial judge to exercise his discretionary power.

TABLE 2.3   Sentence According to Year of Conviction

	No M.R.	M.R. 10<15	M.R. 15<20	M.R. 20<25	M.R. 25<30	M.R. 30(+)
1978	48 (96.0%)	0	2 (4.0%)	0	0	0
1979	47 (94.0%)	1 (2.0%)	2 (4.0%)	0	0	0
1980	46 (92.0%)	0	2 (4.0%)	1 (2 0%)	0	1 (2.0%)
1981	43 (86.0%)	0	3 (6.0%)	3 (6.0%)	1 (2.0%)	0
1982	39 (78.0%)	1 (2.0%)	5 (10.0%)	3 (6.0%)	1 (2.0%)	1 (2.0%)
Totals	223 (89.2%)	2 (0.8%)	14 (5.6%)	7 (2.8%)	2 (0.8%)	2 (0.8%)

There appeared to be some significance between the motive for the offence and the making of a minimum recommendation ($\chi^2 = 0.0279$), though the number of cases in which a recommendation was made was small. All gang feuds and the one terrorist killing resulted in 'simple' life sentences. Where the murder was committed in a fit of temper a recommendation was relatively unlikely, but the converse was true of jealous or revenge killings and, to a lesser extent, murders in the furtherance of theft or gain. All but two of those who gave themselves up to the police received simple life sentences.

The Victims

(i) Their Sex
Earlier studies have indicated that roughly equal numbers of men and women are unlawfully killed. This was certainly true of Gibson's (1975) survey of murders and manslaughters between 1967 and 1971. The Home Office Criminal Statistics for the period 1978 to 1982 show that 53.1 per cent of the victims of offences recorded as homicide were male.[13] 147 (58.8 per cent) of the victims in my murder study were males, which is perhaps slightly more than might have been expected, though not significantly so. The proportion of male victims varied from 52 per cent in 1979 and 1982 to 66 per cent in 1981.

There was some apparent significance between the victim's sex and marital status ($\chi^2 = 0.0085$). Just over half the married and widowed victims were female, whereas more than 70 per cent of the single victims were male. Interestingly, the method of killing also appeared to be related to the victim's sex ($\chi^2 = 0.0028$). Where death was caused by hitting and kicking or by shooting male victims were noticeably more common than females. The converse was true where the murder was by strangulation.

Whether the victim be male or female, it seems that the most common motive for unlawful homicide is some sort of personal emotional reason; that is, the offence is committed in the course of a quarrel or in a fit of temper. In my research this was apparent for 43.5 per cent of male victims and 49.5 per cent of female victims. Gibson (1975) found that 'men were more likely than women to be killed in the course of other crime' (p. 22). All eight of my murders which occurred as the result of gang feuds involved male victims, but there was hardly any proportionate increase in the number of male victims who were killed for theft or gain. Previous research also suggested that there may be a connection between the deceased's sex and the relationship between the parties. Gibson (1975) reported that 'more than half of all male victims were killed by aquaintances, mostly in the course of "normal" murder or common law (involuntary) manslaughter' (p. 18), and 34.5 per cent of female victims of 'normal' murder (aged 16 or over) were killed by their husbands (including 'common law' husbands). My study produced similar results: 69 of the 99 friends killed were male, and 33 of the 38 spouses/cohabitants were female. Most murders of lovers involved female victims (12 out of 19), and the majority of murders of strangers concerned male victims.

At first sight, there is no apparent relationship between the victim's sex and the time at which the offence is committed. Yet more females were killed between 6 a.m. and noon, and more males between 6 p.m. and midnight than might have been expected. Also, female victims were much more likely to be killed in their own home (69.9 per cent), compared to 33.3 per cent of male victims).

(ii) Their Age
Morris and Blom-Cooper (1979) recorded that the largest groups of victims, of people accused of murder, were those aged 15 to 24 (20 per cent), 25 to 34 (15 per cent), 35 to 44 (14 per cent), and 45 to 54 (11 per cent). For the years 1978 to 1982, the Criminal Statistics (1986) show that 27.2 per cent of homicide victims were aged 16 to 29, and a further 30.6 per cent were between 30 and 49. The results of my survey of murder cases, set out in Table 2.4, are generally quite

TABLE 2.4   Age of Victims of Murder

	Number	Relative Frequency	Cumulative Frequency
Less than 1 year	1	0.4%	0.4%
1 to 4 years	5	2.0%	2.4%
5 to 15 years	10	4.0%	6.4%
16 to 29 years	79	31.6%	38.0%
30 to 49 years	83	33.2%	71.2%
50 to 69 years	48	19.2%	90.4%
70 years or more	24	9.6%	100.0%
Totals	100	100.0%	

similar to those produced by the Home Office. During the period 1978 to 1982, the proportion of older victims gradually increased. In 1978 and 1979 there were slightly more victims in the 16 to 29 age-range than in the 30 to 49 group, but the converse was true in the three later years.

In contrast to my results, Morris and Blom-Cooper (1979) discovered that children less than 4 years old were amongst those who were most at risk – 15 per cent of their total sample, which was the second most frequent category along with the 25- to 34-year-olds. The Criminal Statistics (1986), which are similar to Morris and Blom-Cooper's (1975) figures in that they relate to murder and manslaughter, show that from 1978 to 1982 an average of 10.2 per cent of victims were less than five years of age. Children of these tender years seem more likely to be the victims of manslaughter, or perhaps infanticide, than murder.

There is some evidence to suggest that children tend to be killed by people who have lost their tempers. This was the case in Gibson's (1975) analysis, and five of the six victims aged less than five years in my study fell into this category. (There was no clear motive in the sixth case.) As for those aged five to 15 years, five were killed in a fit of rage, two as an act of jealousy or revenge, another two in the furtherance of theft or gain, and one for no apparent motive. It was fairly predictable that all eight gang feuds should involve victims between 16 and 29 years of age. Of greater concern, however, is the fact that 34 of the 72 victims aged 50 or more were killed in the course of theft/gain. At the same time, of course, it is not surprising to find that older people, who are more vulnerable, should feature so prominently in this type of crime.

Gibson (1975) made some interesting observations about the relationship between young victims and their killers. In 'normal' murder, 57 per cent of child victims were killed by their parents, but this was a lesser proportion than in involuntary manslaughter (86 per cent). Gibson (1975) also found that 'Children not killed by their parents were mainly the victims of acquaintances or relatives; only in "normal" murder were any appreciable proportions killed by strangers' (p. 18). The numbers of such victims in my study were obviously very small. The one baby under 12 months was killed by a parent, as were two of the five victims who were less than five years of age. As for the other three, one was killed by another member of the family, and two by friends/acquaintances. The relationship in the ten cases of children aged five to 15 was quite varied – one was killed by a parent, three by some other relative, two by close acquaintances, two by less familiar acquaintances, and two by complete strangers.

Where the victim is 50-years-old or more, it seems that he or she is much less likely to be related to the murderer. Most victims in this age-range were killed either by a friend (45.8 per cent), or by a total stranger (27.8 per cent). Conversely, and quite predictably, most (92.1 per cent) of those who were murdered by their spouse/cohabitant were between 16 and 49, as were a similar proportion (89.5 per cent) of those killed by their lover (or former lover).

Five of the six child victims, (those aged under five), were hit or kicked to death, and whereas those in early or mid adulthood (16 to 49) were more likely to be stabbed or slashed with a sharp instrument, older victims were relatively more likely to be strangled. The relationship between the victim's age and the timing of the offence also seemed to be of some significance, ($X^2 = 0.0153$). All victims under five were killed during the daytime, but a large proportion (34 out of 72) of those aged 50 or over were murdered between 6 p.m. and midnight. Moreover, a disproportionately large number (76.4 per cent) of such victims were killed in their own homes. It was also quite foreseeable that a large number of murders in the street would concern victims in the age-ranges 16 to 29 and 30 to 49 (39 and 28 respectively out of a total of 80).

(iii) Their Occupation
Relatively few offenders were in professional occupations and the same was true of the victims – only 11 merited this description. The largest single group of victims (107) had pursued non-professional jobs. Exactly a fifth were unemployed when they were killed, but

there was also a sizeable group of 82 (nearly a third of the total), who consisted of a mixture of children (including pupils and students), parents and spouses, and old-aged pensioners. Not surprisingly, the proportion of unemployed victims increased from 14 and 16 per cent in 1978 and 1979 (respectively), to 20 to 26 per cent in 1980 to 1982. A disproportionately large number (64 per cent) of these victims were killed during quarrels or in fits of temper, and very few were murdered for gain!

(iv) Their Marital Status
The largest group of my victims – 103 (41.2 per cent) were single. Then came the 94 (37.6 per cent) who were married (though possibly separated), 27 (10.8 per cent) divorcees, and the remaining 26 (10.4 per cent) were widowed. All victims of gang feuds were single. But more worryingly, half the widowed victims were murdered in the course of theft or gain and most of them were killed in their own homes (22 out of 26).

The Relationship between Offenders and their Victims

It is commonly thought that the majority of victims know their killer. Morris and Blom-Cooper (1979) observed:

> Earlier studies of homicide established that murder was overwhelming a domestic crime. More than half of the persons indicted for murder each year have a familial relationship, and up to two-thirds of all have had a personal relationship of some duration and/or intensity with the victim. Only about a quarter of the total number of murder victims have been total strangers to their victims. (p. 10)

The authors acknowledged that their own data was 'inadequate' in that they had no relevant information in almost half the cases they examined. Nonetheless, they stated that:

> . . . family killings could be identified definitely in between at least one third and a half of the total. Taking into account all those cases where there was information indicating some relationship of some duration (within or without the family) between the victim and killer, we calculated that the proportion would be increased by a further 10 to 15 per cent. Even in cases where a relationship was 'not recorded', we think that some of those cases must have included family or close personal relationships. (p. 10)

These remarks generally confirmed Gibson's (1975) results of 'normal' murder between 1967 and 1971 where, for example, 26.5 per cent were killed by strangers, 8 per cent were murdered by their parents, 21.4 per cent by spouses, lovers or other relatives, 5.3 per cent by boyfriends, and 38.1 per cent by 'other associates'.

A comparison of my results for murder between 1978 and 1982 and the Home Office (1986) figures for offences recorded as homicides during the same period is shown in Table 2.5.

TABLE 2.5   *Relationship of Victim to Offender in Murder as Compared with Homicide Generally*[14]

	MURDER		HOMICIDE	
	No.	Relative Frequency	No.	Relative Frequency
Son/daughter	4	1.6%	301	12.4%
Parent	1	0.4%	101	4.2%
Spouse/cohabitant or former spouse/cohabitant	38	15.2%	574	23.7%
Other family	19	7.6%	97	4.0%
Lover or former lover	19	7.6%	123	5.1%
Friend/acquaintance	99	39.6%	580	23.9%
Other associate	14	5.6%	114	4.7%
Police/prison officer	0		11	0.4%
Stranger (act of terrorism)	1	0.4%	24	0.9%
Other stranger	55	22.0%	501	20.7%
Totals	250	100.0%	2426	100.0%

These figures reveal some interesting points of similarity and contrast. In my study 77.6 per cent of victims were known to their killers, and for homicide generally the proportion was 78.0 per cent. The obvious contrast between the two sets of statistics is that in murder more victims are killed by friends/acquaintances, and fewer by close members of the family such as parents, children and spouses/cohabitants, than in homicide generally. Again, it is worth remembering that, although not statistically significant, the figures vary from year to year. For example, I found that the proportion of spouses/cohabitants fluctuated from 10 per cent in 1978, 1980 and 1981, to 24 per cent in 1982; friends from 26 per cent in 1982 to 48 per cent in the previous year, and strangers from 16 per cent in 1978 and 1981 to 28 per cent in 1979.

Three of the four children killed by their parents were hit and kicked to death, and a large number of spouses/cohabitants were strangled or asphyxiated. Significantly though, (p<0.01), where there was a close relationship between the parties the offence was often committed during a quarrel or in a rage; this was true of nearly 60 per cent of cases where the parties were members of the same family and of almost 80 per cent of murders of lovers. Very few cases involving such relationships were committed for gain. In six of the eight gang feuds the parties were complete strangers. Where theft or gain was the apparent motive the victim was most likely to be unknown to, or perhaps an acquaintance of, the killer. Not surprisingly, more than 82 per cent of 'family' murders took place in the victim's home, and more than half of the offences against strangers occurred in the street.

THE METHOD OF KILLING

Earlier studies have indicated that there is much consistency about the method that offenders use to kill their victims. But, as Morris and Blom-Cooper (1979) recognised, there has for some time been considerable public concern about the apparent increase in the use of firearms. Fortunately, the research evidence suggests that this is not a characteristic of homicide. Morris and Blom-Cooper (1979) found that only 378 out of a total of 4110 victims were shot (9.2 per cent).

Table 2.6 provides comparative statistics of the results of my survey with those of Gibson (1975) for 'normal' murder between 1967 and 1971, and with those of the Home Office (1986) for offences recorded as homicide between 1978 and 1982. Where the victim was assaulted in a number of different ways, the method which caused death, either wholly or substantially, is the one which is reflected in the table.

The prevalence of killing by the use of some sort of sharp instrument was also seen in Morris and Blom-Cooper's (1979) survey where between 22 and 40 per cent of those indicted for murder from 1957 to 1977 were alleged to have adopted such a method. Although it was comforting to see that on average only about 8 per cent of murders are carried out by shooting, there appears to be some marked annual fluctuations. The Home Office (1986) statistics for recorded homicides show variations of 3 to 11 per cent (in 1980 and 1978 respectively),[18] and my research produced results varying from 2 per cent in 1982 to 12 per cent in 1979 and 1980. It must, of course, be acknowledged that the figures in my sample were very small so

Murder and Penal Policy

TABLE 2.6   *Method of Killing in Murder and Homicide[15] Generally*

	Murder 1978–82	'Normal' Murder 1967–71	Homicide 1978–82
Sharp instrument	98 (39.2%)	172 (34.7%)	873 (33.3%)
Blunt instrument	48 (19.2%)	87 (17.5%)	309 (11.8%)
Hitting/kicking	22 (8.8%)	42 (8.5%)	403 (15.4%)
Strangulation	53 (21.2%)	122 (24.6%)	466 (17.8%)
Shooting	21 (8.4%)	43 (8.7%)	180 (6.9%)
Explosion	0		17 (0.6%)
Burning	1 (0.4%)		170[16](6.5%)
Drowning	3 (1.2%)	30 (6.0%)	56 (2.1%)
Poison or drugs	3 (1.2%)		59 (2.2%)
Motor vehicle	0		42 (1.6%)
Other	1[17](0.4%)		41 (1.6%)
Not known	0		6 (0.2%)
Totals	250	496	2622

that changes in the frequencies would lead to disporportionate fluctuations in percentages.

Where death is caused by hitting and kicking it is most likely that the offence will have been committed during a quarrel or whilst the offender was in a rage. Most strangulations (nearly 60 per cent) were carried out in these circumstances also. On the other hand, where the victim is shot the most common motive seems to be jealousy or revenge; this was true of 9 out of the 21 shootings in the study.

THE CIRCUMSTANCES SURROUNDING THE KILLING – THE APPARENT MOTIVE

As Gibson (1975) acknowledged, it is always difficult to attribute a motive to an offence; the task invariably involves a degree of subjectivity, the information available may be inadequate, and in some cases there may appear to be more than one particular motive for the defendant's action.

One category of crimes which understandably generates considerable concern is those killings which are committed in the course of furtherance of other serious crimes such as robbery or rape. Morris and Blom-Cooper (1979) noted that the proportion of such offences in the total of murders remains remarkably constant. Over the 20 year period only 379 out of a total of 4710 victims died as a result of such killings (about 8 per cent). (p. 8)

This observation is supported by the Home Office (1986) Criminial Statistics on recorded homicides between 1978 and 1982 which show that 9.8 per cent of offences were carried out in the furtherance of gain.

Table 2.7 shows the appropriate analysis of the cases in my murder study. Where more than one motive was apparent, the case has been categorised according to what seemed to be the dominant consideration.

In the light of Morris and Blom-Cooper's (1979) comments, the discovery that more than a fifth of my murderers killed in the furtherance of theft or gain seems quite alarming. Yet it confirms the impression created by Gibson's (1975) survey where 22.8 per cent of 'normal' murders between 1967 and 1971 bore such a motive. In addition, however, I found that in nine of the 54 cases there was no apparent evidence of the premeditated use of violence. In other words, it seems that the defendant was disturbed whilst committing a theft or burglary and simply struck out with whatever came immediately to hand.

All 54 offenders in this group were male. Nearly a third of them (17) were under 18 years of age when they committed the offence, and just under 45 per cent were between 18 and 29. It is also worth noting that 31 of the 54 were unemployed at the time; (NB 45.6 per

TABLE 2.7 *Surrounding Circumstances or Apparent Motives for Killing*

	Number	Relative Frequency
Rage or quarrel	115	46.0%
Revenge or jealousy	41	16.4%
In furtherance of theft/gain	54	21.6%
Terrorism	1	0.4%
Gang feud	8	3.2%
Escaping arrest	2	0.8%
Other	18	7.2%
Nothing apparent	11	4.4%
Totals	250	100.0%

cent of the total sample were out of work). Generally, those who came within this type of murder had the same sort of previous convictions as those in other categories, though slightly fewer had no convictions at all (14.8 per cent compared to 19.6 per cent in the total sample), and slightly more had convictions for property offences only (35.2 per cent) compared to 29.2 per cent). The ratio of male:female victims of these murders was very similar to that in the sample overall; 59.3 per cent male and 40.7 per cent female.[19] But perhaps the most disturbing feature of this type of murder is the age of many of the victims – 21 of the 54 (38.9 per cent) were aged between 50 and 69, and another 13 (24.1 per cent) were 70 or over. (NB These age-groups constituted 19.2 per cent and 9.6 per cent of the total sample). More than half of the murders committed for this motive were against complete strangers, and in 30 cases the victims were killed in their own homes.

It is, of course, only right that concern should be expressed about these crimes, but it still seems to be the case that a large proportion of unlawful killings are committed during a quarrel or when tempers are high. The Home Office (1986) Criminal Statistics show that 49.5 per cent of recorded homicides between 1976 and 1986 (inclusive) were attributable to 'quarrel, revenge or loss of temper'. Gibson (1975) reported that 35.7 per cent of 'normal' murders were carried out in a 'rage or quarrel', and that a further 15.5 per cent were acts of jealousy or revenge (a similar percentage to that in my sample). It was slightly surprising to find as many as 46 per cent of my murders resulting from fits of temper. However, in some cases there was a sexual element – for example, where the victim made an unwanted homosexual advance to the defendant – and Gibson (1975) may have included such instances in the separate category labelled 'sexual motive' which constituted a further 13.8 per cent.

Gang feuds that lead to murder appear to be quite rare. Only seven of Gibson's (1975) 426 'normal' murders, and no more than 6 per cent of Morris and Blom-Cooper's (1979) cases fell into this category. In six of the eight gang feuds in my research death was caused by stabbing or slashing. Five cases occurred in the early hours of the morning, and the other three between 6 p.m. and midnight.

Eighteen of the cases I examined did not fit clearly into any of the recognised categories of motive and have thus been shown in Table 2.7 as 'Other'. Briefly, their details are as follows:

Case 11 A married couple decided they wanted to move house, and it seems that the husband took charge of the arrangements.

Unfortunately, they could not afford the move, though the wife believed that matters were proceeding satisfactorily. When the removal van did not arrive on the day of the supposed move, she became agitated and her husband, who could not face disappointing her, killed her.

Case 26 The defendant said he had wanted to teach his wife a lesson about the perils of having electrical appliances in the bathroom. He killed her by electrocution, by dropping an electric heater into her bath.

Case 50 With the help of two men, a woman murdered her husband by drowning him. She had known one of her co accused for some time and had had a sexual relationship with him. He had moved in with the woman and her husband, and then the deceased left the matrimonial home. There was evidence that the crime was premeditated; it appears that the husband was regarded as no more than of 'nuisance value'.

Case 53 The defendant, a middle-aged man, was unemployed and had a serious alcohol problem. He blamed immigrants, especially blacks, for bad housing conditions and unemployment, and as an expression of this he strangled a black taxi-driver.

Case 63 In what was described as a brutal and callous murder, a man killed his wife so that he could live with his mistress. Shortly before the offence, the defendant was very upset when his mistress told him that she had been seeing another man. On the night he killed his wife, he had phoned her to discuss whether they should get a divorce.

Case 99 It was alleged that the accused, in a premeditated crime, killed her husband after she discovered that he was a transvestite. She was having an affair with her co-defendant (who was also convicted of the same murder), and she had come to hate the deceased. The defendants gave him some sleeping pills and whilst he was unconscious hit him over the head with a spade, and dropped his body on a main road.

Case 101 A man strangled his landlady with a net curtain. She had said that she wanted to join her recently deceased sister, and the defendant enabled her to do so! But this was not regarded as a 'compassionate' killing in any way. The accused and his victim had argued and she had used violence against him.

Case 116 Described as a 'sexual psychopath', the defendant tried to have sexual intercourse with a teenage girl. He said he heard someone approaching and he thought the girl would scream, and so he killed her, stabbing her in the chest.

Case 138 Two young men who regarded themselves as professional robbers killed someone to prove that they could do it! Their victim was a complete stranger; he was repeatedly stabbed.

Case 151 Despite the apparent lack of any evidence of ill-feeling between them, the defendant killed his brother who was also his business partner. The defence argued that the accused had been attacked by his brother with a knife, and that death had been caused accidently in the course of self-defence.

Case 173 A middle-aged professional man was convicted of murdering his wife so that he could be with his mistress, who was acquitted of any participation in the offence. Death was caused by administering drugs over a period of about eight months. The defendant said the drugs were given because he thought his wife was suffering from a brain tumour. The judge recommended a minimum of 17 years imprisonment.

Case 175 The parties were both East Africans and had been in England for just over two years, but had been told that they could not stay. They became very depressed, and the defendant suggested to his wife that they should commit suicide, but she rejected the idea. He stabbed her and then tried to stab himself.

Case 184 A man killed his second wife only a few days after she had left him, and only a matter of hours after they had agreed to get a divorce. He went to the house where she was staying and, after they talked and had sexual intercourse, he stabbed her and then cut his own wrists.

Case 222 A man killed a young woman who was a total stranger to him. His 'common law' wife had recently left him, and he had become 'anti women'. The offence took place on a building site where he worked; he struck her about the head with a large stone.

Case 231 This case is referred to on page 56 as one of those resulting in a recommendation of a minimum of 25 years imprisonment. The three defendants killed their victim apparently because they knew that he had been convicted of indecently assaulting young girls.

Case 234 This case has also been outlined earlier, on page 51 as an example of a defendant facing more than one charge of murder. It seems that the offender killed his wife and three children because he felt he could not continue his marriage.

Case 236 Two men in their early 20s knocked their victim, a middle-aged man, to the ground and repeatedly kicked him. The defendant was alleged to have suggested the assault to his two co-accused. They chose the deceased because they regarded him as a 'sex case'.

Case 249 A woman killed her lover by narcotic poisoning. She gave him a glass of whisky containing an overdose of sleeping pills. She had wanted to end the relationship, but the deceased had resisted this and had threatened to commit suicide. The accused denied murder on the ground that she lacked 'malice aforethought'. She said she had given the victim a small quantity of the drug to calm him down when he sexually molested her and was violent towards her.

There were no cases in the sample which bore any resemblance to the notion of 'mercy killings', as described by the CLRC (1980).

PREMEDITATION OR PRIOR THOUGHTS OF KILLING

It has already been acknowledged, in the first chapter, that premeditation *per se* is not required by law for a conviction for murder. But it has nevertheless been argued that one way to distinguish those cases which might properly be regarded as the very worst examples of unlawful killing is to look for evidence that the accused had decided at the very least that he was prepared to kill. This readiness to kill should have been exhibited before the fatal assault is committed. It is neither practical nor desirable to specify a minimum time lapse between the two, but the prior thoughts of killing should not occur at substantially the same time as the taking of life.

If this distinction is applied to the cases I examined, it appears that there were 94 clear instances where the prosecution alleged an earlier preparedness to kill, and in a further 27 the allegation was admitted by the defence. In other words, 48.4 per cent of the total sample showed some evidence of this characteristic.

It may be that the nature of the circumstances in which the offence is committed or the apparent motive for the offender's action has a bearing on the likelihood of the presence of some form of premeditation. Table 2.8 provides an analysis of the 121 cases where there was evidence of a willingness to kill.

Not surprisingly, almost all offences committed as an act of jealousy or revenge, and a large proportion of those carried out in the furtherance of theft or gain, were said to have this feature. The group denoted as 'Other' is also well represented. But the fact that there were cases in each of these categories where there was no evidence of

TABLE 2.8   *Prior Readiness to Kill According to Surrounding Circumstances*

	No.	Relative Frequency	percentage of all cases in each group
Rage/quarrel	18	14.9%	15.7%
Revenge/jealousy	37	30.6%	90.2%
Furtherance of gain	45	37.2%	83.3%
Terrorism	1	0.8%	100.0%
Gang feud	1	0.8%	12.5%
Escaping arrest	1	0.8%	50.0%
Other	15	12.4%	83.3%
Nothing apparent	3	2.5%	27.3%
Totals	121	100.0%	

a preparedness to kill serves as a useful reminder of the danger of assuming that cases in a particular category are of equal gravity.

It was also interesting to discover that 45 of the 121 cases (37.2 per cent), were examples of what might be regarded as 'domestic' crimes, in that the offenders and victims were or had been spouses/cohabitants, lovers or closely related, and the offences were committed for reasons arising out of the close relationship between them. 'Domestic' crimes are usually excluded from any notion of the 'very worst' offences, at least insofar as the offender is not treated as a threat to the public. But the fact that they may contain an element of 'preparedness to kill' may cause us to re-assess their heinousness.

WHEN MURDER IS COMMITTED

One of the factors about which there appears to be little or no earlier research is the time of day when murder is committed. Table 2.9 provides the appropriate information for my survey.

TABLE 2.9   *Time of Day When Fatal Act was Committed*

	Number	Relative Frequency
Midnight to 6 a.m.	62	24.8%
6 a.m. to Noon	34	13.6%
Noon to 6 p.m.	57	22.8%
6 p.m. to Midnight	96	38.4%
Other[20]	1	0.4%
Totals	250	100.0%

Over the five-year period from 1978 to 1982 the figures were generally consistent, though about twice as many fatal acts in 1981 were committed from 6 a.m. to noon than in the other years.

WHERE MURDER IS COMMITTED

Again, it seems that very little investigation has been carried out into the location of murder cases. The results of my study are set out in Table 2.10

TABLE 2.10 *Where the Fatal Act was Committed*

	Number	Relative Frequency
Victim's home	121	48.4%
Defendant's home	19	7.6%
In a street/public place	80	32.0%
Victim's/Defendant's workplace	12	4.8%
Other premises	18	7.2%
Totals	250	100.0%

It is, perhaps, rather worrying to find that nearly half the cases occurred within the victim's own home, but it should be pointed out that in 40 of the 121 instances the victim and defendant shared the same home. The 18 cases labelled as 'Other premises' consisted of an interesting variety of locations: five occurred in public houses, one in an off-licence, one each in a remand centre and a prison, one in a polytechnic building, one each in a gentlemen's and ladies' lavatory, one on an underground railway station, and the remaining six were in a farmhouse, cottage, flat, maisonette, washhouse and factory. The figures were generally consistent between 1978 and 1982, although in 1981 there were more cases where the victim's/defendant's workplace was the scene of the crime. Most of the offences committed in the street (59 of the 80), took place between 6 p.m. and 6 a.m. Where the venue was the victim's home, the murder was most likely to have been carried out in a fit of temper or in the pursuit of gain.

HOW THE DEFENDANT WAS APPREHENDED

A total of 32 of the 250 (12.8 per cent) convicted murderers gave themselves up, either by making direct contact with the police or through the actions of a friend or relative. These included one case of a man who was, at the time, serving a ten-year prison sentence for another offence and wanted to 'make a clean breast of things'. His confession, to what was the only 'contract killing' in the sample, was made more than four years after the offence took place. 1979 seems to have been a poor year in that only one person gave himself up, whereas in the other years between six and ten offenders did so. Otherwise, there were no distinct features about the cases where the defendant surrendered himself to the authorities, except that none of the female offenders took this course of action.

NOTES

1. Evelyn Gibson, *Homicide in England and Wales 1967–1971*. Home Office Research Study No. 31. (1975) London. H.M.S.O. This updated two earlier studies, namely E. Gibson and S. Klein, *Murder* (1961) London. H.M.S.O.; and E. Gibson and S. Klein, *Murder 1957 to 1968*. Home Office Research Study No. 3. (1971) London. H.M.S.O.

2. Terence Morris and Louis Blom-Cooper. *Murder in England and Wales Since 1957*. (1979) London. *Observer*. The authors also looked at 764 cases of people indicted for murder between 21 March 1957 and December 1962 – see *A Calendar of Murder* (1964) London. Michael Joseph.

3. Section 1(1) of the Murder (Abolition of Death Penalty) Act 1965. A person who commits murder whilst under the age of 18 will be ordered to be 'detained during Her Majesty's pleasure' – see section 53(1) Children and Young Persons Act 1933. This is similar to life imprisonment, though the offender is detained 'in such a place and under such circumstances as the Secretary of State may direct'.

4. Report of the Royal Commission on Capital Punishment 1949–1953. (1973) London. H.M.S.O., page 330.

5. The word 'adults' here indicates that the offender was aged at least 18 years at the time the offence was committed and was thus sentenced to life imprisonment.

6. This refers to those aged under 18 years at the date of the offence.

7. A further description of the Confidential Memorandum is given in chapter 5.

8. Two groups of offences were distinguished by Gibson – 'normal' murder and 'abnormal homicide'. The latter phrase referred to murders committed by those who were insane at the time, murders where the offender subsequently committed suicide, and offences carried out by people suffering from diminished responsibility under

section 2(1) Homicide Act 1957 and who were convicted of manslaughter. 'Normal' murder thus denotes all remaining murders falling
outside these categories.

9. Section 1(2) Murder (Abolition of Death Penalty) Act 1965.
10. That is, people who come within classes 1 and 2 of the Registrar
    General's Classification of occupations. These include doctors,
    teachers, nurses, company directors, shopkeepers who run their own
    businesses, and police officers.
11. In Great Britain, the number of people out of work were as follows:
    1978: 1 320 750
    1979: 1 234 000
    1980: 1 590 333
    1981: 2 422 416
    1982: 2 808 583
    See Central Statistical Office. Annual Abstract of Statistics. 1986
    edition. No. 122. London. H.M.S.O., page 116.
12. Home Office. Criminal Statistics in England and Wales (1986),
    London. H.M.S.O. Cm.233.
13. See Table 4.6 at page 66.
14. The figures in Table 2.5 exclude cases recorded in the Criminal
    Statistics as 'No suspect'.
15. The figures in Table 2.6 include cases for which there is no suspect
    currently recorded.
16. In 1980 there was an exceptionally high number of recorded homicides
    which occurred in fires.
17. This was a case of death by electrocution.
18. The number of deaths by shooting in 1980 is markedly lower than in
    other years between 1976 and 1986, during which time the proportion
    ranged from 6 to 11 per cent.
19. In Gibson's (1975) study, 64 out of the 97 victims of 'normal' murder
    committed in the course of theft or gain, (64.9 per cent), were male.
20. It was not possible to identify a specific time of day in one case where
    the defendant gradually poisoned his wife over a period of eight
    months.

3 Brief Sketches of the Cases

In the last chapter, an essentially numerical analysis of the data was given which sought to categorise the information in various ways. What follows is a series of very brief sketches of what happened in those cases which have not already been outlined. Each sketch is based on the facts as accepted by the court, though occasionally the arguments put forward by the prosecution and/or defence are also outlined. It is not practicable to provide full accounts of the proceedings, but the intention here is to demonstrate the broad range of incidents which resulted in a conviction for murder.

Case 1 The deceased, an 18-year-old single man, had been having an affair with the defendant's wife. The defendant admitted that he had gone to the victim's flat, but claimed that he had done so purely to frighten his victim and his wife. He said he had taken the gun with him for protection. He also admitted firing the gun, but maintained that this was a reflex action as the result of seeing the deceased's arm move. The defendant did not deny that he had previously planned to kill his wife and her parents, but he had abandoned the idea because it was impractical. The prosecution alleged that the killing – a shot through the head from a range of about 6 inches – was a calculated act of revenge and jealousy.

Case 2 The offence occurred as the result of an argument and a fight in a public street. The deceased, a 16-year-old lad, had a sexual relationship with the defendant's 13-year-old daughter. The defendant incorrectly thought the relationship had ended. One evening he and his wife met the deceased and his friends; they argued and fought, and the defendant stabbed his victim in the chest. Murder was denied on the grounds of either self-defence and/or provocation. The accused had complained to the police that the deceased would not leave his daughter alone, and his wife had wanted the deceased to be charged with raping her daughter (an allegation which the daughter supported), but no formal action had been taken.

Case 3 A man in his mid-30s was killed in his own cottage by two men who had set out to rob him. They thought he had £2000, though in the event they were unable to find the money. Death was caused by multiple stab wounds to the chest, and each defendant blamed the other for committing the fatal acts. They were only remotely acquainted with the deceased, whose cottage was adjacent to the engineering works where the defendants were employed. The trial judge recommended that at least 17 years imprisonment should be served.

Case 4   An unemployed 21-year-old man, known to be a heavy drinker and taking LSD, killed a chef. The defendant's landlady was a casual girl-friend of the deceased. He (the deceased) had been drinking very heavily and had been sent to the landlady's flat. There, it was alleged, he had been obstreporous and abusive, and had disturbed the defendant and his girl-friend. In consequence, an angry struggle took place, and the deceased was stabbed through the heart. The defendant denied liability for murder, claiming that death was accidental and that in any event he had been provoked.

Case 5   An unemployed man in his mid-20s admitted murdering a 38-year-old works manager. It seems they had met casually and that the defendant had been staying at his victim's house for a few days. Death was caused by blows to the deceased's head inflicted by a wooden lamp. The defendant claimed that he had struck out because of the deceased's homosexual advances to him. However, the prosecution alleged that the defendant was a known homo-sexual, though there was no evidence that this was true of the deceased. The police arrested the defendant after he had begun to use the deceased's cheque book only a day or so after the murder.

Case 6   A 74-year-old widow was killed in her own home by two young men who had gone to burgle her house. The deceased was previously unknown to her assailants, and she was killed by blows to her head and face with an axe. The second defendant admitted striking her but claimed that his co-accused had held her down and had also hit her. The co-accused admitted burglary but denied murder.

Case 7   The victim and some friends left a public house, merry but not drunk. The defendant, who was reasonably sober, left the pub soon afterwards, and subsequently overtook the victim. To his friends' amusement the victim began to mimic the defendant's walk. The prosecution alleged that the defendant then verbally challenged the deceased and a struggle ensued and the defendant stabbed his victim with a knife. The defendant claimed that the deceased had originally jumped on him and the two had then struggled. Himself wounded in the leg, the defendant went home and asked his wife to call the police. He admitted the fight but claimed that the deceased had attacked him first from behind and that he had responded purely in self-defence, and this was reflected in his plea at the trial.

Case 8 The murder in this case was the culmination of a history of friction between neighbours. Six months or so earlier the deceased had assaulted the defendant in the street. Then, one afternoon, the deceased's son told his mother that the defendant's cohabitee was going to sue them. There was a discussion between the mother and the defendant who then strapped a knife to his belt for self-protection. Towards the end of the afternoon, the deceased knocked on the defendant's door, and a scuffle broke out between them. The deceased returned home where he collapsed and subsequently died from stab wounds to the chest and stomach. Murder was denied because of provocation.

Case 9 A man killed his wife by hitting her and then manually strangling her. During the 18 months or so prior to the offence, the deceased had left her husband on three occasions and had returned each time. She had told their daughter that she feared that he might be violent towards her. She had had an affair with a younger man and it seems her husband was still jealous about that. After killing his wife in their home, the defendant gave himself up to the police, and confessed to them. He said she had planned to leave him once too often. He denied murder but pleaded guilty to manslaughter on the ground of his diminished responsibility.

Case 10 The defendant, a married man in his late 30s, and known to be a heavy drinker, met his victim, a woman in her late 50s, in a pub. They were both drunk, and they went back to her flat. In the early hours of the morning neighbours heard a woman shouting. Later on the defendant went to a police station and said that he had woken up that morning in a flat in bed with a dead woman. Subsequently, he admitted hitting her, having lost his temper and self-control, but he could not remember stabbing her. The prosecution alleged that they had had an argument during which the deceased had accused the defendant of not being 'man enough', and that this had prompted the fatal attack.

Case 12 The parties met in a pub about two or three hours before the offence occurred. The defendant told a friend that he had killed someone but the friend thought he was only joking. More friends were told and the defendant subsequently gave himself up to the police. He said that he had been picked up by the deceased who had offered him £15 for sex. He also said that he had masturbated the deceased who then refused to pay, at which point the defendant lost his temper, and strangled and stabbed the deceased with a carving knife. The offence occurred in the victim's flat. Again, a plea of guilty to manslaughter on the ground of diminished responsibility was rejected.

Case 13 A man killed his mother's common law husband. The defendant and his wife had lived next door to his mother and his victim for a short time before the offence. Both the defendant and his mother said that the deceased had been very violent on a number of previous occasions. He had beaten the defendant and his younger brother. One evening the defendant and victim went out drinking together. The defendant drank about twice his usual amount and he returned home with a swollen lip. He had had yet another argument with the deceased, who had threatened to kill his younger brother. This was the 'final straw', and he took a shotgun, went next door and shot his victim on the doorstep of his house. His mother phoned the police and he admitted the killing. A plea of guilty to manslaughter because of the deceased's provocation was rejected.

Case 14 A 91-year-old man was killed in his flat one evening, the apparent motive being robbery. The defendant was out of work and this was putting considerable strain on his marriage. He was a neighbour and well-known to his victim, and even had a key to the old man's flat. The police found the body and they discovered some notes which showed that the deceased suspected the defendant of stealing money from him. The defendant later confessed to the murder and also pleaded guilty to robbery.

Case 15 A soldier in his late 20s killed a woman a few years younger than himself, mainly by stabbing her in the chest and abdomen. They had met the previous year and he became infatuated with her. But she had affairs with other men and their relationship deteriorated. Whilst in her flat, they had an argument which developed into a struggle and whilst feelings on both sides were very high, he killed her. Murder was admitted in court.

Case 16 The defendant first met his victim about six months before the offence and they became homosexual lovers. Whilst in the defendant's bed-sitting room they had a row which became a fight, and the victim was stabbed through the heart. Friends of both of them contacted the police when they discovered the deceased was missing. The police found blood on the walls and carpet of the defendant's bed-sit. He admitted killing but claimed that the deceased had attacked him first with a knife. A plea of provocation was rejected. The defendant had got rid of the body too calculatingly – he burned the torso, cut off the head and part of one leg, and buried the rest.

Case 17 A man killed a 62-year-old sub-postmaster whilst carrying out a robbery. Death resulted from asphyxiation using a pillowcase. The girlfriend of a co-defendant told the police that her boyfriend knew someone who was responsible for a murder. The co-defendant admitted stealing a key to the alarm of the sub-post-office and giving it to the defendant and another co-accused. A shotgun was found in the defendant's flat along with other items from the robbery. The defendant admitted gagging his victim, but denied any malice aforethought.

Case 18 A man killed a 78-year-old widow whom he had met on two previous occasions. She had been interested in buying the house that belonged to the defendant's late father. The defendant sexually attacked his victim in her home. She resisted and in a panic he strangled her with her shawl and a wire ligature, so that she would not be able to identify him. Murder was admitted in court.

Case 19 There had been a feud between the families of the two parties for about 18 months or so before the murder took place. The defendant had been beaten about his face, the deceased had threatened to kill him, and they had driven cars at each other. One evening the two men were in a public house, each with their own group of friends. Both sides anticipated trouble, and the defendant got a knife from his car and returned to the pub. A fight broke out between them, each side claiming that it had been initiated by the other. The deceased was stabbed through the heart, in the pub doorway. The denial of liability for murder rested mainly on self-defence, though some provocation was also pleaded.

Case 20 The defendant formed a chapter of Hell's Angels which was resented by a rival chapter in the same vicinity. One evening the defendant and his co-accused discovered that a member of the rival chapter was in the area; they located him, took him to an alleyway, beat him up and threw him in a river. He died from drowning. The police were informed of what had happened by the defendant's girlfriend. At court, a plea of guilty to manslaughter because of a lack of malice aforethought was rejected.

Case 21 The two parties, both single men in their early 30s, lived together in a flat belonging to the defendant's aunt. The defendant claimed that the deceased had tried to rape his aunt and had then made homosexual advances to him. This caused the defendant to lose his temper and strike out. Death was caused by blows struck with a belt, together with punches and kicks. At the trial, the defendant denied inflicting the fatal injuries.

Case 22 An 86-year-old widow was killed by the young man who used to do her gardening. The attack took place at about midnight in her home. A cloth and 75p were stolen! Death resulted from strangulation by hand, and the deceased's cardigan. The defendant admitted liability for murder.

Case 23 A man and his younger brother got involved in a pub fight. Earlier in the evening the deceased and his wife had gone to the pub to celebrate their wedding. The two co-defendants went to the same pub and met a friend there. The defendant winked at a woman in the wedding party, but was asked to stop by the deceased's best man. The defendant was alleged to have kicked away the best man's chair, and a fight ensued, in the course of which the defendant punched and kicked the victim. He died from asphyxiation, having inhaled a lot of his own blood. The defendant's brother came to his aid because he was outnumbered by his opponents. Both were convicted of murder though they had denied the charge, partly on the ground of self-defence, and partly because of a lack of malice aforethought.

Case 24 One afternoon, whilst in a cafe, the defendant thought he was being mocked and ridiculed by a group of people including the deceased. Tempers rose but the defendant left. He returned with a friend about half an hour later allegedly to teach a lesson to those who had laughed at him. A fight took place outside the cafe, during which the defendant was seen to stab the deceased in the chest. At trial, he relied on self-defence.

Case 25 Two trials were needed in this case, because the first jury could not reach a verdict. The defendant, a heavy drinker and drug-user, had rowed with his wife the previous day and, whilst very distressed, had sought help from a psychiatric hospital. On the day of the murder, he and a friend had been drinking for more than seven hours. They were in a pub and were apparently very noisy and abusive. Various people, including the deceased, asked them to be quiet, but to no avail. The deceased then told them to 'belt up' and told the defendant he was 'pissed'. As they were about to leave the pub, the defendant smashed a soda syphon over the deceased's head. A few days later he went to the police station with his solicitor, admitted causing death, but denied malice aforethought.

Case 27 A young man killed his mother-in-law because she nagged him. Initially, he denied the offence, but later admitted killing her by hitting her over the head with a hammer and then stabbing her. He was unemployed, and he said the deceased had berated him for not being good enough for her daughter and not wanting to work for a living. As a result he lost his temper and struck out. The attack took place during the afternoon, in the deceased's kitchen. Manslaughter was pleaded by the defendant on the grounds of provocation and diminished responsibility.

Case 28 A young man manually strangled his seven-year-old niece in her bedroom. He had been drinking and had argued with his wife. He then went to his sister's (the deceased's mother's) house to discuss his marital problems, but she refused to talk to him. Suspicion fell on him when the results of forensic tests became known. The police discovered pubic hairs on his clothes which matched those found between the deceased's thighs. He subsequently admitted trying to have sexual intercourse with her, and putting his hand over her mouth so that she could not be heard. Apparently there was no psychiatric help available for him.

Case 29 A young man killed an elderly woman in a wash-house just up the road from where she lived. About half an hour after she was attacked, the GPO received an anonymous telephone call from a man asking for an ambulance to be sent to the scene of the crime, but the ambulance found no trace of any 'accident'. The police became suspicious of the defendant when they later discovered similarities between the woman's death and an incident about five months earlier when he had hit a tramp. Eventually, the defendant admitted killing the deceased. He said he had been aware that someone was creeping up on him and he had hit out at that person before realising who it was. At the trial, he denied assaulting her but admitted necrophilia with her dead body.

Case 30 A couple who had lived together for about three months before the offence had gone to a night club with a group of friends. The prosecution alleged that just after midnight the man pushed the woman down some stairs, and that she subsequently died from the injuries thereby incurred. The man denied assaulting her, claiming that she had fallen down the stairs, but this was not supported either by the medical evidence or the witnesses. It seems the defendant became very upset because the woman danced with other men.

Case 31 An unemployed man killed his former father-in-law in what appeared to be a motiveless crime. The offence occurred at about 11 p.m. in the deceased's home. The defendant was seen, less than half an hour later, by two police officers who noticed that he had blood on his hands. He admitted killing the deceased; his only explanation was, 'because I'm a lunatic'! A plea of diminished responsibility was rejected.

Case 32 After she called him 'queer', a man killed his former financée by hitting her about the head with an axe at about 4 o'clock in the morning in her home. Their relationship had ended just a few months earlier but the defendant continued to pester the deceased and had allegedly been violent towards her. The offence was witnessed by the deceased's son. The previous evening, her boyfriend had heard the defendant threatening to kill her. The defendant denied murder, seeming to rely on a mixture of provocation, lack of malice aforethought, and diminished responsibility. He said that when called 'queer', he had completely lost control of himself.

Case 33 Another man killed his former lover: this time he stabbed her in the chest with a screwdriver whilst they were in his flat. Whilst their relationship had lasted they had intermittently lived together. They were both described as very 'promiscuous'. In his statement the defendant said that the deceased, who was almost 20 years his senior, disliked his associations with women of his own age and had been violent to one of them. The prosecution alleged that the offence was the result of his jealousy at the fact that the deceased intended to marry another man. But the defence pleaded provocation on the basis that the deceased had initially attacked the accused with the screwdriver.

Case 34 Notwithstanding a plea of guilty to murder and various other crimes of violence the judge made a recommendation that at least 15 years imprisonment be served in this case. The parties had known each other for about 15 years and the defendant had worked part-time for the deceased for more than ten years. The offence occurred just after 4 p.m. in the deceased's workshop where it was alleged the defendant knew that large sums of money were kept. Initially, the police arrested another man for the murder, but he told them that the defendant had planned to rob the deceased and said the defendant had taken a gun from him on the day of the offence. The victim had been shot in the chest, and the workshop had then been set on fire.

Case 35 A man strangled a woman who was a friend of his and who had attended his wedding. The prosecution claimed that it was the result of a frenzied and perverted sexual attack, that took place in a country lane in the very early hours of the morning. The defendant pleaded provocation and lack of malice aforethought – he said that the deceased had wanted to have sex with him, that she had become hysterical and threatened to accuse him of rape. He panicked and killed her.

Case 36 Early one evening the victim left home to make her usual visit to her mother's house. Five hours or so later, the police found her body in a lane. The prosecution alleged that having returned from her mother's house at about 5.45 p.m. the deceased had rowed with her husband, accusing him of wasting petrol by coming to meet her at the bus stop. Their daughter said she heard them shouting at each other. Subsequently, the husband admitted killing his wife, though offering no specific explanation. Death was caused by strangulation by ligature. Murder was denied through lack of malice aforethought.

Case 37 Two young men were convicted of the murder of a third man outside a night club, in the early hours of the morning. The two defendants had gone to the club after the pubs closed, and they met the deceased. It seems there was a minor argument between the defendant and the deceased. The body was later found by a

14-year-old schoolboy at the site of a new railway station. The police questioned the co-defendant and he implicated the accused, who subsequently admitted killing the deceased though not intending to do so. Denying murder, the defendant said he lost his temper, hit and kicked the deceased and dropped him over a bridge.

Case 38 The two parties in this case were well-known to each other, having worked for the same firm. The deceased's wife had left him and moved in with the defendant. Shortly before the offence, the deceased and his wife began to attempt a reconciliation. At about 10.20 p.m. they went to the defendant's flat and told him of the reconciliation. Feeling ill, the wife went to the bathroom, leaving the two men alone together. When she returned she found that her husband was very unwell, and later saw the defendant removing her husband's body from the room. The corpse was discovered just before midday the next day. The defendant subsequently admitted strangling the deceased (with a clothes-line), because of his jealousy.

Case 39 The defendant's former wife was the sister-in-law of the deceased. By all accounts the defendant's divorce had not gone at all smoothly, and there was a history of 'aggravation' between the parties. The defendant had blamed the deceased and his family for not being allowed to see his son as he had wished. He went to the deceased's flat one evening, they argued, and he stabbed his victim several times in the chest and abdomen with a knife. The offence was witnessed by the deceased's wife. At the trial, murder was denied; the defendant claimed that the killing was accidental and that the deceased had lunged at him.

Case 40 A man in his early 20s killed the mother of one of his childhood friends. The defendant was burgling her house when she disturbed him and recognised who he was. He stabbed her and then strangled her with her cardigan. Murder was admitted.

Case 41 A few months before the offence, the victim travelled abroad to his birthplace and whilst he was away the defendant moved in with the victim's cohabitee. When he returned the victim was very upset and threatened the defendant on a number of occasions. In the early hours of one morning the victim came to the flat where the defendant lived with his (the victim's) former girlfriend, and refused to go away. Subsequently, there was a scuffle in the street outside, during which the defendant stabbed the victim. The defendant admitted the stabbing, but said that the victim had brought the knife, and he denied murder on the grounds that he had only acted in self-defence and that he had been badly provoked.

Case 42 The two parties were teenagers who had been to the same junior school but had attended separate secondary schools. About four months before the murder the defendant had been set upon by a group of youths, one of whom was believed to be the deceased. It was alleged that that caused the defendant to hold a grudge against the deceased, so that revenge was the motive for the murder. During the hours leading to it, the defendant and the deceased had been drinking heavily, with friends. The defendant later admitted to a friend that he had hit someone in a park, and the deceased's body was then discovered. The police alleged that the defendant confessed to killing for revenge, but at the trial the defendant said he could not remember making a confession. He denied acting with malice aforethought, and claimed that he had kicked out at the deceased in self-defence.

Case 43 A teenage apprentice bricklayer killed a 64-year-old widower in the early hours of the morning. The defendant was burgling his victim's home, after he had spent the evening at a discotheque where he had consumed several pints of beer. He was disturbed by the deceased and he struck out with a hammer – death was caused by multiple blows to the head. Murder was denied through lack of malice aforethought, on the basis that the defendant had reacted without thinking.

Case 44 A 17-year-old boy stabbed his girlfriend whom he had known for about four weeks. They had had sexual intercourse and at his trial the defendant said that the girl had laughed at him and indicated his lack of sexual prowess, and claimed that he could not satisfy her. In the hours before the offence, the defendant had been drinking in a pub with some friends and had been taking drugs. One of his friends said that the defendant had threatened to do something to the deceased because she was getting on his nerves, and that he had a knife. The offence took place just before midnight, near a canal bridge. Murder was denied because of the deceased's provocation.

Case 45 A 14-year-old boy, who had twice run away from home, pleaded guilty to the murder of an 81-year-old widower. About

6.30 p.m. the defendant was playing football near the deceased's house. He went to fetch the ball when it was kicked into the deceased's yard, and saw £5 on the table in the living room. The defendant entered the house and took the £5 note, but was disturbed by the deceased. He pushed his victim to the ground and hit him with a poker, before stabbing him with a pair of scissors. He then stole a wallet containing £85, collected the ball and left.

Case 46 Four defendants were being held in custody on remand awaiting trial in respect of other alleged offences. Their victim was also on remand charged with indecently assaulting a seven-year-old girl. It appears that within the cells the defendants held a 'mock trial' of the deceased, and hung him as a punishment. The prosecution argued that the hanging was planned, but the defendant resisted this, claiming that there had been no intent to kill and that the 'mock trial' had got out of hand.

Case 47 A taxi driver was shot in the neck at close range in his car just after 9 p.m. There were two defendants – a 16-year-old who was ordered to be detained during Her Majesty's pleasure and a man in his mid-20s whom the judge recommended should serve at least 25 years imprisonment. Each blamed the other for the shooting, though the judge apparently believed the younger defendant who had pleaded guilty to manslaughter on the ground that he had not expected any violence to be used. The motive was robbery.

Case 48 In an apparently motiveless crime, a student killed his 23-month-old brother. The victim had been taken to hospital suffering from a broken leg, broken arms, facial sores and bruises, about two months before the offences. The doctors were not convinced that these injuries were accidental, but no formal action was taken. The deceased was again taken to hospital after falling down some steps, with severe head injuries. When interviewed by the police, the defendant admitted hitting and kicking his baby brother, but at his trial he claimed he had only made these admissions as a result of threats of violence against him by the police.

Case 49 A woman who had attempted suicide, had a defective personality and who was said to be pathologically over-dependent on her mother, struck another woman over the head with a claw-hammer. Again, there was no obvious motive for the attack. A charge of theft was pending against her; she was finding it very difficult to get a job and she thought her mother was soon to die from cancer. The murder took place at about 9.30 a.m. in a shop where the victim worked. Liability for murder was denied at trial on the ground that she lacked malice aforethought. She admitted carrying out the attack, but claimed that she could recall nothing about it.

Case 51 An air hostess was killed whilst walking in a country park. Her killer had seen her on four previous occasions and had asked her out, but she had refused. On this occasion, he tried to have sexual intercourse with her, but she resisted. He became angry, knocked her to the ground, strangled her and then struck her about the head with a stone. Murder was admitted.

Case 52 A man and a woman, both in their 30s, were accused of murder in the course of a robbery. She was convicted of manslaughter and sentenced to four years' imprisonment. The two co-accused had been drinking in a pub and were heard to admit to being short of money. They saw their victim, a middle-aged man, enter the pub and it was alleged they decided to rob him. The offence occurred in an alleyway by a hotel at about 11 o'clock at night: the deceased was hit with a stone, and then strangled with a tie. Although he was alleged to have made a full confession to the police, the defendant denied this at his trial, claiming that the victim was still alive when he left him and that someone else must have killed him.

Case 54 A man killed his 'common law' wife in their flat by stabbing her. He was said to be educationally retarded, and had been drinking heavily. He may also have been taking drugs. Their relationship had been deteriorating, particularly as a result of his suspicions that she was having affairs with other men. He was anxious that his son should not be adversely affected by her 'promiscuous' behaviour. Murder was admitted at the trial.

Case 55 The defendant and his 'common law' wife, both said to be alcoholics, had a history of numerous violent arguments. Four days or so after she died, the defendant went to his doctor and told him that he could not waken his wife. They then went to the defendant's flat where they found her decomposed body. The defendant initially told the police that he had discovered his wife in that state on his return from work, though he later admitted that he had hit her. The prosecution alleged that both defendant and victim had been drinking, that they had had yet another violent quarrel and that he had repeatedly kicked her about the head. At trial, he pleaded guilty to manslaughter only, on the ground that he had lacked malice aforethought.

Case 56 About ten months or so before the murder, about 68 turkeys (valued about £500) had been stolen from his father's small-holding and the defendant was convinced that the deceased was involved in this theft. In an act of revenge, the defendant and his co-accused went to the deceased's caravan in the early hours one morning, and the defendant shot his victim from a range of about ten feet. The shooting was admitted but the defence argued that the gun had gone off accidentally – the accused had intended only to frighten.

Case 57 An 18-year-old man strangled a ten-year-old boy with a belt. The boy had noticed the defendant sitting on the doorstep with a dog, and he went over to stroke the dog. The boy was invited inside and they went into the defendant's bedroom. When the defendant began to interfere with him sexually, the boy struggled and screamed, and was thereupon strangled. They were not previously known to each other. At the trial, murder was admitted.

Case 58 All three parties in this case were prisoners in a Category B prison. The accused and his co-defendant were said to be homo-sexuals, and they were aggrieved at the fact that their victim had been convicted of raping a 13-year-old girl. The co-defendant was, at the time, serving a life-sentence for murdering a homosexual acquaintance and, as a result of this later offence, was given 15 years' imprisonment for manslaughter. They enticed the deceased into the co-defendant's cell and struck him over the head with a metal bed leg. Both admitted their responsibility at trial.

Case 59 The defendant, said to be a sexual psychopath, a 'A Walter Mitty' character, met his victim in a pub only two or three hours before the fatal attack. He repeatedly hit her over with a claw-hammer in the very early hours of the morning, after they had been drinking in the pub. The attack occurred by the gates to the engineering works where the defendant worked. He subsequently confessed to the police, not only his guilt for this offence but also for other attacks on women. At his trial, he denied murder, on the basis of his diminished responsibility.

Case 60 A man described as having a disturbed emotional development, killed a woman in what was thought to have been a drunken
quarrel. About 18 months before the murder, he met the victim's
sister and they periodically had sexual intercourse. After a year or
so he moved in with her, but they had a number of disputes, and
the relationship between the defendant and deceased was severely
strained. Less than a month before the murder, the deceased
attacked the defendant after a drunken argument. A week or so
later the victim's sister complained that she had been raped and
grievously injured by the defendant, though charges to this effect
were withdrawn. The events leading to the murder began when the
defendant took some librium tablets and then went out drinking.
He met the deceased in the pub and they left together at closing
time. Just before midnight they were seen in the street, apparently
in a very amorous mood. Thereafter, the prosecution alleged they
returned to her house, quarrelled, and the defendant stabbed her
and then set fire to the house. At trial, murder was denied on the
ground that the defendant was too drunk to have acted with malice
aforethought.

Case 61 In what was believed to be an intended robbery, two young
men killed a third man after they had all been to a discotheque at a
restaurant. The offence took place at about 1.30 or 2 o'clock in the
morning in the street not far from the deceased's home. He was
only very slightly acquainted with his attackers. The police said that
the defendants had admitted they had beaten the deceased about the
head with an iron bar. At the trial the co-accused, who was treated as
a psychopath, pleaded guilty to murder, but the defendant denied
guilt, saying that he had only helped to move the body.

Case 62 A man was killed shortly after 11.30 p.m. in or just outside
some public toilets. The two co-accused had been drinking with
friends in a pub. After leaving the pub they met the deceased in the
toilets where, according to the defendant, the deceased made homosexual advances to them. The accused lost his temper and struck out.
They kicked the victim, particularly about the head, from which he
later died. The co-defendant was sentenced to six years' imprisonment for manslaughter. The defendant denied murder on the grounds
of provocation and lack of malice aforethought.

Case 64 A man gave himself up to the police after manually
strangling his wife. Both had been drinking heavily and they began

to quarrel. The prosecution alleged that her husband had made excessive sexual demands on her and had been violent towards her. The defendant denied murder through lack of malice aforethought. He said he had been worried that his wife might leave him – she had compared his sexual prowess with that of a former lover. The offence occurred at about 4 a.m. in their flat.

Case 65 In a fit of temper, a young man killed the three-year-old daughter of his 'common law' wife. The deceased had been wetting and dirtying her bed and this had irritated and annoyed the defendant – he began to hit her – he said he could not help himself. It seems that on the relevant occasion he had been drinking, lost his temper and punched the little girl mainly about the head and face. He admitted the killing to the police but denied murder at trial, claiming that because of the stress he had been under, he had lacked malice aforethought.

Case 66 The defendant met the deceased in a pub one lunch time. They left the pub and moved on to a club where they continued drinking, and were later seen in an off-licence together. Thereafter they went to the victim's house when, according to the defendant, the victim made homosexual advances to him and in a fit of temper he strangled the deceased with a piece of cord. He then took a wallet and left. Initially, the defendant denied murder, but he changed his plea to one of guilty during the trial.

Case 67 A woman was stabbed twice in the chest by her former cohabitee. Just after lunch the defendant went to his victim's house. He left, but soon returned, and the parties were seen by a neighbour talking to each other. Screams were then heard from the deceased's house and a neighbour saw the defendant lying on the ground with blood stains on his clothing. On the way to hospital he said he had stabbed the victim because she did not love him anymore, and he had tried to burn both of them. He had been badly depressed and had become particularly upset when the deceased confirmed the failure of their relationship. At his trial, the defendant admitted manslaughter only because of his diminished responsibility.

Case 68 A man killed a 14-year-old girl who worked, in the evenings, at the same factory as he did. It was alleged that he had molested her on a number of previous occasions. The evidence suggested that she had been killed on factory premises at about 7 p.m. The prosecution claimed that the defendant strangled her and then drove out to the country and dumped her body in a lane and hit her several times with an axe. The defendant denied all responsibility saying that at the time he had been repairing his car, but this was not supported by forensic evidence which showed, for example, that woollen fibres on his clothing matched those on the deceased.

Case 69 In the early hours of the morning, a man killed his estranged wife by stabbing her several times in the throat with a kitchen knife. He drove to her home, and attacked her whilst she was in bed. Murder was denied on the basis of her provocation. The defendant said that his wife had taunted him by claiming that he was not the father of their children, and that he was still very upset by these taunts when he killed her.

Case 70 The defendant thought that his former 'common law' wife was having an affair with the deceased. A week or so before the murder the defendant confronted her about this and assaulted her. Three days later the defendant's flat was burgled, and he told the police that he suspected that the deceased was the burglar. The murder occurred just after 3.00 p.m. in the defendant's flat. He said that he thought the deceased had a gun and intended to kill him and had stabbed his victim in self-defence. The deceased had a reputation for being violent. But the prosecution alleged that the offence was an act of jealousy or revenge arising out of the ill-feeling between the parties over the defendant's former common law wife.

Case 71 The precise motive in this case was unclear. It was suggested that the murders were committed either while the defendant was attempting to obtain drugs or while he was under the influence of drugs or suffering from withdrawal symptoms. The victims were the wife and daughter of a restaurant proprietor: they were repeatedly stabbed, mainly in the neck and chest. The offences occurred at about 12.40 a.m. in the flat above the restaurant. At one time the defendant admitted carrying out the attacks but he later retracted this and denied any involvement in it at his trial.

Case 72 In the heat of an argument with her, a man killed his mother-in-law by suffocating her. It was suggested that shortly before the killing, he had been drinking quite heavily. In the early hours of the morning, the police received a 999 call indicating that there had been a burglary at the deceased's house. When they arrived a few minutes later they discovered her body. Subsequently, the defendant confessed to the killing, saying he had been 'riled' by his mother-in-law. At his trial he denied murder on the basis of a lack of malice aforethought.

Case 73 The offence took place at a party at the defendant's house. At about 2 a.m. the atmosphere was soured when the defendant had an argument with his wife, and this led to a scuffle. The victim, a man in his late 20s, tried to calm things down, but he was then stabbed by the defendant. When questioned by the police, the defendant initially claimed the deceased had accidentally fallen on some broken glass but he later admitted the stabbing. At trial, murder was denied on the ground of provocation.

Case 74 The defendant, an unemployed man in his mid-20s, killed another man, of similar age, in what appears to have been a robbery that 'went wrong'. The parties were acquainted with each other, though they could not be described as friends. The defendant knew that the deceased would have money on him because it was 'pay day'. Just before midnight the defendant struck the victim over the head with a brick: the attack occurred on a garage site. Articles belonging to the deceased were later found in the defendant's house. Liability for murder was admitted.

Case 75 A man was recommended to serve at least 15 years imprisonment for killing a 16-year-old girl. Whilst on his way to work one morning, he accosted her in the street. He 'fancied' her but she rejected his advances. He said he had intended to have sexual intercourse with her. (His wife was pregnant and was not able to have sex.) On being rejected he lost his temper and strangled her. He then stole some money from her and dragged her body into a river. At his trial, the defendant admitted murder.

Case 76 The defendant met his female victim in a pub one evening, and they both consumed considerable quantities of alcohol. In the early hours of the morning they took a taxi to the defendant's lodgings. There was no apparent motive for what subsequently happened. The defendant assaulted her and then stabbed her in the chest and dumped her body in a dustbin. Although he admitted killing the deceased the defendant denied liability for murder on the ground of diminished responsibility.

Case 78: One afternoon, an 83-year-old widow was killed in her flat. A plastic bag was placed over her head and she was manually strangled. The defendant's mother was the warden of the flats where the deceased lived, and through her information was acquired that made the deceased a potential victim of robbery. The defendant and his female co-accused (who was also convicted of murder and robbery), broke into the flat but they unexpectedly encountered the deceased. She screamed, and they killed her. Murder was denied because of lack of malice aforethought.

Case 79 Although the deceased had obtained a judicial separation order against her husband, they still lived in the same house. He was described as an alcoholic, and their relationship had also been fraught with money problems. At about midnight, he shot her in the head whilst she was in bed. He did not deny that he had murdered her.

Case 80 A man killed his homosexual lover by repeatedly stabbing him in the chest and abdomen with a flick-knife. The offence took place in their bed-sit one evening. The defendant denied acting with malice aforethought and also pleaded provocation. The victim had called him a 'bastard' and, said the defendant, attacked him first. Although there was evidence of provocation, it seems that the defendant had retaliated in an unreasonably violent fashion.

Case 81 A woman died as the result of being beaten about the head with a pick-axe handle by her husband. Their marriage had obviously deteriorated as the result of a number of problems, including a shortage of money and his heavy drinking. They had a very heated argument one morning, largely about the defendant's wish to install his mistress, whom he thought was pregnant by him, in a flat. The police said the defendant admitted that he had planned the offence, and he pleaded guilty to murder at his trial.

Case 82 The parties first met about seven months before the murder took place, buying and selling various commodities, including guns and houses. One evening, whilst they were at the defendant's farm, they argued when the defendant accused the deceased of cheating him in a particular deal. The argument led to a fight, and the defendant shot his victim six times from close range.

Case 83 Two young men were convicted of murdering an older man by repeatedly stabbing him. The three of them met in a cafe at about 3 o'clock one morning, and they went back to the deceased's house where they drank and took drugs. The prosecution alleged the two defendants decided to rob their victim, who was a homosexual. The defendant engaged the deceased in 'love play' and the co-accused stabbed him in the back. They both then stabbed him several times. At their trial, each defendant blamed the other.

Case 84 The defendant and deceased ran rival mini-cab businesses. Three years or so before the murder, the defendant was employed by the deceased as a mini-cab driver, but after about 12 months he left and set up his own business. Thereafter, there was constant aggravation between them, trying to steal each other's customers and drivers. The deceased thought the defendant was blocking his radio frequency and he went (with his wife) to the defendant's office to confront him about it. They had a heated discussion which led to a scuffle in the street and the deceased was stabbed in the chest. The defendant helped to take him to hospital, but he later died. At his trial, the defendant denied murder, saying that the stabbing was accidental.

Case 85 A man killed the husband of a woman (the co-accused) with whom he was having an affair. The deceased and co-accused were alcoholics, and the defendant was a 'reformed' alcoholic, who did voluntary work for alcoholics. He had volunteered to help the deceased and his wife, and he subsequently formed a romantic relationship with her. The defendant was upset by the fact that the deceased assaulted his wife when he was drunk. It was also believed that, having suspected his wife was having an affair, the deceased threatened her with a large kitchen knife. Early one evening, the defendant went to the deceased's house and found the co-accused in a distressed state. It seems that the defendant then lost his temper and struck the deceased with a club-hammer before handing it to his co-accused who 'finished her husband off'. The defendant denied murder at the trial, and his co-accused was convicted of manslaughter on the ground of her diminished responsibility.

Case 86 Just before 1.30 a.m. the defendant, an unemployed man in his early 20s, was beaten up outside a discotheque. He went home, collected a gun, and returned to the discotheque. He and his co-accused thought that the deceased was responsible for the assault and they followed him when he drove off. In revenge for the assault, the defendant shot the deceased and was then driven away by his co-accused. The defendant denied murder because he had been too drunk to have acted with malice aforethought. His co-accused was convicted of manslaughter.

Case 87   Having been asked whether he had stolen £51 from her purse, the defendant hit his victim – a 70-year-old widow – over the head with an iron bar and then strangled her with a scarf. The defendant, an unemployed man in his late 20s, had been a friend of the old lady for some months. But when challenged about stealing from her, he lost control of himself and attacked her. He did not deny murdering her.

Case 88 The defendant, a man in his mid-20s, was unemployed, as was his victim, a woman in her early 50s. They had first met in a pub about six weeks before the murder occurred. The defendant and his girlfriend visited the deceased's house late one afternoon, and they all drank cider. Having decided to steal some money from the gas and electricity meters, the defendant sent his girlfriend out to get some more cider, and whilst she was gone he attacked his victim so that there would be no witnesses to his theft. He strangled her with a scarf. Murder was admitted.

Case 89 A man killed his former 'common law' wife. They had lived together as man and wife for about five years, but she left him the day before they were to be married. This happened about eight months before she was killed. Nevertheless, she still visited him and slept with him. Early one afternoon, they argued, mainly because he thought that she wanted to terminate their relationship completely. In a fit of temper he strangled her with a pair of tights. The defendant admitted the killing, but pleaded provocation.

Case 90 Having spent the evening drinking, the two defendants, both young men, decided to commit a burglary. They broke into the victim's home and attacked her whilst she was in her bed, and made off with £500 and two bottles of brandy. The deceased, an 89-year-old widow, was punched in the face and died from shock and inhaling her own blood. The defendant pleaded guilty to murder, and his slightly younger co-accused was convicted of burglary.

Case 91 The marriage between the defendant and his victim had deteriorated considerably. She had obtained a judicial separation order from him and had obtained a non-molestation order against him. After they separated, she had custody of the children, though the defendant was given access to them. As the result of his behaviour towards the eldest daughter, his wife wanted to prevent the defendant from seeing her, at least for a time. The defendant thereupon decided to confront his wife about the situation, which was complicated by the fact that he was jealous and suspected her infidelity. He attacked her whilst she was in bed, stabbing her in the abdomen. He gave himself up to the police about an hour later. Murder was denied, firstly because he said he lacked malice aforethought, and secondly on the ground that he had not caused his wife's death. She had been taken to hospital and put on a life-support machine. After various tests were carried out, the machine was disconnected and the wife was pronounced dead. The defendant argued that death was caused by switching off the machine, and not by his assault on her.

Case 92 A teenager was ordered to be detained during Her Majesty's pleasure, for the murder of a complete stranger. A street fight broke out in the early hours of the morning after provocative and threatening words had been exchanged between two groups of young men. One youth was seen to lunge at the deceased who died from stab wounds to the neck inflicted with broken glass. The defendant admitted being involved in the affray, and the police said he had confessed to the murder. At his trial, he denied stabbing the deceased and claimed that he had only confessed because the police had persuaded him that it would be in his best interests to do so.

Case 93 A teenage schoolboy was shot in the head when, it was alleged, he disturbed four men who were burgling a farmhouse. Two defendants were given recommendations of at least 25 years imprisonment, one was ordered to be detained during Her Majesty's pleasure (all for murder), and the fourth was sentenced to 12 years for manslaughter. Liability for the offence was denied by the defendants.

Case 94 An unemployed teenager, from a broken home and said to have a drink problem, stabbed a man of 60 years of age in the street outside the deceased's flat. The defendant had intended to rob his victim, but the old man resisted and a struggle ensued between them. A plea of not guilty to murder on the basis of lack of malice aforethought was entered by the defendant.

Case 95 The defendant and deceased, both teenage youths, met in a pub. They argued when the defendant would not let his victim borrow his bike. In the course of the argument the defendant was seen to snatch the victim's knife. The deceased punched the defendant and then ran off with the defendant in pursuit. At about 10.30 p.m. the defendant paid his victim for the knife and they were seen to go into an alley 'to settle things'. The prosecution alleged that the defendant then stabbed the deceased and made off. At his trial, the defendant said that he had been provoked and attacked by his victim and that he had only acted in self-defence.

Case 96 A middle-aged man was stabbed in the stomach by a teenager who, with two other youths, was carrying out a robbery. (The other two were convicted of manslaughter and robbery.) The offence took place in the victim's shop at about 6.40 p.m. The deceased resisted the robbery, and tried to prevent the defendant from getting away. They struggled and the defendant stabbed him whilst trying to make good his escape. Murder was denied because of an absence of malice aforethought.

Case 97 A middle-aged woman was shot in the head by a youth who was a friend of her son. Again the offence was the result of an intended robbery which had 'gone wrong'. The defendant said that he had taken the gun solely to frighten her and that it had gone off accidentally.

Case 98 A teenager, described as a heavy drinker, stabbed his victim in the chest. Yet again, the motive was robbery, and the defendant claimed that the killing was unintended. It only happened because the deceased resisted the robbery and the defendant panicked in his efforts to get away. The victim was a man in his mid-20s, a complete stranger to his attacker. The offence occurred at about 11.30 p.m. in the street. A co-defendant was acquitted of manslaughter.

Case 100 After a heated argument, a woman killed her 14-year-old son by stabbing him in the face and chest. When she discovered that he was in trouble with the police, the defendant lost her self-control, and struck out. She pleaded provocation at her trial.

Case 102 The defendant had been drinking heavily and he had gone to his victim's house because he was interested in buying his scooter. The two parties were bare acquaintances in that the defendant had known the deceased's late son. In the event they argued about whether the scooter needed a de-coke, and in the heat of the moment the defendant stabbed the deceased through the heart. He later went to the police and made a full confession.

Case 103 This case might be described as a crime of passion. A young man killed his former girlfriend in what seems to have been an act of jealousy. She had ended their relationship only about a week before the offence, and she resumed a former relationship with a man who was the natural father of her illegitimate child. After drinking a couple of pints of beer, the defendant went to her house and shot her and her new boyfriend. Fortunately, the boyfriend lived.

Case 104 The defendant was an unemployed man in his late 20s, and the victim was a retired man of 67. They were both said to be homosexual, and had known each other for 13 or 14 years. Indeed, they had lived together on one or two occasions. The deceased became very jealous when the defendant announced his plans to remarry, and threatened to tell the defendant's finacée of his homosexual past. One evening, at the deceased's house, they had an argument about the situation and the defendant in effect suffocated the old man. The defendant denied acting with malice aforethought, intending only to incapacitate.

Case 105 A man killed his cohabitee just after midnight, after they had had a row. Initially, the defendant told the police that the woman had been assaulted by her husband, but fortunately at that stage she was still alive and able to tell the police that this was not true. The police said that a few hours later the defendant admitted making the attack and claimed that she had refused to leave when he had asked her to do so. At the trial the defendant again denied attacking the deceased and said her husband had visited their flat and killed her. Death was caused by stab wounds to the chest and stomach.

Case 106 A middle-aged man out of work and described as a psychopath and chronic alcoholic, stabbed his landlord. They had both been drinking during the evening, and they had an argument about food and the state of the house. The deceased told the defendant to leave. The latter thereupon picked up a knife, took a swipe at the deceased's dog, missed and stabbed the deceased in the stomach instead. The deceased and his dog left the room, followed by the defendant and they went out into the street where the defendant inflicted a second, and fatal stab wound on his landlord. Just after a week later, the defendant gave himself up to the police. He admitted losing his temper but said he could not remember the second stabbing. Murder was denied on the grounds of provocation and an absence of malice aforethought.

Case 107 A woman was strangled with the cord from her dressing-gown by the man with whom she had had a casual relationship for about six months. The offence, which took place in her flat, occurred – according to the defendant – after she had had a tantrum and they had quarrelled with one another. He admitted killing her, but said that it happened in the heat of the moment. A plea of guilty to manslaughter on the ground of diminished responsibility was entered at the trial.

Case 108 The parties were both men in their early/mid-20s and had worked for the defendant's brother-in-law. They had disliked each other for some time. The offence arose during a party, as the result of an argument between defendant and deceased. The argument led to a fight and the defendant inflicted multiple stab wounds on the deceased. This was said to be in retaliation against the deceased who was trying to gore the defendant's good eye. At the trial, the defence claimed that death was accidental, there had been no intention to kill, and that in any event the accused had been severely provoked.

Case 109 This was the one 'terrorist murder'. A man in his mid-20s, ostensibly a language student, shot a journalist who shared the same nationality as his attacker. The offence occurred in the street, just after lunchtime, and the deceased was shot from close range. The defendant and his co-accused both pleaded guilty to murder.

Case 110 In the early hours of the morning, on their way home from a nightclub, the defendant and his two co-accused mistook four young men for people with whom they had argued. They set upon them with large spirit-levels and a brick hod. The victim was a man in his mid-20s who turned out to be a total stranger to the defendants. At the trial, each defendant, denied making the attack.

Case 111 A man and his two sons were convicted of murder. They had spent the afternoon drinking and had had an argument with their victim, a man of 50 years of age. The argument subsided and the defendants pretended to resume their previous cordial relationship with the deceased. They gave him a lift to a greyhound race-track, but on the way they stopped, punched and kicked him and then stabbed him in the chest and abdomen. The defendant and one of his sons blamed the other son for the stabbing, but he said he had no recollection of what had happened.

Case 112 An unemployed man and his two co-accused obtained entry to a flat by posing as police officers. Their intention was to rob the occupants. The man who lived in the flat was hit over the head with a replica revolver by one of the co-accused and that prompted his wife (who was aged 61) to attack the defendant. They struggled and she was shot in the chest. The defendant denied liability for murder on the ground that he was too drunk to have fully appreciated what he was doing – he had consumed a large quantity of alcohol and had taken other drugs.

Case 113 A man shot a 70-year-old farmer whom he had described as his best friend and for whom he and his wife had worked (on a casual basis) for some years. The defendant and his wife went to the deceased's home one evening so that the wife could do some clerical work. They had been drinking during the evening, and the defendant then left the room, only to return shortly afterwards with a shotgun. He shot his victim from a range of only two or three feet; the offence probably occurred just before midnight. When questioned by the police, and at his trial, the defendant said he could not remember the shooting because of the effect of the alcohol. There was no apparent motive for the crime.

Case 114 Two months or so before the murder took place, two of the three co-defendants were thought to have conspired to steal a consignment of goods from a vehicle driven by the deceased. The deceased was subsequently arrested by the police in connection with the theft and he implicated one of the co-defendants. Early one afternoon two co-defendants took the deceased to a derelict hut in a deserted docklands area where they beat and stabbed him to death. The third co-defendant was accused of assisting them after they had committed the murder. At their trial, the two alleged murderers each blamed the other for carrying out the fatal assault. The obvious motive was revenge.

Case 115 A man killed his estranged wife, stabbing her mainly in the head, neck and chest. They had separated about five months earlier, and she had obtained an injunction excluding him from the matrimonial home. The defendant became jealous when he suspected that his wife was having affairs with other men. It was alleged that he hid in an outhouse for some 12 hours and when his wife came out of the house he chased her up the garden path and stabbed her. At his trial, he pleaded diminished responsibility based on his emotional jealousy.

Case 118 The victim in this case was the defendant's seven-month-old son. The conditions in which the young defendant and his 'common law' wife were living were undeniably very stressful. During the months leading up to the offence he had found it increasingly difficult to cope with the situation, a predicament which had only been exacerbated by the baby's persistent crying. One evening, he lost his temper and struck the little boy. He called for an ambulance, but the child died on the way to hospital. The prosecution alleged that he swung the baby by his legs, causing him to hit his head against a hard surface. The defendant denied this, but admitted punching him twice. Liability for murder was denied at the trial, on the ground that he had not acted with malice aforethought.

Case 119 About a month before the murder took place, the deceased's elder son unexpectedly disappeared along with the defendant's sister. The deceased's family were accused of encouraging the relationship between them by the accused and his family. In what was clearly regarded by the prosecution as an act of revenge, the defendant repeatedly stabbed his victim in the chest and abdomen about 8 o'clock one morning, in the street. Responsibility for the killing was denied throughout the investigation and trial, but the judge recommended that at least 18 years imprisonment should be served before the defendant's release.

Case 121 A man who had been working on the central heating system in his victim's home, killed a 50-year-old woman by hitting her over the head with a cosh and a 2 lb weight. The offence occurred when she returned from work, just after 2 p.m. The defendant was described as being depressed, in debt and had been sleeping rough. The motive for the attack was money, which he took from the deceased's handbag. At his trial, he admitted burglary, but denied murder. He said he had panicked and had not acted with malice aforethought.

Case 122 As a result of an argument, a man killed his mother's 'common law' husband, at about 8 o'clock one evening. The defendant initially argued with his mother whom he thought had been 'picking on' his sister. The deceased intervened, to support his cohabitee, which led to his quarrel with the defendant. They fought each other, the defendant knocked his victim to the ground and kicked him about the head. At the trial, murder was denied on the ground of the deceased's provocation.

Case 123 The defendant was a young man in his early 20s who shared the same lodging as the deceased, a 71-year-old pensioner. Having spent the evening drinking quite heavily, the defendant was approached by the old man who made homosexual advances to him. This caused the defendant to lose his temper and he struck his victim about the head and then stabbed him. Again, responsibility for murder was denied because of the deceased's provocation.

Case 124 The deceased, a 16-year-old girl, was a friend of the defendant's girlfriend. She was walking home one evening, at about 10.15 to 10.30 p.m., along a footpath in a field when she met him. He questioned her about his girlfriend whom he suspected was seeing other young men. He became very angry and grabbed her around her throat, which caused her to collapse. The defendant panicked and bundled her over a fence into a ditch where she subsequently drowned. At the trial, the prosecution rejected the defendant's plea of guilty to manslaughter because of a lack of malice aforethought.

Case 125 An unemployed man in his mid-20s was convicted of murdering his father. The defendant was described as a heavy drinker who had attempted suicide on six occasions and was in need of psychiatric treatment. His father, said to be mentally defective, was regarded as a strict disciplinarian who had beaten his wife and children. The relationship between the parties predictably had been very poor, and the prosecution claimed that the defendant had been obsessed with the idea of killing his father. The defence said that after arguing with his brother, the defendant was followed by his father who grabbed him around the throat. The defendant then got a knife from the kitchen and stabbed his father once in the abdomen. A plea of diminished responsibility was made at the trial.

Case 126 Another unemployed man, in his late 20s, killed a woman of similar age, in the early hours of the morning. They both lived in bed-sits in the same building, and had known each other for about three years. The defendant visited the woman in her room, and thought she wanted to have sexual intercourse with him. But she rejected his advances and he was overcome with what was described as a 'sexual frenzy' and he manually strangled her. He had drunk a considerable amount of alcohol during the hours preceding the attack. Liability for murder was admitted by the defence.

Case 127 The three defendants in this case consisted of two young men and a middle-aged woman. The victim was a night-watchman of a building site, in his mid-60s, a former lover of the woman. At her suggestion, the two men went to the building site to carry out a robbery. Both of them had been drinking during the evening prior to the offence, which occurred between 11.30 p.m. and midnight. They hit the night-watchman several times over the head with a brick, and stole £191. They denied murder because of a lack of malice aforethought.

Case 128 The defendant, unemployed, in his early 30s, was described as a heavy drinker. He killed one of his drinking companions, a middle-aged man, after they had a drunken quarrel about money. The offence seems to have taken place just before midnight, in the defendant's flat – apparently, the deceased had been staying there with him. Death was caused by a number of stab wounds mainly in the chest and back. At his trial, the defendant sought to rely on the deceased's provocation.

Case 129 In what was clearly a burglary that had 'gone wrong', a man killed an elderly widow by hitting her over the head with an iron bar and strangling her with a ligature. The defendant, who was unemployed at the time, broke into the house but was disturbed by the old lady. In his panic, he attacked her and then set fire to the house to try to conceal what had happened. The offence occurred at about 11 o'clock in the morning. At the trial, the defendant admitted the burglary, but denied both murder and arson.

Case 130 The deceased, a man in his late 20s, had been staying with the defendant, who was of a similar age. They carried out three burglaries together, but early one morning they had a fierce argument about a post office robbery. This culminated in the defendant hitting the deceased several times over the head with a hammer. The offence came to light after the defendant took his victim (who was then still alive) to the hospital, and an ambulance driver contacted the police. Again, murder was denied at the trial; the defendant relied on his victim's provocation.

Case 131 The defendant returned home quite late at night, having spent much of the evening drinking. His cohabitee, a widow in her mid-60s, told him to leave, and this led to a heated argument. He put her into a bath of scalding hot water and hit her about the head with a bottle. The following morning, the defendant went to the police station and told them that he had found his cohabitee dead at their home. But he could not give the police satisfactory explanations about the bloodstains and hair in the bath; and later admitted the killing. At his trial, the defendant denied murder on the basis of his intoxication.

Case 132 There was no obvious motive for the murder in this case. The defendant was one of a number of football supporters, at an away fixture. On the way to the match, he made what appeared to be an unprovoked attack on a group of supporters of the home team. The offence occurred at about 7.30 p.m. in the street. The defendant, who had been drinking, stabbed the deceased several times in the chest. The police said that he admitted carrying out the attack, but at his trial the defendant said that he had not acted with malice aforethought.

Case 133 A man killed his former cohabitee by stabbing her in the chest with a bayonet. They had separated about six weeks previously, but the defendant was jealous of the men with whom he thought she was associating. One evening, they were both in a public house and he followed her upstairs and then carried out the fatal attack. He confessed to the killing when questioned by the police, but denied murder at his trial on the ground of diminished responsibility.

Case 134 The two defendants, men in their mid-20s, both received recommendations that they should serve a minimum of 15 years imprisonment. One of them thought he had been deceived into giving the deceased some money, for which they decided to take revenge. In the early hours of the morning, they attacked him in the street, and struck him over the head with a piece of scaffolding pipe. At their trial, they each blamed the other for carrying out the assault, but both were convicted of murder and robbery.

Case 135 This case also occurred in the early hours of the morning, in the street, when two groups of people who had been at separate

New Year parties, began to fight with one another. Those concerned were mainly in their 30s, and it is not clear what had initially caused them to fight. The defence said that the fatal attack was in response to an assault on a woman who was at the defendant's party. Two men were charged with murder, on the basis that they had struck the deceased with a carlock and kicked him about the head. One defendant denied any involvement in this attack, while the other admitted hitting the deceased but insisted that he had not killed him.

Case 136 The murder in this case was only discovered when the defendant, who was serving a ten-year sentence for robbery, decided to 'make a clean breast of things'. He admitted that about four years previously he had been hired to carry out what is often called a 'contract killing'. His victim was a man who was a well known member of the criminal underworld and was believed to have been involved in an unlawful homicide. The defendant shot him in the chest, in the street.

Case 137 The two defendants, both men in their early 20s, met their victim only a few minutes before he was killed. An argument occurred between them, which was initiated by the defendant's verbal abuse. Tempers were lost and a fight ensued, during which the victim was beaten and kicked to death. This happened at about 2 o'clock in the morning, in a public car park. The defendant denied murder on the grounds that he had been provoked and had not acted with malice aforethought. His co-accused was acquitted of manslaughter.

Case 139 A young woman accused her husband of having an affair with another woman, and they began to argue about it. They then went for a walk, the argument was resumed and he assaulted her. He hit her over the head with a metal bar. The offence occurred just before 7.30 in the evening. The defendant said that his wife had attacked him first by trying to knee him in the groin, and this had precipitated his fatal assault on her. He pleaded provocation at his trial.

Case 140 Both parties were men in their early 40s. They were known to one another, but could not be described as friends. After drinking throughout the evening in a pub, they had an argument when the defendant accused the deceased of maltreating him. The argument led to a fight, in the course of which the defendant stabbed his victim in the chest. This happened at about 10.30 p.m. At his trial, the defendant denied murder, on the grounds of provocation and self-defence, but there seems to have been no other evidence to corroborate his claim that the deceased had attacked him first.

Case 141 The defendant, a man in his early 20s, was a friend of his victim and her husband. One morning, he was talking to her, in her home, about his financial problems and he thought that she was nagging him unjustly, and blaming him for his difficulties. It seems that he became so annoyed and angry at this that he attacked her, hitting her with a poker and stabbing her in the chest. He admitted his liability for murder.

Case 142 A teenage boy admitted murdering his grandfather who lived next door to him. Apparently, they argued with one another, and the boy lost his temper, and stabbed his grandfather with a pair of scissors. The offence took place at about 5.30 p.m. in the deceased's house.

Case 143 Defendant and victim in this case were both sixth-formers at the same school. Their families were members of the same religious sect, but there was a fierce political division within the sect and the defendant said that his family had been physically attacked and intimidated by those who adopted opposing views. He said he carried a knife with him because he fully expected to be attacked himself. He was confronted by the deceased and other boys one lunch time, on a football pitch at their school, and he slashed his victim in the stomach. He then telephoned the police and told them what had happened. At his trial, his main plea was one of provocation, though occasionally he seemed to be saying that he acted in self-defence.

Case 144 This offence arose out of an affray at a discotheque. The defendant was an unemployed teenager, and his victim was a polytechnic student. Both had been drinking considerable amounts of alcohol. The deceased was said to have poked fun at the defendant who reacted angrily, and a scuffle broke out between them. Death was caused by a stab wound to the heart. The assault took place just after midnight, in one of the polytechnic buildings. The defendant denied inflicting the fatal wound, though he admitted 'stabbing' the deceased with a mouth organ.

Case 145 The three defendants, two in their mid-20s and one teenager, were male prostitutes, and their victim, an unemployed man in his early 20s, was a homosexual. He refused to pay them for their services. They argued and fought, and they hit him about the head with some sort of blunt instrument. This occurred at about one o'clock in the morning, in the street. Each defendant blamed the others, but they were all convicted of murder.

Case 147 The two defendants, teenage boys, said their victim, a middle-aged man, had offered them money in return for homosexual favours. They followed him to a wood, where they intended to rob him. He made homosexual advances to them, whereupon they attacked him with sticks and a brick. This happened at about 4.15 in the afternoon. Both defendants denied acting with malice aforethought, but both were convicted of murder.

Case 148 Whilst on his way to work one morning, the defendant accosted a woman whom he knew only by sight and forced her into her house. He took her into a bedroom, intending to have sexual intercourse with her. She told him that this was impossible because she was pregnant. At that point he began to leave, but he became frightened that she would report what had happened to the police and so he stabbed her repeatedly with a knife. He denied murder on the ground of diminished responsibility, but was convicted and ordered to be detained during Her Majesty's pleasure.

Case 149 In what was quite evidently an act of jealousy, a young woman killed her husband's mistress, by stabbing her with a bread knife. The prosecution case was that the defendant had deliberately set out to kill her victim. The attack took place at about 7.15 in the evening, in the street outside the deceased's house. At her trial, the defendant pleaded self-defence, though it seems that during the hearing the main issue was whether or not she had been provoked to kill. She alleged that after she had confronted the victim, there was an argument and a struggle between them, in the course of which the fatal wound was inflicted.

Case 150 A woman, her cohabitee (and co-defendant), and her former cohabitee (the victim), lived in the same flat. They had all been drinking during the course of the evening. In the early hours of the following morning, an argument occurred between the woman and the deceased. The co-defendant entered the room and, thinking that the deceased was about to attack his cohabitee, he stabbed him with a fork in the neck and face, and punched and kicked him. Then both defendants pushed the deceased over the edge of a fire-escape. At their trial they denied being guilty of murder. The woman said that because of the effect of the alcohol she had consumed, she did not act with malice aforethought. Her co-defendant sought to rely on self-defence. Both were convicted.

Case 152 A young man admitted murdering an elderly lady early one evening in her house. He knew her quite well, having carried out some repairs to her house and performed various odd jobs for her. He and his wife also visited the old lady socially. It seems that he lost his temper when she refused to lend him £10. He pushed her down, threw a bottle at her and hit her with a poker. The defendant then bent the poker but could not strangle her with it, so he pushed a metal fire-place against her throat with his foot.

Case 153 This case is quite similar to the previous one in some respects. A young man killed an elderly widower by stabbing him in the chest. The two were acquainted with one another, and the offence occurred when the defendant visited the old man one afternoon, in order to borrow some money. An argument ensued between them, in the course of which the fatal wounds were inflicted. The defendant gave himself up to the police just over 24 hours later. At his trial, he sought to rely on the deceased's provocation and, in any event, he denied acting with malice aforethought.

Case 156 Although the defendant had done some work for him, the deceased was not satisfied with the quality of the workmanship and refused to pay the bill. One morning, the defendant went to the deceased's workplace, only to find that he was not there. But he bound and gagged the deceased's clerk and locked him in the toilet. The clerk subsequently heard the deceased arrive, and the defendant threatened to kill him (the deceased) and set fire to the premises. Death was caused by gagging the victim, which the defendant admitted to the police. At his trial, however, he denied responsibility for the offence.

Case 157 The defendant was a young unemployed man who had been drinking heavily on the evening of the offence. He and his friends left the pub and attacked the victim, an 18-year-old man who was a complete stranger, in the street. The defendant stabbed him in the back while he was lying on the ground and stole a wallet from the deceased's friend. At his trial, the defendant denied murder because of his intoxication. He said that he had only confessed to the police because one of his friends had told him that he had stabbed the deceased – he had no recollection of what happened.

Case 158 Both in the early 20s, the defendant was a soldier, home on leave, and the deceased was unemployed. They met in a pub one evening, and the defendant offered the deceased a bed for the night. In the early hours of the following morning, the defendant woke to find his victim standing by his (the defendant's) bed with the defendant's wallet in his hand. He immediately seized the deceased and manually strangled him. Very soon afterwards, he contacted his superior officer in the army and the police, and told them what had happened. He later said that he had also suspected that the deceased was about to make a homosexual advance to him before he was killed. At his trial, the defendant sought to rely on provocation to reduce the offence to manslaughter. He said he had buggered the deceased who then threatened to blackmail him.

Case 159 An unemployed man in his mid-20s killed an elderly lady for whom he had carried out various domestic jobs in the previous months. It seems that she thought he had stolen more than £2000 from her and she threatened to tell the police about her suspicions. They argued and he killed her. He hit her on the head with a hammer and then suffocated her. Having killed her, the defendant hid her body under the floorboards of her house. The body remained there for about four months. At this trial, the defendant did not deny his liability for murder.

Case 160 Two men were charged with the murder of a man in his early 60s. Both defendants were heavy drinkers – the defendant was said to be an alcoholic – and they were owed £150 or thereabouts by the old man. The co-defendant, who was subsequently acquitted of murder, lodged with the deceased. At about 5 p.m., the defendants asked the old man to repay the money he owed, but he was abusive in his refusal. The defendant thereupon lost his temper and stabbed him with a kitchen knife several times, mainly in the throat and chest. He then took £30 and the deceased's spectacles. At his trial, he sought to rely on the old man's provocation.

Case 161 The victim in this case was the accused's uncle. The defendant was heavily in debt, and he spent much of the previous evening drinking with his girlfriend and became quite upset having spent much of the time talking about his financial problems. In the early hours of the following morning, he broke into his uncle's house intending to steal some jewellery. But his uncle disturbed him, and he lashed out and stabbed him. He pleaded guilty to manslaughter only because he said he had not intended to kill: he had acted in the heat of the moment.

Case 162 The defendant, an unemployed 19-year-old, suggested to two of his friends, that they should go to the victim's house and assault him. It seems that the defendant was very angry because he believed that the victim had overcharged him for some drugs. Before going to the house, the defendant had been drinking and had taken some LSD tablets. The fatal attack was carried out at about one o'clock in the morning: the deceased was stabbed in the chest and neck. The following day, the defendant gave himself up to the police, and he admitted responsibility for murder in court.

Case 163 Another unemployed 19-year-old killed one of his friends by attacking him with an axe and, having failed to burn the body, he then hid it in a cupboard of a derelict property. The offence took place at about 1.15 a.m. in the defendant's house. It seems that they had been out drinking during the previous evening and returned to the defendant's house, intending to sleep there. The defendant admitted carrying out the fatal assault, but said that the deceased had wanted to go to bed with him and this led to an argument and they had then fought each other. At his trial, he sought to rely on diminished responsibility.

Case 166 As the result of an argument about money, an unemployed man in his early/mid-20s, killed a middle-aged man by hitting him several times about the head and body with a hammer. The defendant had been lodging with the deceased for several weeks prior to the offence. Just before lunchtime one day, the defendant asked his victim for the money that was due, they quarrelled and the defendant lost his temper because the deceased refused to pay the debt. At court, the defence sought to rely on provocation to reduce the offence to manslaughter.

Case 167 The prosecution alleged that the defendant murdered his brother-in-law. It was said that the deceased rightly suspected that his wife was having an affair with the defendant and that the latter intended to kill him. During the evening prior to the murder, the deceased had been drinking and he went to the defendant's flat to confront him about his suspicions. In the early hours of the next morning, the defendant drove him to a car park where he cut his throat with a razor. Ostensibly, the defendant had been giving his victim a lift home. When questioned by the police about the attack, the defendant said that the deceased was blackmailing him, and that he (the defendant) had been attacked initially by his victim. But at his trial, he said that he had only admitted the killing because of police oppression, and denied any responsibility for the offence.

Case 169 The defendant and victim in this case were known to each other, though they could not be described as friends. A friend of the accused had a girlfriend/cohabitee whose sister was the deceased's girlfriend. The deceased agreed to persuade the accused's friend to stop beating his girlfriend. (Both the defendant and his friend were subsequently convicted of rape.) Thus the deceased went to a pub one evening where he accosted the defendant and his friend. They argued and a fight broke out between them, and the deceased was stabbed in the stomach. The defendant denied liability for murder on the grounds of the deceased's provocation and a lack of any malice aforethought.

Case 170 A man killed his former mistress by repeatedly stabbing her in the neck and body. They had separated several months before the offence took place. At about 10 o'clock in the evening, he broke into her flat and they had a very heated argument. The defendant then took a carving knife from a kitchen drawer and chased his former mistress out of the flat to a nearby off-licence, where he stabbed her. He admitted killing her but sought to rely on the partial defence of provocation. The essential legal issue appears to have been whether he had retaliated in an unreasonably violent and aggressive fashion.

Case 171 Two young men, both unemployed, had a drunken fight in the street in the early hours of the morning. They had been drinking for most of the previous day, and in the evening, along with a mutual friend, they went to a dance hall. The friend felt unwell and so all three left and took a taxi home. The deceased and his friend both felt very sick and wanted to get out of the taxi, but this was resisted by the defendant who became very angry. Nevertheless, they all got out of the taxi about a quarter of a mile before their destination. Whilst the friend walked on ahead, the defendant and the deceased continued to argue and this led to the fatal struggle between them. At his trial, the defendant admitted the killing, but denied acting with malice aforethought because of his intoxication.

Case 172 The accused and his victim in this case were both vagrants. They had had a rather casual relationship for about 12 months, but she had always 'encouraged' other men and this had clearly upset the defendant. The two of them and another man spent one lunchtime drinking together in a pub. The deceased and the other man then left, and the defendant followed them. After hearing them trying unsuccessfully to have sexual intercourse in some public toilets, the defendant attacked the woman and stabbed her in the throat. He later tried to rely on her provocation to reduce his guilt to manslaughter.

Case 174 An unemployed man in his late 20s was convicted of murdering a 2½-year-old boy. The defendant lived with the boy's family and looked after him whilst his mother was at work. The prosecution argued that the defendant had assaulted him on previous occasions, though this was denied. Death was caused by a violent blow(s) to the abdomen. The defendant said that the boy had died after an accident in a playground – he had fallen off a 'rocking boat', been struck by the handlebars and then on to the concrete floor.

Case 177 The defendant and the deceased had both been having an affair with the same woman. The defendant and his brother went to the woman's flat. The deceased challenged the defendant that if he laid his hands on the woman, he would kill him. Thereupon the defendant lunged at his victim, there was a struggle and the deceased was stabbed in the neck. Before he eventually collapsed through loss of blood, the deceased chased after the attacker. The incident took place just after 8.15 p.m. At his trial, the defendant denied murder because of his lack of malice aforethought.

Case 178 There was no obvious motive for this murder, though at one point it was suggested that one of the two defendants planned to rob the deceased. All three were young men in their early 20s, and they had been drinking together in a pub. The defendants lay in wait for the deceased and attacked him when he was on his way home from the pub. His throat was slashed and he was stabbed in the chest and abdomen. It seems that one of the defendants at least had planned to plead diminished responsibility, but at the trial they relied on an absence of an intention to kill. Both were convicted of murder.

Case 179 Defendant and deceased were described as very good friends! They had spent the evening drinking together in a working men's club and were said to be 'merry' but not drunk. They went back to the defendant's house where they intended to stay the night. An argument ensued between them when the deceased accused his friend of stealing £30. This the defendant strenuously denied, but it appears that he lost his temper and struck out hitting his friend five times over the head with a hammer. A few hours later, he gave himself up to the police. He pleaded guilty to murder.

Case 180 Two men in their early/mid-20s robbed a betting shop one morning, stealing £176. The manager of the shop refused to tell them the combination of the safe, and the defendant stabbed him in the face and body. Although he initially denied liability for murder, the defendant changed his plea to guilty during the trial and was recommended to serve at least 15 years imprisonment. His co-accused was also convicted of murder, but no minimum recommendation was made.

Case 181 The defendant killed his former 'common law' wife by manually strangling her in the house where they used to live together. Their relationship had deteriorated four or five years earlier. Just over a week before the offence, she told him that she had got married. This apparently upset him very much: he said he could not stand the thought of her new husband being the 'father' of their daughter. One morning he went to her house, they argued and he attacked her. After strangling her (which was the fatal act), he hit her over the head with an ashtray and cut her throat. Later on, after confessing what he had done to two colleagues, he gave himself up to the police. He also said that he had tried to kill himself by drinking bleach, but there was no medical evidence to support this. At trial, he sought to rely on her provocation.

Case 182 A middle-aged tramp killed an elderly caretaker of a convent. The convent had been vacated by the nuns during the Christmas holidays, and one morning the defendant broke into it intending to steal. But he was disturbed by the caretaker, and he strangled the old man with his (the deceased's) scarf. When subsequently questioned by police, he admitted committing the burglary but denied murder. He said he had panicked and killed the caretaker in the heat of the moment. This was also the essence of his case in court.

Case 183 The two defendants first encountered their victim when they were all drinking in the same pub. They met again whilst on their way home, and it seems that the deceased started an argument with them. Indeed, the defendants said that he attacked them first. In any event, they knocked him to the ground and repeatedly kicked him, mainly about the head and neck. They robbed him of a small amount of money and then ran off. To the police and at their trial, the defendants denied acting with malice aforethought. They also alleged they had been provoked by the deceased who was known to be argumentative, especially when he had been drinking.

Case 185 Two young men in their early 20s were charged with the murder of a 74-year-old man. The deceased had lived with the mother of one of the accused, but that relationship had ended and he had moved into his own flat. They knew that he would have money in his possession, and at about 7.30 p.m. they visited him, taking with them a nylon bar. The co-accused went into the flat initially to give the old man a message, and came out. Then the defendant went in, repeatedly hit the old man about the head and neck with the bar, took his wallet and left. They both pleaded guilty to manslaughter at the start of the court hearing, though the co-accused changed his plea to guilty of murder during the trial. Both were ultimately convicted of murder and robbery (stealing £259).

Case 186 The defendant's 'common law' wife left him about three months before the offence. He was very upset about the situation, and said he still loved her and their children, but could not get them back. At about 7 o'clock one morning, he asked a neighbour for a knife with which to kill his wife! About two hours later he went to where she was living, taking a knife with him. They had an argument, and he stabbed her and immediately surrendered himself to the police. He did not deny that he had murdered her.

Case 187 An unemployed man in his early 20s, described as educationally very subnormal, killed a security guard. The offence took place between 7.30 and 8 a.m. on the premises where the deceased lived and worked. He was hit over the head with a fire extinguisher; cash, and a watch and a pair of hand cuffs were stolen. The defendant pleaded provocation and diminished responsibility.

Case 188 Another unemployed man in his early 20s killed his 14-year-old sister-in-law. She and her brother were temporarily staying with the defendant, whilst work was being done on their home. The night before the offence she had been drinking alcohol, had become tearful, and had sexual intercourse with the defendant after he comforted her. The next morning, he went to her bedroom to wake her (though the prosecution said he wanted to have sex with her again), and she called him a bastard. They struggled, and he pinned her with her face down to the bed and manually strangled her. It was further alleged that either during or after the struggle, he buggered her. The defendant hid the girl's body in his wardrobe for six days, but when it began to decompose he moved it to the bathroom where he tried to dismember it. At court, he pleaded guilty to manslaughter on the basis that he had not acted with malice aforethought.

Case 190 Three brothers, from a broken home, in their late teens/early 20s, attacked a man who was a complete stranger to them outside a wine bar. The defendants and their friends had had a good deal to drink in the wine bar, but there was no obvious motive for their assault on the deceased, a man in his late 30s. They cut his throat with a piece of broken glass. All three defendants were convicted of murder, despite their claims that because of their intoxication they had not acted with malice aforethought.

Case 191 The parties met in a pub a few days before the offence, and the deceased invited the defendant to share his flat. The clear implication was that this invitation was made because the deceased hoped to form a homosexual relationship with the defendant. In the early hours one morning, the defendant awoke to find the deceased trying to bugger him. The defendant was so outraged that he grabbed hold of a bedside lamp and struck the deceased several times over the head. Later in the day, he took various items of property (valued at £2872) before leaving the flat. He subsequently admitted the theft, but denied murder, mainly on the grounds of provocation and a lack of malice aforethought.

Case 192 An unemployed teenager who was said to have 'psychiatric problems', killed a 79-year-old woman whom he had known since his childhood. He entered her house early one afternoon, looking for money. When she disturbed him, he hit her over the head with a log of wood and then impaled a hay fork in her neck. When questioned by them later in the day, the police said that he admitted the attack, but at his trial the defendant said the old lady was already dead when he first entered her house.

Case 193 Another unemployed teenager broke into his neighbour's house and stole a modest amount of money. This occurred at about 9.30 a.m. The deceased, a 69-year-old widow, found him in her bedroom, and he attacked her with a spanner and a knife, and left. Later in the day, he returned with a butcher's knife, stabbed the old lady several times and jumped on her body to try to prevent identification. He confessed what he had done to the police and admitted liability for murder in court.

Case 194 As in the previous cases, the defendant was an out-of-work teenager. One lunchtime, he was walking home across some playing fields when he saw a woman (aged 59) and he decided to snatch her handbag. He struck her on the back of the head with his fist and manually strangled her. Both to the police and at his trial, the defendant confessed to the robbery and admitted killing the woman, though he denied acting with malice aforethought.

Case 195 Yet another unemployed teenager killed a middle-aged taxi-driver, by stabbing him through the heart. The prosecution alleged that the essential motive for the attack was robbery, whereas the defendant said they had argued about the proper fare and the deceased had threatened him with a knife. The fatal wound was inflicted in the ensuing struggle. The defendant also denied responsibility for murder because he had been drinking and had taken marijuana prior to the offence.

Case 196 An out-of-work 16-year-old visited his grandmother one morning, intending to borrow some stereo equipment. It was alleged that she refused to lend him the equipment and they argued with one another. He then stabbed her in the abdomen and set fire to her body. When questioned by the police that evening, and at the subsequent court hearing, the defendant admitted seeing his grandmother but said she was still alive when he left her.

Case 197 Two teenagers were charged with the murder of a 12-year-old schoolboy, though one of them was subsequently acquitted.

The case for the prosecution was that the defendant suspected that the deceased had stolen some money from him and had decided to teach him a lesson! He shot the boy in the back, roped concrete blocks to his body and then threw him in a burn. (His co-accused thought he was only joking and did not intend to carry out the threat). The defendant admitted killing the boy, but said he had not intended to kill.

Case 198 The defendant and the deceased were both teenagers. They went to a party one evening and obviously consumed a fair amount of alcohol. They had an argument and a minor scuffle quite early in the proceedings. The prosecution alleged that the defendant then deliberately got a gun in order to kill his victim, who was shot in the chest at close range. The defendant made no effort to conceal himself, and admitted the shooting when questioned by the police. At his trial, he denied liability for murder because of his intoxication.

Case 199 The defendant was the former mistress of her victim's husband. In what was clearly felt by the prosecution to be an act of revenge, she engaged the co-defendant, a man ten years her junior, to carry out the killing. The attack on the deceased, who died from stab wounds, took place at her home at about 9.30 a.m. The police said that the defendant had confessed her guilt to them. But at the trial both defendants denied murder, and both were convicted and sentenced to life imprisonment.

Case 200 A woman in her mid-30s killed her 'common law' husband with whom she had lived for about two years. Her principal explanation for hitting him over the head with a sledgehammer was that he had made unreasonable sexual demands on her and they had frequently quarrelled with each other. The assault took place at about 11 p.m. whilst the deceased was in bed. Initially, the defendant secreted the body in a box room, but after a week she and her daughter moved it to an outside toilet, where it was discovered some three months later. At her trial the defendant sought to rely on the deceased's provocation.

Case 201 The deceased was the step-father of the defendant's wife. The defendant, an unemployed man in his mid-30s, was separated from his wife, a situation about which he was very upset. He also felt that the deceased had been responsible for aggravating his marital problems. Having consumed quite a considerable quantity of alcohol, he went to the deceased's house intending, he said, to commit suicide. Just before midnight he shot the deceased in the chest. The police said he made a full confession, but he pleaded not guilty at court.

Case 202 The defendant, a man in his early 20s, who had been drinking, was called a 'bastard' and a 'drunken cunt' by his victim, a man of 82 years of age. This incident occurred at about 10.30 p.m. in the grounds of an old people's home. The defendant was particularly sensitive about the word 'bastard' because members of his family referred to him as being illegitimate. When verbally abused by the old man, he apparently lost his self-control and punched and kicked him several times, especially about the head. A short while after the attack, he was seen by a police patrol car and he gave himself up and admitted the assault. At court, he pleaded guilty to manslaughter, on the basis of the deceased's provocation and because he had not acted with malice aforethought. One possible explanation for the offence was that the defendant was in effect directing the anger that he felt towards his father at others and the word 'bastard' had triggered off an angry attack.

Case 203 The two men involved in this case were homosexuals and had lived together, 'on and off', for about a two-year period prior to the offence. The defendant had been drinking heavily during the evening and had taken cannabis. Just before midnight they had an argument which was sparked off when the deceased nagged the accused about relationships with other men. The defendant lost his temper and struck the deceased over the head with a hammer several times. About two weeks later, he saw his solicitor and the two of them went to the police station where he explained what had happened. When indicted for murder, the defendant sought to rely on his intoxication to reduce his liability to manslaughter.

Case 204 A 21-year-old unemployed man was convicted of murdering his 11-year-old female cousin. (There were two co-defendants, one of whom pleaded guilty to manslaughter on the basis of diminished responsibility, for which he was sentenced to four years imprisonment.) The defendant had been befriended by the girl's mother and they lived in separate flats in the same block. Early one evening, the defendants entered the mother's flat and they were in the process of stealing some money from her desk when they were disturbed by the girl. When she threatened to tell her mother, the defendant hit her over the head with a small wooden stool and then strangled her with a piece of wire. They stole £4700 cash and set fire to the flat. When questioned by the police the two main defendants implicated each other. The accused denied liability for murder in court, arguing that the fatal assault had been inflicted by his co-defendant.

Case 206 A young man who had taken an overdose and was in the habit of drinking heavily, was recommended to serve at least 12 years for murdering his fiancée. They had quarrelled a number of times, especially about what she regarded as his financial irresponsibility. Indeed, their relationship had deteriorated so much that she wanted what was called 'a trial separation', but he wanted their engagement to continue. Just before 10 o'clock one evening they quarrelled again and he stabbed her twice in the chest. He had lost his temper when she refused to talk to him anymore. A hour or so later, he surrendered himself to the police, and pleaded guilty to murder in court.

Case 207 Two men in their mid-30s were convicted of the murder of a 66-year-old man whom they knew socially, and the judge recommended that they should each serve at least 15 years in prison. They went to his flat at about 7.15 one evening, knowing that he would have money there. In the course of robbing him, they punched and kicked him, fracturing his skull amongst other injuries. They denied liability for murder on the ground that they had been drinking before the offence and thus had not acted with malice aforethought.

Case 208 A man killed his wife by strangulation. She had moved out of their home some two weeks earlier and had gone to live in her mother's flat. She had filed a divorce petition which was based on his alleged adultery. Early one morning he went to visit her, and they argued about money and their other matrimonial problems. When subsequently questioned by the police he admitted killing his wife but denied that the offence was premeditated. He denied culpability for murder at his trial.

Case 209 The defendant in his early 40s and out of work, admitted murdering his 'common law' wife. Their relationship had been deteriorating for some time and they had quarrelled on numerous occasions. In the course of an argument about eight o'clock in the morning, the defendant lost his temper and strangled her with a plastic clothes line. He subsequently told his social worker's superior what had happened and asked her to contact the police.

Case 210 A man in his late 50s, in and out of work, killed his 80-year-old mother-in-law by strangling her with a pair of tights. The defendant and his wife lived in the deceased's house. He had become very depressed after his son had committed suicide, and he was an alcoholic. It seems that his mother-in-law had been persistently nagging him about his inability to properly support his family. In the end, about 8.30 in the evening, the defendant lost his temper and killed her. He immediately telephoned the police and explained what he had done, and suggested that he had been provoked by her nagging. At his trial, he sought to rely on diminished responsibility, though a plea to this effect was rejected by the prosecution.

Case 212 A 21-year-old unemployed man was convicted of murdering his girlfriend. They were walking home from a pub late in the evening. She refused to have sexual intercourse with him and he lost his temper and assaulted her. The offence took place around midnight in a field; the defendant kicked and stamped on her, mainly about the head and upper body. The defendant told the police that he began to kick her and could not stop himself. At his trial, his plea of guilty to manslaughter by reason of diminished responsibility was rejected by the prosecution.

Case 213 A man killed his wife about 10.15 one evening by stabbing her repeatedly, especially in the neck. The deceased had had numerous affairs with other men, and had tried to persuade her husband to leave their home. She refused to cook for him and constantly moaned at him. He had become very depressed and drank quite heavily. In the end, he 'couldn't take any more', and killed her. Half an hour or so after the attack, he confessed to the matron of the home where his mother lived and she (the matron) contacted the police. He admitted to the police what had happened and said he had intended to kill himself but lacked the courage to do so. At court, he sought to rely on his wife's provocation, but this failed, apparently because he had not lost his self control when he killed her.

Case 214 The two defendants – brothers-in-law in their early 20s – were convicted of murdering a 57-year-old woman who was a former workmate of one of them. They knew that she lived alone and that she would be given her wages on a particular day. They visited her home one evening, intending to rob her. One of the defendants unsuccessfully tried to strangle her, and the other then beat her and slashed her wrists, so that she would not be able to identify them. He pleaded guilty to murder, but his co-accused sought to blame him entirely for her death. The judge recommended that they should each serve at least 15 years in prison.

Case 216 There were five defendants, three men – two of whom were convicted of murder – and two women, one of whom was the former wife of the victim. The principal defendant was having an affair with her, and in the early hours of the day on which the offence was committed they argued with the deceased about his behaviour towards his ex-wife. The prosecution alleged that as a result of this row she decided to have her former husband assaulted and sent messages through her son and daughter (two of the co-defendants), to her lover and the other accused who was convicted of murder, who was the boyfriend of one of the victim's daughters. Her plan was to take the deceased to a pub that evening and to have him assaulted on his way home. In the event, he was attacked, at about 10.45 p.m., in a passage by the side of his house. Two of the defendants struck him over the head with a hammer. At the trial, they each sought to attribute most of the responsibility to the other.

Case 217 A man in his early 30s was convicted of murdering his lover's husband by stabbing him in the chest. The motive for the offence was money. The defendant's workmate was convicted of manslaughter and robbery for his part in the venture (for which he was sentenced to nine years and six years imprisonment respectively), and his lover was acquitted of murder/manslaughter but given five years for robbery. It was argued that, with her knowledge and support, the other two planned to ambush her husband and steal the takings from his business. The defendant was in considerable financial difficulties at the time. The assault took place at about 9.30 p.m. outside the deceased's home. The two male defendants each claimed that the fatal wounds had been inflicted by the other.

Case 218 An unemployed man in his mid-20s killed another unemployed man who was about ten years older. The deceased had been living with the defendant's brother and sister-in-law for about three weeks prior to the offence. When told that the deceased was having an affair with his sister-in-law, the defendant flew into a rage, and went out and stabbed his victim in the chest. This occurred at about 1.30 p.m. in a local pub. He then gave himself up to the police and told them what had happened. At the trial, he sought to rely on the deceased's provocation, but this seems to have been rejected essentially on the unreasonableness of the defendant's reaction.

Case 219 The defendant, an unemployed alcoholic, killed his former 'common law' wife. She had asked him to leave their flat about two weeks earlier, and he had been drinking in the hours leading up to the assault. In the early hours of the morning, he hit her over the head several times with a hammer whilst she was asleep, and then had sexual intercourse with her. He admitted his liability for her murder.

Case 220 A man killed his estranged wife by strangling her with a cardigan. The prosecution alleged that she had complained that her husband had been physically violent towards her, and that she had custody of their children. Apparently, the defendant believed that she had carried out her threat to tell her solicitor that he had raped her. Subsequently, after admitting to the police that he had killed her, he said that he had gone to see his wife to persuade her to admit to her solicitor that she had lied to him. The attack took place at about 3.00 a.m. At his trial, the defendant denied murder on the basis of his wife's provocation.

Case 221 An unemployed man in his mid-20s admitted murdering his homosexual lover, by beating and strangling him. One evening, in the deceased's flat they argued about the amount of alcohol the defendant had been drinking. It seems that he lost his temper and made the fatal assault. The trial judge recommended that he should be detained in custody for at least 15 years.

Case 223 An unemployed 60-year-old defendant killed a middle-aged man with whom he shared a bedroom in the same lodgings. A few hours later the defendant told the police what he had done, and told them about the deceased's snoring and dirty habits. The defendant complained that he had endured them for the four years they had shared a room together, and simply could not control his anger any more. In a fit of temper, just after 1.00 a.m. he manually strangled his victim. At the trial, he pleaded provocation.

Case 224 A man in his early 30s, out of work, killed the woman with whom he had been living for about two months. Their relationship deteriorated as a result of arguments about money and because of his jealousy of her other friends. He was due to leave the flat where they had been living only a day or so after he killed her. Death was caused by a stab wound to the abdomen inflicted by a kitchen knife. They had quarrelled yet again, and he lashed out in a temper. Her body was discovered about 18 months later. The police said that he confessed to them that he had killed her, though he denied acting with malice aforethought. But at his trial, the defendant said he could not remember being questioned by the police and denied any responsibility for the offence.

Case 225 Two young men were accused of murdering a third man at a party, in the early hours of the morning. There was an argument, possibly about drugs or about some stolen property, and this erupted into a fight involving a number of individuals. The principal defendant was later alleged to have said that someone gave him a knife and told him to use it, though he subsequently denied any responsibility for the killing. His co-accused pleaded guilty to manslaughter. The deceased, an unemployed man in his mid-20s, was a complete stranger to the defendants.

Case 226 A 19-year-old, out-of-work defendant, admitted murdering a clergyman who was in his mid-60s. The assault took place just before 6 p.m. on an industrial estate. The defendant, a homosexual, said that the deceased had been too forceful in his advances, and he (the accused) had consequently reacted in a fit of rage. He strangled his victim by ligature and hit him in the face with a stone. When questioned by the police, he admitted killing the deceased, and showed them where to find the body.

Case 227 There were three young defendants in this case, two men and a 15-year-old girl. Only the men were charged with murder. They attacked a 50-year-old man, a total stranger to them, in a public lavatory early one evening. Their motive was robbery and they both admitted committing that offence. The police said that they also admitted carrying out the fatal attack – one used a knife, the other a claw-hammer. One of the defendants was convicted of murder, though he claimed to have lacked malice aforethought because he had taken some drugs. His co-accused was convicted of manslaughter, for which he was sentenced to seven years imprisonment.

Case 228 A young man who was about to lose his job, killed an elderly widower whilst burgling his house. Immediately before embarking upon the burglary, the defendant had been drinking in a local pub. He was in the process of looking for things to steal from the house when he was disturbed by the deceased. When the old man indicated that he recognised him, the defendant panicked and lashed out with a bread knife, stabbing his victim in the chest. He confessed to the police, and pleaded guilty at his trial.

Case 229 The defendant was an unemployed teenager. His victim with whom he was acquainted, made homosexual advances to him which caused him to lose his temper. He smashed a bottle over the deceased's head, cut his neck with a piece of broken glass and nearly strangled him. A few days after the attack, the defendant went with his parents to the police and admitted the assault. At his trial, he sought to rely on the deceased's provocation, but the court seems to have taken the view that he acted too coolly.

Case 230 Just after midnight, the defendant was disturbed whilst in the process of syphoning some petrol from a van on factory premises. He was an unemployed man in his mid-30s, and was described as 'educationally subnormal'. His victim was a police constable. When disturbed, the defendant lashed out in a panic, and stabbed the constable in the chest. He pleaded not guilty to murder on the ground that he had not intended to seriously injure anyone.

Case 232 A 19-year-old man, out of work, killed his cohabitee's 17-month-old baby. The police said he had admitted to them that the baby had been crying, seemingly incessantly, and he had lost his temper and punched him in the stomach. The baby's liver was ruptured and he died from internal bleeding. In court, the defendant denied any responsibility for the death, and blamed his cohabitee.

Case 233 The prosecution alleged that the defendant, a young soldier, flagged down a car driven by the deceased, a woman in her early 20s. They drove to a village and he raped her. In retaliation, she tried to attack him with a knife. They struggled, he disarmed her, bound and gagged her and stabbed her several times. The assault occurred at about midnight in her car. The defendant admitted to the police that he had stabbed her, but he claimed that she had consented to having sex with him and then 'went wild', attacking him first. This was reflected in the pleas he entered when the charges were put to him in court.

Case 238 A man was convicted of murdering his bigamous wife, by strangling her with a belt. They had had a number of sporadic rows, the last of which was sparked off when she told him that she had aborted their child by using a knitting needle. This row happened in the early hours of the morning. She left the house, and he followed her. While she was walking through a park, he attacked and killed her. The police said that the defendant had said to them that he had strangled her, but claimed that his assault was the result of her provocation. This was also the essence of the defence case at trial.

Case 239 The defendant was a young man in his mid-20s, out of work, and described as a heavy drinker and suffering from depression. He was convicted of murdering his grandfather, with whom he lived. The defendant had consumed quite a large amount of alcohol and had taken some tablets just before the crime was committed. The deceased criticised his grandson about his drinking habits and they began to argue. The defendant was told the leave the flat, and he thereupon attacked his grandfather, hitting him with a heavy vase and then jumping on his chest. This was at about 8.15 in the evening. The following morning the defendant phoned the police and told them that he had returned home to find his grandfather's body. But the police said that he subsequently confessed his guilt to them, and he pleaded guilty at the court hearing.

Case 240 A unemployed man, in his mid-30s, was convicted of murdering the woman with whom he had been living for about two and a half years. It seems that they returned home from a pub at about midnight; she went to the kitchen and he sat down to read a book. They started to argue when she accused him of not paying attention to her. She suspected that he was having an affair with another woman, though the defendant denied this. She then hit him and berated him for his heavy drinking and borrowing money. The argument thereupon became much more heated and he stabbed her in the neck and abdomen. Soon afterwards, the defendant phoned the police and told them what had happened, and he subsequently surrendered himself to them. At his trial, he denied murder primarily because of his intoxication, though the defence also appear to have raised the issue of the deceased's provocation.

Case 241 The defendant pleaded guilty to murder, robbery and rape, against the same victim. He arrived at her house one afternoon, posing as a prospective house-purchaser, but the deceased disturbed him whilst he was attempting to steal from her purse. He forced her to go upstairs, and bound and raped her. Then he strangled her with a belt and ties, and left with her purse (containing £19 and a credit card).

Case 242 Two groups of youths were verbally abusing each other on an underground station late one evening. This led to a fight between them and a 19-year-old man was stabbed in the chest. There were three defendants; two were convicted of murder and the third admitted disposing of the murder weapon. The two principal defendants denied liability for murder on the grounds that they were drunk, and had been glue-sniffing, and also that they had acted in self-defence. Both were ordered to be detained during Her Majesty's pleasure.

Case 243 One evening at about 7.15 p.m. a 17-year-old lad broke into a house and demanded money from the occupant, a 67-year-old woman. (Her husband was ill in hospital at the time.) When she became hysterical, he struck her over the head several times with the butt of an air rifle. He took her wrist watch, and left. He was subsequently arrested after the police had traced the stolen watch. The police said that he admitted carrying out the fatal attack on the old lady, though at court the defendant denied acting with malice aforethought.

Case 244 The defendant was made redundant on the morning of the offence, and had some 'farewell' drinks with his friends at lunchtime. He thought he had been badly treated by his former employers and was, understandably, very depressed. But at about 3 o'clock in the afternoon he broke into his next-door neighbour's house, intending to burgle it. His neighbour was a woman aged 77 years. When she disturbed him he lashed out at her, stabbing her many times in the chest, neck and head. He admitted killing her, but pleaded diminished responsibility, though there appears to have been no medical evidence to support this. The judge ordered that he be detained during Her Majesty's pleasure.

Case 245 Initially, three men faced criminal charges in this case – the defendant, his co-accused and the co-accused's brother – but the brother was too ill to be tried and he later died. The victim, a middle-aged man, first met the co-accused and his brother and sister about 14 months before the offence. He, the victim, persuaded the sister to have sexual intercourse with him for money, but their relationship had ended. Nevertheless, the co-accused and his brother used to steal property – especially meat – from the deceased's house. Late one evening the three defendants were in the process of stealing more meat when their victim disturbed them. He was struck on the head and neck with the butt of a gun. The defendant and co-accused admitted the burglary, but said that the fatal assault had been committed by the accused's brother who allegedly accepted sole responsibility for the killing. But the defendant and his co-accused were both convicted of murder.

Case 246 The defendant, an unemployed 16-year-old, pleaded guilty to the murder of a 17-year-old girl. The prosecution put the case thus: the defendant went out with his girlfriend, while her sister spent the evening with the deceased. All four then met near the girlfriend's house, the two sisters went inside, leaving the defendant to walk his victim home (at her request). The accused said that when she put her hands on his genitals he became very angry and beat her with his hands and feet and a brick. He denied any sort of sexual interference with her, though his fingerprints were found amongst blood on her breasts, and her knickers and tights had been pulled down and her blouse and bra disarranged. The assault happened just before 11.45 p.m., outside a block of flats.

Case 247 Two 16-year-olds were ordered to be detained during Her Majesty's pleasure. The main defendant and the victim, a 15-year-old boy, were pupils in the same school. It seems that for some months the deceased had been pressing the defendant for repayment of a debt and had threatened him with violence. The defendant then decided to kill him and enlisted his co-accused's help. They lured their victim to a golf course early one evening, ostensibly for the purpose of glue-sniffing. There the deceased was beaten with a pick-axe handle and stabbed with a knife – these weapons allegedly having been hidden at the scene on the previous day. Both defendants admitted their responsibility for the murder.

Case 248 A 16-year-old schoolgirl, (who was said to be from a broken home, to be depressed, and to have twice taken an overdose), and her younger boyfriend, were convicted of murdering her 18-month-old niece. The baby had been persistently crying and screaming, and this was getting on the nerves of the two defendants. Early one afternoon they visited the baby's bedroom; the boy punched and kicked her, and his girlfriend did likewise and threw her niece across the room. When questioned by the police they both admitted assault, but at the trial the defendant said that her boyfriend was solely responsible for the killing of the baby.

Case 250 A woman, her brother and her lodger were convicted of murdering her husband in what was said to be a well-planned offence. The principal reason was the deceased's ill-treatment of his wife and son. The two male defendants strangled him with a rope and then tried to stab him. The police said that all three defendants admitted their responsibility in the offence when questioned, but at the trial the woman denied being involved.

4 Future Definitions and Concepts of Murder

Not surprisingly, the study confirms that murder remains an extremely diverse crime, not merely in its external characteristics, but also in the gravity of the cases that it encompasses. There is no simple description of the people who are convicted of murder, or of their victims or the surrounding circumstances. It would be convenient if categories of murder and murderers could be readily identified, but only superficial classification appears to be possible. It was relatively uncommon to find any statistical significance in the correlation between even two factors. Admittedly, there were some instances of cases bearing certain characteristics – for example, there were several murders committed by young men, many of whom were unemployed, who apparently killed for financial gain, and many of their victims were late-middle-aged or elderly people, killed in their own homes. But many other young male murderers committed very different offences and many of them had a job; many victims aged 50 or more were killed by older offenders, and for seemingly different reasons.

The numbers of murders seem to be increasing but only very gradually; the Home Office Criminal Statistics (1986) show 108 recorded convictions in 1976 and 173 in 1985, though the figures fluctuate from year to year. Yet the overall impression is that the nature of murder remains largely unchanged; the vast majority of murderers are male, they usually know their victims, killing with a sharp instrument is still the most common method, and nearly half of the murders are carried out in a fit of temper. It is, of course, encouraging to find that those committed in the furtherance of theft or gain, about which there is understandable concern, continue to represent no more than about 22 per cent of the total number. The obvious apparent change is that fewer convicted murderers in the sample had no previous convictions and more of them had a prior record of violence than their predecessors. At the same time, it is worth remembering that the number of people convicted of criminal offences in England and Wales during the period 1978 to 1982 increased by 24.6 per cent compared to 1967 to 1971, and there were more than three and a half times as many recorded crimes of violence against the person between 1978–82 than during the years relating to Gibson's (1975) survey.

The apparent motive for the commission of a crime can provide an indication of its gravity, for a person who kills, say as an act of revenge, may deserve greater condemnation than one who lashed out in a fit of rage. In this study, in cases in the former category, the judge was much more likely to make a minimum recommendation of an above-average period of imprisonment than in those of the latter variety. But it would be dangerous to suggest that the seriousness of a case can be assessed in such a simplistic manner. Murders in the course of theft or robbery are usually considered to be particularly serious, especially when compared to 'domestic' killings. One of the reasons for this is that it is thought that large numbers of offences of financial or property gain are committed by professional criminals after calmly calculating the pros and cons of the offence. But this study had demonstrated that crimes in this category do not always follow this pattern. Whilst nearly 80 per cent of the 54 murderers who killed in the furtherance of theft or gain had previous convictions for property offences, eight had no convictions at all and three others had been convicted of minor traffic or drugs offences only. More than two-fifths had never received a custodial sentence, and only 11 had been given a sentence of 12 months imprisonment or more. Nearly a third (17 of the 54) were under 18 years of age when the offence was carried out.

Moreover, this group of murders should be divided into those where the offender killed with an instrument which he had taken with him, having previously decided that he would use it if necessary, and those where he grabbed hold of the first thing that came to hand and struck out at his victim. A planned offence in which the offender coolly defies the law is more blameworthy than one which is committed impulsively or on the spur of the moment. In cases where a person carries a weapon such as a gun, knife or iron bar the court is likely to infer that some form of violence has been contemplated. Any unlawful killing is a very serious matter but, for example, the burglar who is disturbed and – panic-stricken – kills on the spur of the moment surely deserves less condemnation than the robber who sets out with a knife or gun with which he is prepared to kill or grievously injure.

The term 'domestic murder' is often used to denote cases in which the defendant has, strictly speaking, fulfilled the legal requirements of murder but it ought not to be considered as one of the very worst offences. It is a term which cannot be defined with any great degree of confidence, though it is possible to identify cases where the parties were closely related, familially or domestically, and the offence was committed because of familial or domestic problems. A wide variety of situations may arise in this category, some of which are well-known stereotypes – the man who kills his wife's lover, or the husband who kills his wife because their relationship has deteriorated and he cannot stand the thought of losing her. The notion of 'domestic murder' may also denote instances where there has been a long-running feud, either between members of the same family, or between different families. It might include cases where a parent or guardian has killed a baby or child because, say, the victim had been crying incessantly and the defendant simply lost his temper. It might even apply where one man makes an unwanted homosexual advance to a friend who hits out in anger and disgust. The example may be tenuous, but it illustrates the potential elasticity of the concept of 'domestic murder'.

If a broad interpretation, as described in the preceding paragraph, is given to this notion, there were 113 'domestic' offences in the sample (45.2 per cent). At first sight this may seem to be a lower proportion than might have been expected, but it is not significantly different from Gibson's (1975) survey. Indeed, it has already been pointed out in chapter 2 that, in the light of Morris and Blom-Cooper's (1979) study and the Home Office's Criminal Statistics (1986), large numbers of cases where the parties were closely members of the same family result in convictions for manslaughter rather than murder. This research has clearly demonstrated, however, that some cases which might bear the 'domestic' label nonetheless merit considerable condemnation. Whilst there are instances where the offender was provoked so that there is a minimal degree of mitigation, insufficient to reduce liability to manslaughter, there are others where the offence was carried out quite deliberately and there are no apparent extenuating circumstances. In this respect, certain so-called 'domestic' murders may attract the same censure revulsion as the most heinous examples of murders committed in the furtherance of gain.

It is very tempting to point to the depravity of an offence in order to assess its gravity, and this explains why, for example, sexual or sadistic killings of children are regarded with such outrage and revulsion. Killing elderly people in the course of burglary or robbery is also treated as an illustration of great moral wickedness. But there are strong objections to the adoption of depravity or moral wickedness as the criteria for determining whether an offence is one of the very worst examples of its type. Firstly, they are vague concepts and people may vary in the level of moral condemnation they attach to a particular crime. Secondly, and more importantly, people's abhorrence of certain offences, such as those against the young and the old, is a response to the external elements of the facts rather than to an analysis of what led to them. Little effort is made to look behind the facts and see how they came about.

The young and the elderly are both vulnerable in that they are less able to protect themselves against attackers, and thus offences against them are considered to be morally more culpable than those against other individuals. Crimes against law-enforcement officers such as the police are often said to be particularly blameworthy because they are seen as a symbolic rejection of law and order. This is, of course based on the assumption that the offender is aware of his victim's occupation. Fortunately, it seems that fatal attacks on such people are rare. But it would be unwise to determine the heinousness of a crime simply by reference to the vulnerability of the victim or the apparent symbolism of the act.

Whether or not an unlawful killing should be regarded as a heinous offence is a question which must reflect the degree of culpability that attaches to it. Crimes that exhibit greater blameworthiness will attract increased moral censure, but to assess culpability it is necessary to take account of an offender's responsibility for his actions. All the surrounding circumstances of a crime should be considered, especially the situation which led to its execution and the state of mind of the offender. Thus, provocation or substantial abnormality of mind may reduce to manslaughter what would otherwise have been treated as murder. In both instances it may be said that the defendant's behaviour was not entirely voluntary, and the extent to which the individual chose to embark upon a course of conduct is a vital factor in determining the level of his culpability. Yet the notion of choice here may be interpreted in a variety of ways. Distinctions can and should be drawn between, at one extreme, cases of carefully considered choice and, at the other extreme, those where a person merely responds to the immediate situation. In each case the individual 'chose' to act in that the brain sent messages to and controlled the physical actions, and there was no insanity or other mental deficiency which affected the voluntariness of the behaviour. But the law should reflect these variations so that a man who commits a crime 'in the heat of the moment' is not attributed with the same level of responsibility as one who acts more deliberately. Again, however, it should be acknowledged that a person who kills in the heat of the moment, such as in the course of a quarrel, may, prior to the quarrel, have considered the situation and decided that he was prepared to kill. The fact that he carried out the fatal attack whilst in a very agitated or emotional state of mind does not automatically preclude the possibility of some earlier thoughts about what he might do.

There appear to be two ways in which the law might be reformed: either (i) retain the present general definition of murder but identify separate categories according to whether or not there was any evidence of 'forethought'; or (ii) redefine the legal definition of murder so that it encompasses only those cases which contain any prior willingness to kill, and treat 'spontaneous' killings as manslaughter. Reckless killings and unlawful homicides where the offender intended to seriously injure but no more, would also be manslaughter. (A third alternative is the substitution of a single offence of 'unlawful homicide' for murder and manslaughter, but this appears to be unacceptable in view of the response received by the CLRC.) The first option would partly resemble the law in many states in the USA, where the purpose of differentiating between degrees of murder is to apply more severe punishment to what are regarded as the more serious cases. Thus, a further dimension to this first option is that the mandatory life sentence should be retained where there was 'forethought', but spontaneous murders should carry only a maximum of life imprisonment. It may be recalled that the change from a mandatory to a maximum of life imprisonment in New South Wales has been very satisfactory, with no apparent ill-effects. Alternatively, of course, the more heinous offences might attract capital punishment, and 'lesser' murders be dealt with by way of a mandatory life sentence, but this is probably a less politically viable suggestion in that it is unlikely to be adopted by Parliament.

One obvious benefit to be derived from distinguishing cases where there is a preparedness to kill from those of a spontaneous nature is that some substance would be injected into the term 'malice aforethought'. To a large extent, this type of distinction can be seen in the differentiation made in the United States between first and second degree murder. There are essentially three varieties of murder in the first degree, namely (i) cases where there was an intent to kill accompanied by premeditation and deliberation; (ii) murder in the course of four or five specific felonies (usually including arson, rape, burglary and robbery); and (iii) murder by lying in wait, by poison and by torture. It is usually only in some of the murders in the course of listed felonies that there need be no evidence of forethought. Second degree murder, which should generally attract a lesser penalty, encompasses intent-to-kill murder where there is no premeditation, intent-to-seriously-injure murder whether or not there is premeditation, murder where the defendant knew or ought to have known there was a very high risk of death, and murder in the course of non-listed felonies (such as abortion). In (i) the phrase 'premeditation and deliberation' is interpreted as requiring that the offender 'with a cool mind' reflected upon the situation at least for a short period before he killed. The fatal act may have been committed immediately after the formation of the intent to kill, and the intent itself may precede or follow the premeditation and deliberation. Admittedly, there have been cases where the premeditation consisted of only a brief moment's thought, but these have been criticised as blurring the distinction between first and second degree murder.

The element of premeditation and deliberation must be proved in addition to the intent to kill, and it may have to be inferred from the evidence. For this purpose, three categories of evidence are significant: (i) evidence of 'planning activity', which is concerned with facts about how and what the defendant did before the killing which indicate that he was engaged in activities that were directed towards the killing. This may take the form of prior possession of the murder weapon, a surreptitious approach of the victim, or taking the prospective victim to a place where other people are unlikely to intrude; (ii) 'motive' may be inferred from evidence about the defendant's prior relationship and conduct with the victim. This may consist of personal violence by the defendant against the deceased, plans or wishes on the part of the defendant which would be facilitated by the victim's death, or previous conduct by the victim which angered the defendant; (iii) the nature of the killing may itself suggest that it was carried out in accordance with some form of preconceived design. The fatal wounds may be deliberately directed at vital areas of the body.

The notion of 'premeditation and deliberation', may seem rather vague, and the admission and assessment of evidence in a court of law is a less than wholly scientific process, but it is surely not beyond the realms of practicality that steps can be taken to determine whether or not a particular defendant 'coolly reflected' before he killed. This is not to suggest that we should simply adopt the approach which prevails in many of the American states, as outlined above, but we ought to look upon it as indicating the way in which our existing laws might be reformed.

The second option, whereby killings in the heat of the moment would be regarded as manslaughter, has the immediate benefit that all murders would have a common characteristic, namely prior willingness to kill. 'Malice aforethought' is interpreted so widely by the courts that it cannot realistically be seen as a regular feature of murder. Confining murder to those cases where there is evidence of 'cool reflection' would enhance the stigma that the offence would attract, and it would provide clear justification for ascribing to it a unique sentence. Such a change in the law would go a long way towards dealing with the criticism that the legal definition is so wide that some murders are less heinous than other offences, as was recognised by Lord Kilbrandon in Hyam's case in 1974. Lord Windlesham, Chairman of the Parole Board, was recently reported to have argued that less serious murders should not result in the imposition of a life sentence; (see *The Times*, 16 August 1988), and a House of Lords Select Committee has been set up to consider, amongst other things, whether the current mandatory penalty for murder should be replaced by a maximum of life imprisonment. In some cases a determinate sentence is more appropriate, and the clear implication is that other offences which do merit life imprisonment should be regarded as more serious.

In the absence of any mitigating circumstances such as provocation or diminished responsibility, the dividing line between murder and (involuntary) manslaughter would be moved so that more cases would fall within the latter group of offences. It may be objected that, as a result of this adjustment, a man may, for example, be unsuccessful in pleading provocation which would reduce his offence to voluntary manslaughter, and yet be convicted of involuntary manslaughter because he killed on the spur of the moment. Such an outcome ought not, however, to be seen as anomalous or undesirable, for manslaughter would continue to carry a maximum of life imprisonment and the culpability of an offender can be measured in the penalty imposed by the court. Furthermore, there would be no diminution in the condemnation of crimes that hitherto have been, at least legally, regarded as murder. It is quite possible that the status of manslaughter as a serious crime would be reinforced, so that those convicted of it would not be thought to 'have got off lightly'. The very word 'manslaughter' tends to create images of horrific killings, and the law should not be slow to recognise and reflect this.

The second option seems preferable to the first, principally because it fulfills the desire to preserve the stigma that should attach to murder. A system which identifies different degrees or categories of murder may be hard-pressed to achieve this result. The essential need is that the law be amended so as to ensure that murder denotes the very worst examples of unlawful homicide and that the stigma is maintained. Insofar as it is impossible to draw clinical divisions between offences, some anomalies are inevitable, but the requirement of prior consideration and preparedness to kill is likely to assist the courts in reaching verdicts which more precisely reflect the nature of the facts.

The retention of the mandatory life sentence can only be justified if murder is treated as a uniquely and heinous offence, and it is submitted that this can only be achieved if the above suggestion is put into effect. Only by giving real substance to the concept of malice aforethought can the stigma of murder be maintained. The present law, as it is interpreted by the courts, permits far too wide a range of cases to fall within its definition, many of which merit less condemnation than other crimes (such as robbery and rape) carrying discretionary life sentences.

Part II

The Management of Life-Sentence Prisoners

5 Life Imprisonment: Policy and Practice

INTRODUCTION

A sentence of life imprisonment is mandatory where an offender commits the crime of murder and at the time of doing so is aged 21 years or over.[1] At the same time as imposing such a penalty the sentencing judge has a discretionary power to make a recommendation to the Home Secretary that the offender should serve a minimum period of time in custody before being released.[2] Life imprisonment is also the maximum sentence which may be imposed for a number of other serious offences such as manslaughter, robbery, rape, aggravated burglary and arson.

In the case of a person who commits murder and who was under the age of 18 years at the time of the offence, the appropriate order for the sentencing judge to make is that he be 'detained during her Majesty's pleasure'.[3] This is similar to life imprisonment, though the offender is detained 'in such a place and under such circumstances as the Secretary of State may direct'. Likewise, those aged under 17 when they commit offences other than murder for which a life sentence may be imposed on an adult may be ordered to be detained for life.[4] This type of sentence is effectively the same as detention during Her Majesty's pleasure.

If, on the other hand, a person commits murder when he is under the age of 21, he should be sentenced to 'custody for life' unless he is liable to be detained during Her Majesty's pleasure.[5] If the court thinks it is appropriate to do, it may impose a similar sentence on a person aged at least 17 years but under 21 who commits any other offence for which a life sentence may be passed in respect of an adult.[6] 'Custody for life' is similar to life imprisonment except that, '... the Secretary of State may from time to time direct that an offender ... who is female, or who is male and under 22 years of age, is to be detained in a youth custody centre instead of prison.[7]

Although offenders who are sentenced to life imprisonment (including those detained during Her Majesty's pleasure or serving custody for life), represent a relatively small proportion of the total prison population, there has been a steady increase in their numbers in recent years. The average population of life sentence prisoners in England and Wales rose from 1123 in 1976 to 2201 in 1986.[8] Those convicted of murder generally make up about 75 per cent of the lifer population, and it is clear that there has also been a correspondingly steady increase in the number of convicted murderers (from 931 in 1976, to 1706 in 1986).

About 10 per cent of lifers have committed manslaughter, and the remainder have been convicted of 'non-homicide' offences. There has also been an increase in the average length of time served in prison. In the early 1970s lifers were generally detained between eight and nine years, but by the mid-1980s the appropriate figure was about ten and a half years.[9]

CURRENT POLICY

The 'Revised Strategy'

As a result of the increasing size of the population of life sentence prisoners and the consequential problems of the management of them, the Prison Department formulated a new policy embodied in what was known as the 'Revised Strategy'. The basic principles of this are now set out in Prison Department Circular 2/1989.

Prior to the introduction of this new policy, the practice had been for a lifer to be transferred from the local prison, shortly after conviction, to a training prison and he would spend the major part of the period of detention there. When it was decided to release him, the lifer would usually be moved either to an open prison or to a hostel under the Pre-Release Employment Scheme (PRES)[10] from which he would be released on licence. Alternatively, he might even be released directly from the training prison after a period on an outside working party. It was thus possible that the whole of his period of detention would have been spent in just two institutions – the local prison and the training prison.

There were a limited number of prisons which accommodated life sentence prisoners – only six in the mid-1960s – and with a steadily increasing lifer population, it was evident that more prisons would have to take lifers. Moreover, it was considered undesirable that a lifer should spend such a lengthy period in one institution. The indications were that this tended to lead to the lifer becoming dependent upon the institution, and it was a poor preparation for his release.

The 'Revised Strategy' adopted by the Prison Department is based on certain underlying principles. Firstly, it is felt that lifers should be treated as a separate group. The prison system should recognise that they have special needs because of the indeterminacy of their sentence and the resulting psychological and practical problems. At the same time it is not considered appropriate to physically separate them from determinate sentence prisoners, nor to grant them additional rights and privileges. Many governers have argued that lifers would actually benefit from mixing with fixed-term prisoners, particularly when there is a probability of the lifer being released in the near future. Whilst they should not enjoy extra privileges, lifers should normally be accommodated in single cells.

A second feature of the new policy is that the system should give lifers a sense of purpose and direction. One aspect of this is that they will begin their sentence in secure conditions and gradually progress towards a more liberal environment. After sentence, adult male lifers should be allocated to a main centre – namely, Wakefield prison, Wormwood Scrubs or Gartree. H Wing at Durham Prison operates as an effective main centre for female lifers. The initial allocation of young male lifers is normally to Aylesbury, Swinfen Hall or Castington.

Invariably, the lifer will spend the early part of his imprisonment in a closed institution. But the Prison Department accepts that such an environment is not appropriate for testing and assessing the prisoner's suitability for release. The lifer's behaviour in a closed prison clearly should not be used as a basis for determining his likely response when released. It is felt that both in the interests of society generally and of the individual prisoner, lifers should spend part of their custodial sentence in low security institutions, that is, semi-open and open prisons. There, the lifer is to be given the opportunity and encouragement to assume greater responsibility for himself. It is only in such comparatively liberal conditions that he can make decisions for himself and it is thus possible to make a more realistic estimate of how the lifer is likely to behave if and when he is released. Given that a critical factor in determining whether to release a prisoner is the safety of the public, pre-release preparation should be as thorough and varied as possible.

However, the structure of the prison system for female offenders is more simplistic than for their male counterparts in that there are no semi-open establishments for women. They will be transferred directly from a closed institution to open conditions. The reason for this is at least partly historical, for female lifers were regarded as generally less culpable and were expected to serve shorter periods in detention. Since they spent less time in closed/secure conditions, they experienced fewer problems of adjustment when moved to open establishments. More recently, though, this distinction between male and female lifers has disappeared, yet it is not intended that semi-open prisons for women should be created. This is not simply because of the relatively small number of female lifers. Bearing in mind the more limited types of accommodation in the female system, P4 Division (which is responsible for the allocation of female and certain young lifers) emphasises the quality of life and the care provided within a prison by the nature of the regime and the attitude of staff and their relationships with lifers, rather than the physical manifestations of security. For example, a closed prison for females may be operated in a manner which has more resemblance to a Category C,[11] semi-open establishment for men, than a Category B prison. More effort is to be put into staff training, in the assessment and counselling of lifers and detailed career-planning and monitoring so as to improve the quality of the lifers' experience of detention.

In contrast, P2 Division (the life-sentence section of the Prison Department) emphasises the desirability of transferring lifers to semi-open prisons as soon as it is felt safe to do so, in order to enhance the opportunity to assess their suitability for release. Thus, in recent years there has been an expansion of these establishments.

Another characteristic of life imprisonment and one which is of central importance to the sense of purpose and direction, is that lifers, other than Category A prisoners, should have career plans. These are written records which should try to reflect the sort of progression towards less secure conditions mentioned earlier. Prisoners should not spend lengthy periods in any one establishment. Indeed this greater movement of lifers through the system should have the advantage of indicating to the lifer the progress he is making towards release.

The Revised Strategy also recognises that lifers are a heterogeneous group, each having his own problems and posing a variety of areas of concern. Thus, the process of release should to some extent be a flexible one so as to take account of the needs and circumstances of individual cases. In a very few cases, it is unlikely that the prisoner will ever be released, either because the gravity of the offence requires a very long detention, or because of the need to protect the public, or perhaps simply because he was at an advanced age when sentenced. Nonetheless, such lifers will be accommodated with other prisoners within the same prison structure.

Progress Through A Life Sentence and Review Procedures

A person who is remanded in custody, having been charged with an offence which might result, on conviction, in a life sentence being imposed, will usually be detained in a remand centre of a local prison. The governor of the prison or remand centre sends information (about the accused and the alleged offence) to P3 Division so that a decision can be made as to the appropriate provisional security category of the individual who is held on remand. After conviction and sentence, the files of all adult male non-Category A lifers are sent to the Regional Director in the region where the local prison is situated, who then allocates the lifer to one of the three main centres – Wakefield, Wormwood Scrubs (D Wing), or Gartree. When making this allocation, various factors will be taken into account, such as the feasibility of visits, and the desirability to separate the prisoner from co-defendants. The allocation and management of all Category A prisoners is the responsibility of P3 Division of the Prison Department. The initial allocation of these prisoners is to a main centre or a dispersal prison. Female Category A lifers are allocated to H Wing of Durham prison. As for female and young offender non-Category A lifers, their files are passed to P4 Division for their initial allocation.

A lifer's case will be reviewed quite frequently during the course of the sentence, and some of the reviews will be especially significant. For example, those undertaken by the local review committee (LRC) and the Parole Board are concerned with whether or not they should recommend release on life licence. In any event, a review of one sort or another will be made every 12 months, simply to monitor the lifer's progress. Uniform officers and governor-grade staff (that is, the governor or those formerly described as the deputy or assistant governor) will comment on his behaviour since the previous review and they may well have interviewed him before preparing their reports.

The Confidential Memorandum

After all stages of any appeal have been completed, P2 Division prepares a summary of each case, known as the 'Confidential

Memorandum'. This document summarises all the available information about the offence and its surrounding circumstances. These summaries tend to conform to the same structure, and they provide personal details (including previous convictions and punishments) of the offender and victim, the events leading up to the offence and the crime itself, the defendant's statements to the police, medical reports (especially those relating to the offender), the trial and extracts from letters sent by the trial judge to the Home Secretary. A copy of the Confidential Memorandum is sent to the prison where the lifer is located to assist the governor and his staff in the preparation of reports which are required throughout the sentence.

'F75' Reports
The governor is informed by P2 Division when what are called 'F75' reports are required. These are concerned with the lifer's conduct in prison, the nature of his relationships with other prisoners and staff, the situation regarding his family and other outside contacts, and his eventual prospects for rehabilitation and release. They also contain staff opinions on his appropriate dispersal, such as transfer to another institution, possibly to less secure conditions, in order to assist P2 Division in assessing the next stage of his imprisonment. F75 reports are prepared by governor-grade staff, a medical officer, the chaplain and the prison probation officer. They will be called for from the prison at intervals of not more than three years. Additional reports – such as those prepared by the lifer's case officer, psychologists or others with a special knowledge of the lifer – may also be forwarded to P2 Division.

Fixing the first parole review date

Until a few years ago, the first major formal review of a life-sentence case was by what was known as the Joint Committee which was set up in 1973 and consisted of the Chairman and Vice-Chairman of the Parole Board (the latter was invariably a High Court judge), a psychiatrist from the Parole Board, and two senior officials from P2 Division. The main function of this Committee was to recommend to the Home Secretary a future date at which the lifer's first formal parole review should be undertaken by the Local Review Committee (LRC) of the prison in which he would be then held. This consultation between the Joint Committee and the Home Secretary normally took place after the lifer had served about three years in prison. To assist in the making of its recommendation, the Committee had before it a copy of the Confidential Memorandum and the first F75 reports prepared on the lifer by the prison. If it felt unable to recommend a date when the case should be reviewed for release – perhaps because it was clear that the lifer could not be released for several years – the Committee would fix a further date for the case to be brought before them again.

On 30 November 1983 the then Home Secretary, Mr Leon Brittan, stated in a written answer to the House of Commons that he had disbanded the Joint Committee, so that decisions about the date of the first formal parole reviews are now taken by the Home Secretary after consultation with the Lord Chief Justice and, if possible, the trial judge.[12] The judiciary must be asked for their views on the tariff period – that is the length of time to be served in prison to meet the needs of retribution and deterrence. The first review by the LRC takes place three years before the expiry of the tariff period. Originally this consultation would take place when the lifer had served about three years of his time in custody.[13]

However, the timing of this first formal review of life-sentence prisoners has had to be amended as the result of the decision of the Divisional Court's judgment in the case of *Rv, Secretary of State for the Home Department ex parte Handscomb and others*.[14] There, Lord Justice Watkins described the practice of waiting three or possibly four years before undertaking a review as 'irrational' and 'unreasonable'. Instead the judiciary should be consulted for their views on the appropriate tariff 'immediately after a life sentence has been passed'. No explanation for delaying the consultation was offered to the court and his Lordship could think of no advantages in doing so. Indeed, he felt there was good reasons for immediate reviews:

The facts of the case and the impression the prisoner has made upon the trial judge will be fresh in his mind. Both he and the Lord Chief Justice (within a short time, I feel sure) could provide the Home Secretary with the tariff. Thus, at the very outset of custody, the Home Secretary could set in motion the process of selecting the date for the first review and likewise of causing those who advise him to watch for signs of special circumstances or exceptional progress. . . . There may be in some cases advantage arising from obtaining the tariff very soon after sentence is passed which will be of benefit to a prisoner, in that release on parole will be accelerated for him.

Under the 1983 system, the delay in obtaining the judicial view on tariff, 'must lead, in almost every case, to the equivalent of 9 years' fixed term sentence (3 years before request to the judges, 3 years' review process including consideration by the Parole Board assuming reference to a local review committee immediately after receiving the initial judicial view, and 3 years' notional remission) (per Lord Justice Watkins). Although these comments relate primarily to discretionary life sentences, they can also be applied to mandatory sentences. It is possible, albeit not particularly commonplace, that it might be felt to be appropriate for a convicted murderer to be released from prison on licence before he has served, say, nine years in custody.

According to the revised procedures announced by the current Home Secretary, consultation with the judiciary should take place 'as soon as practicable after the imposition of the sentence'.[15] This is to apply to all life sentences, both discretionary and mandatory.[16] Under the 1983 policy it was theoretically possible to bring forward the consultation with the judiciary for the determination of tariff in very exceptional cases – although the Divisional Court was not given any criteria for identifying the exceptions. The court was told that in 1984 there were nearly 2000 life sentence prisoners in custody, but only five cases had been identified where there had been an accelerated request for initial judicial review and two of those related to offenders under 17 years of age.

Lord Justice Watkins' judgment has also had implications for the process of determining the tariff. Where the life-sentence is discretionary, the tariff is the determinate sentence that would have been passed but for the element of mental instability and/or public risk. Henceforth, the Home Secretary must accept the judicial view on tariff: no other factors can be taken into account, otherwise the Home Secretary may effectively be re-sentencing the offender. In murder cases, however, life imprisonment is mandatory, so that the notional equivalent fixed-term sentence does not arise. In these cases, the Home Secretary had announced that he will continue to consider other factors – such as the need to maintain public confidence in the penal system – as well as the views of the judiciary.

These new arrangements apply to all those sentenced to life imprisonment on or after 1 October 1987. At the time of the introduction of these revised procedures, there were – of course – some life sentence prisoners who had not been given a date for their first review by the local review committee. Here P2 Division had to set about obtaining the views of the judiciary immediately so that LRC dates could be determined. As at 1 October 1987 there was also another group of life-sentence prisoners in respect of whom adjustments may have been necessary in the light of the Handscomb decision. Those who had received discretionary life sentence who had a first LRC date had to be re-examined to consider whether the date of their first LRC review conformed with the judicial views on tariff. Where appropriate, the LRC dates had to be altered.

Although adjustments have had to be made after the Handscomb case, Lord Justice Watkins acknowledged that the 'broad concept of the [1983] policy is unassailable'. It had been held to be lawful by the House of Lords in the case of *In re Findlay*.[17] The amendments to the timing of the consultation with the judiciary and the determination of tariff were necessary though, to prevent potential injustice.

All prisoners should be informed,[18] at an early stage, of the date of their first review by the LRC, which will normally take place three years before the expiry of the tariff period. The setting of the LRC review three years' before the expiry of the tariff period is to provide a reasonable time in which to prepare and test the prisoner – for example, in an open prison and/or the Pre-Release Employment Scheme – before release is finally authorised by the Home Secretary. It should be emphasised that, at this stage – the first formal review – the only issue for consideration is that of tariff. The other major factor in releasing life-sentence prisoners is that of risk, but this is something which is regularly assessed by those who submit reports on the prisoners and it is therefore a matter for the Parole Board when making recommendations to the Home Secretary. However, in cases where the prisoner is likely to serve more than 20 years, the first LRC review will be held after he has spent 17 years in custody.[19]

Twenty-year minimum categories

At this point, it may be recalled that in October 1983, the then Home Secretary announced at the Conservative Party Conference, and formally confirmed in a written answer to the House of Commons on 30 November 1983, that in four categories of murder he would henceforth use his discretion so that the offenders should expect to serve at least 20 years in custody.[20] These categories are: murders of police or prison officers, terrorist murderers, sexual or sadistic murderers of children, and murderers by firearm in the course of robbery. The Home Secretary continued that: '... there will be cases where the gravity of the offence requires a still longer period. Other murders, outside these categories may merit no less punishment to mark the seriousness of the offence'.

Career Plans

When the first LRC date has been fixed. P2 or, as the case may be P4 Division then prepare a 'career plan'.[21] According to a Circular sent by P2 Division to the governors to all lifer establishments. 'The purpose of the career plan is to indicate the man's likely progression through the system, to identify training and treatment needs and to highlight particular areas of concern'. The principles underlying a lifer's progression are stated as being: (i) that he should be allocated to the lowest appropriate level of security – where possible, allocation will be made on the basis of proximity to the lifer's home, thereby facilitating visits, although training and treatment requirements, available facilities at specific prisons, and vacancies also have to be taken into account; (ii) those in dispersal and other Category B establishments should be moved to a Category C prison well before the first LRC review; (iii) virtually all lifers should be released via an open prison and the Pre-Release Employment Scheme. Staff at the main centre are strongly urged to offer advice on identifying particular training and treatment needs and to make appropriate recommendations. They are encouraged to adopt a team approach.

As a result of the Handscomb case, career plans should be available earlier than they used to be. Where the date of the first LRC review has been set at four to six years after the date when the lifer was first remanded in prison, the F.75 reports should be drafted when he has served 18 months. The career plan will then be prepared, unless the lifer is to stay at the main centre, in which case his career plan should be drawn up three years into his sentence. If the first LRC date is set at more than six years after the first remand date, the plan should also be available at the three-year stage. The vast majority of convicted murderers will come within one of these two categories. Other lifers, though, may be in a slightly different position, for if the first LRC date is set for less than four years after the first remand date, the career plan should be prepared after the views of the Parole Board have been disclosed. In practice, it is likely that plans will be available at about the three-year mark.

The plan is filed at P2 Division and a copy should be sent to the main centre, together with a note of the first LRC review date. The career plan should be kept with the Confidential Memorandum.[22]

The confidentiality of the plan may appear to be a rather ambiguous issue. On the one hand, the Prison Department Circular Z/1989 states:

> . . .[it] is a restricted document in the sense that it should not be shown or copied to any prisoner. The reason for this is that planning at such an early stage can only be tentative and the career is liable to be amended at later stages of sentence for a variety of reasons. So much will depend not only on the prisoner's subsequent behaviour but also on other incidents and events inside and outside the system that it would be unhelpful to enter into any firm commitment or 'contract'. (para. 33)

But the Circular immediately goes on to state that:

> This does not mean, however, that the plan should not be discussed with the lifer in general terms. Indeed, unless there are good reasons for doing otherwise . . . this should be done – at the same time as the prisoner is given his LRC review date – so as to convey to him that some thought has been given to his likely progression through the system; that there will be stages and targets for the assessment of progress, and that his domestic and other needs are recognised so far as possible. (para. 34)

The essence of career plans is to indicate to both staff and lifers the likely shape of the sentence, how the prisoner is expected to work with staff, and the particular matters of concern – such as whether he has a drink problem or whether he can behave responsibly when put under stress – which need to be carefully examined. Staff are requested to discuss possible moves to different prisons with lifers, to identify their preferences and alternatives, and to report on these issues to P2 Division. The career plans should be read in conjunction with the Confidential Memorandum and F75 reports which are made by staff at the prisons in which the lifer is accommodated. In this respect, the plan is to be regarded as a form of checklist when making subsequent assessments of the prisoner's progress.

Moving to different prisons

Instructions for the transfer of prisoners from one prison to another are issued by the Prison Department. There are a variety of possible reasons for moving a prisoner to a different establishment. Obviously, the career plan must be kept in mind and the desire to accommodate the prisoner in the lowest level of security. At the same time, it is thought to be undesirable to keep a prisoner in a particular prison for more than a few years. To do otherwise would incur the risk that he might become rather 'stale' in the same environment, living in the same routine for too long. Moreover, the prisoner needs to be given new challenges and changes in lifestyle which will inevitably accompany a move to a different prison even though he may remain in the same security category. As the Prison Department acknowledges in its Circular:

> Conditions in terms of physical amenities, flexibility of regime etc., vary a good deal between lifer establishments, and there are some well-known anomalies. It may sometimes be difficult for a prisoner moving from what he or she may have regarded as a 'comfortable number' to more spartan and superficially regimented conditions to equate the move with progress towards release. There may be similar difficulties in connection with accessibility for domestic visits. (para. 42)

Where lifers do express their discontent as a result of a transfer to a different prison, staff are requested to remind them that the primary aim is their release from custody and that this might entail apparently short-term sacrifices. Moreover, one of the objectives of the penal system is to put the prisoner in as wide a variety of situations as possible and to assess his response. In this way the system can maximise the information upon which a decision can ultimately be made regarding the release of the prisoner and the risk to the public.

A prisoner may also be transferred for disciplinary reasons. He may have committed disciplinary offences as a consequence of which it is felt that he should be kept in a more secure establishment where he will have less opportunity to offend. Cases sometimes arise in which the behaviour of a group of prisoners gives cause for concern and staff take the view that the appropriate course of action is to separate them by moving some of them to different prisons. Here it may be that the group of prisoners are jointly committing disciplinary offences. Alternatively, a prisoner may feel threatened in some way by fellow inmates and the only long-term solution is to transfer him to another prison.

A young offender, (often referred to as a YP), who was aged less than 18 years when the offence was committed will normally be detained in a youth custody centre, but he cannot remain there beyond the age of 22. He must then be transferred to a prison which accommodates adult prisoners. It is felt that this age-related policy reduces the danger of collusion between staff and inmates whereby a prisoner seeks to remain in a particular regime, and it minimises the danger of premature reclassification. It also permits a degree of flexibility in that there are some months available in which to prepare some immature YPs for adult prison life.

The Local Review Committee and the Parole Board

The situation regarding each life sentence prisoner should be reviewed at regular intervals – preferably every six months according to the Prison Department's Circular 2/1989, para. 44 – in order to assess his progress. The boards carrying out these reviews should be multi-disciplinary, comprising representatives from all departments in the prison and thus able to comment on the lifer's physical and mental health and his attitude to his offence, his sentence and his plans for the future. The Prison Department encourages the attendance at some stage of the proceedings at review boards of the prisoner, for this 'can go a long way towards breaking down prisoner's natural suspicion of collective authority, and establishing open and honest relationships' (para. 45).

Reviews by the LRC are governed by the Local Review Committee Rules, Rule 5 of which states that 'the local review committee shall review the case of any prisoner if directed to do so by the Secretary of State'. The appropriate governor is notified by P2 Division of the date of the first and subsequent LRC reviews. The timing of any LRC review will be based on the tariff for the particular offence and the need for the lifer to have been in the prison long enough to have settled down and for staff to have had sufficient time to get to know and assess him. The review will be undertaken even though the prisoner may indicate that he does not wish his case to be reviewed.

The Committee, which includes members of the Board of Visitors and other lay outsiders, will be provided with all the current and earlier F-75 reports and any earlier decisions of a LRC. The prisoner may make his own submission to them either in writing or verbally in an interview with a member of the committee. The LRC should make a formal recommendation regarding the prisoner's release, setting out the grounds for the recommendation as fully as possible. The case is passed to the Prison Department and P2 Division undertakes further consultation – for example, the Directorate of the Prison Medical Service is approached for comments on the prisoner's mental condition and whether he should be treated as a potential danger to society.

All this information, including the latest remarks made by the DPMS, is then sent to the Parole Board. The Board, which must include a High Court judge and a psychiatrist, and preferably a probation officer, considers the case, with professional advisers present from the Prison Department. They may recommend that the prisoner be released on licence or further detention. If the latter, the Board will state when the next review should take place. On the other hand, if the Board recommends release, the papers are sent to the Lord Chief Justice and the trial judge for their comments. The criteria for selection for parole are set out in Appendix B, p. 297. Where, after consultation with the judiciary, release on licence is proposed and where the Board recommend further review after transfer to an open prison, the case must be submitted to the Secretary of State for his consideration. The authority of a Home Office Minister is required before a lifer can be moved to open conditions. In addition, where a prisoner has been detained for more than ten years and the Parole Board have not yet recommended release, Ministers must be informed. The prisoner is informed of the result of the review, but if he is not to be released, he will not be given any reasons for his continued detention. There is no right of appeal against the decision to refuse parole. It is feared that the giving of such explanation might be abused by the prisoner in his efforts to secure release. This is regarded as an example of the effects of the paramouncy of the need to protect the public.

The final stages before release

The Home Secretary may or may not accept the recommendations of the Parole Board. Under Section 61 Criminal Justice Act 1967 only he can authorise the release of a lifer on licence. In 1986 374 lifers were considered by the Parole Board, of which 115 were recommended as suitable for release 'on dates ranging from the immediate future to two years ahead'.[23] The Home Secretary did not accept 12 recommendations for release and a further 19 cases were still being considered by the end of 1986.

When a lifer receives a provisional date for his release on licence, the system should make the appropriate preparations either by transferring him to an open prison or by giving him increasing experience outside the prison or both. This may take the form of shopping visits to a nearby town where the prisoner is accompanied by a member of staff. It might also include working and/or studying outside the prison. Lifers who have been given a provisional release date are eligible for short periods of home leave when they are within nine months of that date. This usually enables them to spend the weekend away from the prison with their family. The vast majority of prisoners will spend some time in open conditions towards the end of their detention. The time spent in these less secure regimes and the experience gained whilst the prisoner is outside the prison boundaries not only forms part of the preparations for his release, but also provides further evidence of his suitability for release. If his conduct even at this stage gives cause for concern his provisional release date may be withdrawn and he may also be transferred to a less liberal regime.

It is now standard practice for lifers to be released on licence via the Pre-Release Employment Scheme (PRES). Usually the last six months will be spent in this way, but in some cases the period is nine months. The prisoner lives in a prison hostel and should pursue ordinary employment in the community, returning to the hostel in the evenings by a prescribed time. He must pay a contribution from his wages towards his board and lodging, and is encouraged to resume responsibility for the maintenance of his family. Weekend leave from the hostel, which is usually conditional upon the prisoner having obtained a job, may assist in the renewal of relationships with family and friends and acquaintances.

Again, the time spent on PRES helps to test suitability for release. But it also provides an opportunity for the prisoner to readjust to a 'normal working routine' and to equip himself financially and socially for life outside the prison system. Life sentence prisoners are given priority over other categories of prisoner for PRES vacancies. However, the Prison Department Circular 2/1989 acknowledges that, 'the national employment situation has made it necessary to adopt a broader approach and other, prison-based schemes designed to provide useful experience and testing, such as Job Familiarisation, Community Work, full-time education, and where available, suitable outside training courses, all have something to contribute, and local initiatives in these fields can be considered' (para. 53).

One of the most important matters concerning a lifer as he approaches release is his resettlement plans and arrangements. Where he has strong family connections or other ties, such arrangements may not be problematic. But where he has no relationships of this nature difficulties are more likely to arise. The prisoner's plans and arrangements which he makes for his release are regarded as very significant by the Parole Board, and the Chairman has stated that the views of the outside probation officer are usually treated as most important of all.[24] Naturally, prison staff are encouraged to monitor resettlement plans; if they are felt to be unsatisfactory, the release date may be deferred.

Life Licence

The standard form of the life licence (which is reproduced in Appendix A, p. 296) is a simple set of rules. They require the lifer:

  (i) to place himself under the supervision of whichever probation officer is nominated.
 (ii) report to the probation officer on release and to keep in touch with him or her in accordance with the officer's instructions;
(iii) to receive visits at his home at the request of the probation officer;
 (iv) to live and work only where approved by the probation officer and to notify him/her of any changes of address or loss of job;
  (v) not to travel outside Great Britain without the probation officer's prior permission.

After consultation with the Parole Board, other conditions may be added according to the circumstances of particular cases – for example, the need for medical or psychiatric supervision, or prohibiting the licensee from communicating with a specified person, or attempting to do so. Superficially, the idea of attaching conditions to the licence may seem very attractive – such as abstinence of alcohol, or the imposition of a curfew. But any conditions must be enforceable, and the probation service has tended to oppose the stipulation of a long list of conditions because of the difficulties of enforcement and because of possible adverse effects on the supervisory relationship generally.

The licence remains in force for the whole of the remainder of the prisoner's life. The supervisory probation officer submits regular reports to the Home Office. Usually, after a minimum of four years, if the licensee has settled well, without giving any cause for concern, and the supervising officer so recommends, the licence conditions are cancelled. Otherwise they are retained for as long as it is thought necessary. But the licence continues in operation, and it may be revoked by the Home Secretary at any time on the recommendation of the Parole Board. According to the Prison Department's Circular 2/1989, 'A licence would not normally be revoked if the licensee had committed a minor offence unrelated to that which led to the life sentence, but it would always be if any conduct gave reason for thinking that the licensee might again be a danger to the public generally or any member of it' (para. 58). If the licence is revoked the licensee is immediately recalled to prison to continue his life sentence. He will be given an opportunity to make representations to the Parole Board, who may order his immediate release. If not, the question of release is assessed in the same way as the initial release of a life sentence prisoner.

Prison life for lifers

With the possible exception of Kingston prison, life sentence prisoners are not detained in an environment which is physically separated from other inmates who are serving determinate sentences. Kingston prison is an exception; it is a specialised training prison catering solely for lifers. In any event, lifers are not subjected to a special regime simply because of the indeterminacy of their sentence. The nature of the regime to which prisoners are subjected is determined primarily by their security categorisation.

Notwithstanding the violent nature of their offences, not all lifers constitute a security risk. Yet, in a survey of the lifer population, Brown (1979) found that:

> ... the 'low risk' life prisoners are exceptions, and the general rule is that life prisoners are held in higher security conditions than other prisoners. In general, a lifer will not be classified as 'C' or 'D' until he has served several years of his sentence, but will be categorised initially as 'B'....[25]

The median periods served before being transferred to lower security establishments were four to six years for Category 'C' and six to eight years for Category D (see p.10).

Roger Sapsford (1983) described the predicament of life sentence prisoners thus:

> Lifers are exposed to the same kind of regime as other prisoners with its extreme emphasis on routine, its requirements of obedience to prison officers and to rules laid down by others and its

tendency to make the prisoner dependent on staff even for trivial facilities. They are housed, many of them, in the same noisy, overcrowded, depressingly Victorian prisons of which a Minister of State at the Home Office said that:–

The statistics have little meaning until one has entered a small cell in one of our ancient gaols and seen and even smelled, the effect of these men living in an oppressive claustrophobic atmosphere. (Lord Harris, the Guardian, 8 November 1978).[26]

Whilst it is true that there are some more modern prisons housing lifers where the accommodation is perhaps slightly less oppressive than as pictured above, it is nevertheless the case that Sapsford's description is generally indicative of the situation in which many prisoners still find themselves.

Fitzgerald and Sim (1982) portrayed this image of dreariness and indignity in the following account of a typical day in prison:

Each morning about six o'clock, and after the first count of the day, the cells are unlocked. In the next two hours, the 'slop out', wash, make their beds, clean the cells, and eat breakfast. 'Slopping out' is one of the most symbolic practices of modern prisons. Prisoners carry their piss-pots down the landing, and queue up to empty them in the recess. . . . Razor blades are handed out and collected back each morning. If a prisoner wishes to grow or shave off a moustache he has to seek permission from the governors. Applications to see the governor, doctor or social worker must be made during this period. Applications are made through the principal officer, who decides whether or not a prisoner will see the governor. Before eight o'clock prisoners who are going to work-shops line up outside their cells. They are counted out of the wing, marched over to and counted out of the workshop and marched back into the wing . . . for dinner. They are counted again . . . [In the early afternoon] they line up for work and are counted and marched back. . . . When moving from one part of the prison to another, prisoners are always escorted and formally handed over to the officer in charge. After tea, prisoners are . . . locked in their cells for a 'quiet hour' which is historically provided as a space for personal reflection. It also coincides with the time staff take tea. In the early evening, prisoners may be unlocked for a recreation period, when they can associate with others, attend evening classes, watch television, read papers, and play games such as darts, snooker, chess and table tennis. . . . The majority either stay in their cells, watch television, or simply walk around the [wing] . . . talking with friends. . . . By about nine o'clock prisoners are back in their cells. . . . Officers begin to lock up, counting as they go from cell to cell. About ten o'clock the lights go out. Throughout the night, the patrolling officer will look through the peep-hole of each cell to check that the occupants are inside and asleep. For top-security prisoners, the cell light burns all night.[27]

This may be an accurate reflection of life in many prisons, though penal establishments vary, and some of the specific characteristics identified by Fitzgerald and Sim do not apply, for example, to lower security prisons. As stated earlier, life-sentence prisoners are entitled to be accommodated in a single cell. Clearly the quality of life in penal institutions will depend to a large extent on the variety and nature of the facilities available in them. In the course of their sentence prisoners may carry out work – usually of a menial or routine nature – in different types of workshop. They may be offered certain vocational training courses over a period of weeks or months, and it is possible that prisoners will acquire skills which will assist or enable them to obtain employment when they are released. Educational courses, on a full-time or part-time basis, are also available in many prisons, though there may not be one which is suitable or sufficiently interesting for a prisoner at the particular prison in which he is detained.[28] The prison service as a whole contains a wide range of courses, from very basic education – teaching prisoners to read and write – to Open University degree courses (at a limited number of establishments). Similarly, the range of options open to a prisoner to pursue hobbies, sporting activities and other forms of recreation will differ from one prison to another. To some extent, these matters are constrained by the Prison Rules, although it is fair to say that the way in which governors interpret them should also be taken into account.

COMMENTS AND CRITICISMS

Notwithstanding the efforts of the Prison Department to develop a policy for the management of life-sentence prisoners, a number of critical observations and reservations have been made, both from academics and those 'working in the field', which should not be overlooked. What follows is intended as an indication of the main areas of concern.

The Confidential Memorandum

Regrettably it has been the case that some lifers spend considerably longer than three years in the main centre; the delay being caused by the simple fact that the reports and the Confidential Memorandum have not been prepared by the appropriate time. For example, having stated that there are cases where it takes nearly four years instead of the desired three, John Staples – the then Deputy Governor at Holloway Prison – commented:

> This has caused considerable stress to lifers in Main Centres and embarrassment to staff. But so far away from the impact of such decisions are those who make them that this has been insufficiently appreciated.[29]

Fixing the First Parole Review Date and the 1983 Policy

Commenting on the pre-1983 system for determining the first LRC date, Maguire *et al.* (1984)[30] remarked:

> Getting a date was regarded as an opportunity to prove over the next few years their fitness for release and as a 'message' from the authorities that progress in prison would give them a good chance of parole. By contrast, failure to get a date left the prisoner in a state of uncertainty, with no clear light at the end of the tunnel. (p. 253)

At the time of carrying out their research, Maguire *et al.* reported that 50 per cent of lifers were given a date for their first LRC review as a result of their initial Joint Committee hearing. The LRC dates were usually set at least three years into the future. 'The remainder had to wait sometimes for several years, for reconsideration' (at p. 253). The researchers summarised the old system as follows:

> ... while there is little doubt that the amount of time actually served by lifers, particularly those who did not arouse worries about dangerousness, could not be understood without reference to the strong constraints of a judicial tariff system, this is by no means the whole story. Several other parties had the possibility, in individual cases, of exercising a significant influence upon the release decision. (pp. 264, 265).

Maguire *et al.* (1984) have made a number of observations and comments about the post-1983 system. One benefit to the prisoner is that he should not now be kept 'in the dark' about the minimum period he can expect to serve. 'Most will have reason to expect that, if they can dispel any concerns about the danger they pose to the public and avoid disciplinary trouble in prison, they will have a very good chance of release when they have served a specified number of years' (p. 265).

However, many of the authors' comments about the new system are highly critical. For example, lifers will have a much reduced chance to 'beat the tariff'. The research showed that in several cases the LRC and the Parole Board recommended release at a time earlier than that suggested by the Lord Chief Justice, and that the Home Secretary accepted some of these recommendations. Yet, whilst acknowledging that the Home Secretary may, at a later stage in the sentence, bring forward the first LRC date,[31] the authors felt that, '. . . past experience . . . suggests that the Prison Department officials who advise him are reluctant to support release significantly in advance of the L.C.J's recommended minimum period, and therefore it is unlikely that many review dates will, in fact, be brought forward' (p. 265).

The dangers of this are aptly illustrated in the recently published report of the Parliamentary All-Party Penal Affairs Group, where the comments of a life sentence prisoner on the new policy were as follows:

> Some extremely long review dates have been sent back by the Home Office in what are quite clearly and explicitly seen by many staff as 'political decisions'. . . . In general, the new policy's evident harshness has been destructive of prison morale and has encouraged more bitterness than I have seen in five years of prison life. One man in his early 30s has taken his own life: others are heard to discuss the idea of suicide without the customary smile to lessen its seriousness. It is a reawakened spectre. In prison there has always been some constructive atmosphere, even among lifers who are, after all, statistically one of the 'safest' bets for a law-abiding life as future free citizens. Recently however, I see a kind of bitter hopelessness.[32]

One of the broader implications of the new system was that the influence of the LRCs and the Parole Board became significantly reduced. Cases are first reviewed by the LRC and then the Parole Board three years before the expiry of the tariff period. But Maguire *et al.* (1984) discovered that only very rarely did the Parole Board feel that the Lord Chief Justice's recommendations were too lenient and did not seek to delay the release of prisoners who were not regarded as a danger to society. The role of the Board thus appeared to be one of largely 'rubber stamping' the views of the judiciary in these cases. At the same time, it is only right to acknowledge that the Parole Board should retain a significant role in determining the release of prisoners who are seen as dangerous. Here again though, the researchers found that the Board were 'very reluctant to act against the recommendations of the D.P.M.S.[33] who provide authoritative medical assessments of risk' (p. 266).

Another worrying feature of the post-1983 system is that the influence of an important group of people involved in the assessment of lifers has also been reduced – viz. the staff in the prisons accommodating lifers. Traditionally, considerable interest was taken in the lifer's 'progress' through prison, and in this respect attention was paid to such matters as his relationships with other prisoners and staff, his work, hobbies and recreational activities, and how he coped with problems and stressful situations. The new heightened emphasis on tariff may well mean that less significance is to be attached to these issues when fixing release dates. As Maguire *et al.* (1984) remarked:

> It may be that performance in prison in reality made relatively little difference to the release of many prisoners; certainly, the research suggests that most non-dangerous lifers served a tariff period, and that it was only in cases where they offended seriously against prison discipline (or, conversely, reacted exceptionally well) that there was any significant variation. On the other hand, the fact that progress in prison could make some difference, was a positive element, both for lifers, in that it gave them some hope of earning earlier release through their own efforts, and for prison staff, who could feel that their work with lifers and their report-writing might have a real influence in the ultimate decision. No doubt, too, it played a part in easing control problems. (p. 266)

The extent to which any or all of these fears is well founded obviously remains to be seen. But certainly the Parliamentary All-Party Penal Affairs Group had sufficiently strong reservations about the new policy to lead them to call for a return to the system that operated before 1983 when the Joint Committee set the first review date by the LRC (para. 81).

In essence, as Maguire *et al.* pointed out, it is the judiciary who will have a much more influential role in determining the minimum lengths of sentence which lifers will serve. As a result of the emphasis placed on 'the requirements of retribution and deterrence', tariff will be the primary criteria for setting a release date. Only after they have served the 'time for the crime' will other factors relating to their suitability for release become relevant. The broad conclusions to be drawn from this were forcibly put:

> Life sentences remain the only prison sentences for which sentencers do not, in effect, determine the minimum and maximum term, [except ... in the small proportion of cases ... where the trial judge makes a formal minimum recommendation ....], and there seems to be no logical reason why this anomaly should not be removed. However, it seems much more satisfactory to remove it by *allowing judges to pass determinate sentences for murder in open court*, rather than by confidential recommendations sent to the Home Secretary. The crucial difference is that an offender given a long determinate sentence for rape, robbery, or other major crime has a right to appeal. A lifer who receives a parole review date set at, say 15 years has no appeal. (p. 267)

The Twenty Year Minimum Category

Having reviewed the recent statistics relating to these categories of prisoners, the Parliamentary All-Party Penal Affairs Group (para. 98) reported that there is likely to be a substantial difference to the length of time served by those convicted of murder by shooting in the furtherance of theft. There will be less impact in cases of those who murder police or prison officers and sexual or sadistic murderers of children. The Group were unable to assess the effects in relation to terrorist murderers. Lifers who already had a provisional release date before the new policy was introduced have not had them deferred or cancelled. But it is reported that four prisoners whose release in the fairly near future would not have been in line with the Home Secretary's view of the gravity of the offence were returned from open to closed conditions. One prisoner indicated that his release had been put back about four years. Fears of such effects of the reassessment of cases following the introduction of the new policy were expressed by the British Association of Social Workers. The Group felt it was significant that the number of cases in which the Home Secretary rejected the Parole Board's recommendation for release of lifers on licence, which fluctuated between three and seven between 1977 and 1982, rose to 15 in 1983.

Whilst accepting that many lifers who fall within the categories identified by the Home Secretary should remain in custody for very lengthy periods, it was argued that all cases should be considered on their individual merits and that it is wrong to operate a 'blanket policy'. These prisoners vary tremendously, and the detention for at least 20 years 'of a prisoner who could safely be released after a lesser period will do nothing to reduce violent crime' (para. 102). Inevitably, therefore, the Group proposed that the new policy should be discontinued. The implications of continuing the Home Secretary's policy of imprisoning certain murderers for at least 20 years were pointed out by Maguire *et al.* (1984), that a new kind of tariff will be introduced which is not judicial in origin. The effect of the new policy is summarised thus:

> . . . the Secretary of State could be said . . . to be usurping the role of the Lord Chief Justice as stipulator of the minimum period necessary to serve the interests of justice. While it is certainly the Home Secretary's right to deny a lifer release on any grounds he chooses, it has always been implicitly assumed that he will in a sense dilute his own power by consulting other parties with particular expertise and taking note of their opinions. It is not inconceivable that the L.C.J. would in fact recommend a minimum period of considerably *less* than 20 years for some of these crimes, based upon commensurability with his tariff scale for other types of murder. If so, would such recommendations be consistently ignored? (p. 267)

The Local Review Committee and the Parole Board

It has long been recognised that prisoners resent the fact that they are not told why they are denied parole, and there is no shortage of support for their claim to be given more information. For example, the Prison Reform Trust has talked of 'great tension, suspicion and bad feeling' resulting from the present system. Greater feedback to prisoners about the reasons for refusing to recommend release on licence would, according to the Trust, 'have a great and welcome effect on the administration of the life sentence'. The importance of this issue to lifers was described by John Staples (1981) thus:

> There are grave difficulties about giving reasons for Board decisions and, perhaps, these have to be accepted for fixed term prisoners. But for lifers, the decision is so much more significant

and the reaction likely to be more acute. There is no fall back date for the lifer to draw comfort from, no date of release beyond which he cannot be held. Such a peculiar disadvantage demands extraordinary treatment. (p. 7)

Predictably, perhaps, the majority of the Parliamentary All-Party Penal Affairs Group has recommended that prisoners should be made aware of the reasons for the conclusions reached at the end of the review (para. 91).

Prison Reports

At this point it is worth making some brief comments about the quality of the information which forms the basis on which prisoners are reviewed and their suitability for release is assessed. The extent to which the documentation provides a full and accurate picture from which constructive and reliable decisions can be made is clearly of immense importance. Yet Dr John Coker, who carried out research into all 239 lifers who were released between 1960–64 and 1970–74, has identified and discussed some of the common criticisms of prison records[34]: viz,

   (i) Reports of life sentence prisoners are usually subjective and judgmental, reflecting the staff's perception of the interaction between themselves and the prisoner.
  (ii) There is a danger that an opinion about a prisoner may be formed at an early stage in the process by a member of staff reading the dossier and that the rest of the documents is used, perhaps subsequently, to support the original view.
 (iii) There is also a danger that old material is simply repeated; that labels tend to stick.
  (iv) Although some efforts have been made to organise the material by using standardised forms, this has done little to improve the verification of the material.

Coker then remarks that the net result of these criticisms is 'not perhaps as bad as might seem to be the case'. By the time they are considered for parole, most lifers will have been moved from one prison to another, and these changes of environment and personnel provide fresh starts for the prisoners and a more widely-based staff view which may not be as subjective and well-worn as indicated above. Then again, the author admits that labels do tend to stick, and regardless of their accuracy it may be some time before their impact is diminished. As Maguire *et al.* (1984) observed:

> The acquisition of a 'label' of dangerousness was a complex affair, and might stem from the offence, indications of instability, or even failure to conform to disciplinary codes in prison. On the other hand, however it had been acquired, most prisoners were likely to lose the label at somewhere around the 10 year point in their sentence. They then stood a fair (although still below average) chance of release. (pp. 262, 263)

The ultimate importance of the information in the prisoner's dossier is, of course, the fact that it is used in the prediction of how he is likely to behave if released. Moreover, it is equally clear that behaviour in prison cannot be assumed to be a reliable indication of future conduct outside prison.[35] Yet O'Leary and Glaser (1972) commented that prisoners who show educational progress and achievement whilst in prison are more likely to be treated favourably in their parole application than those who do not.[36]

A further criticism by Coker (1985) is that the prisoner is not given sight of the documentation and is thus prevented from challenging any factual inaccuracies or opinions. In its *Review of Parole in England and Wales* (1981), the Home Office sought to justify the withholding of the dossier from the prisoner on the ground that disclosure might lead to 'non-committal reporting and reluctance by L.R.Cs and the Parole Board to take risks on this suspect information' (p. 20). Naturally, numerous factors may have a bearing on this issue, such as ethical considerations, or the fear of intimidation by prisoners. At the same time, it may well be that some staff who disagree with the policy of secrecy may ignore it surreptitiously or at least give broad hints to the prisoners.

Very little has been published about what prisoners feel about the unavailability of their records. Coker (1985) cites the example of a group of prisoners who, when shown their probation reports complained of factual errors and challenged the opinions of probation officers. John McVicar who was not a lifer but served a cumulative sentence of 26 years' imprisonment, discovered his file during a prison riot:

> I was surprised to learn that I was a member of the 'Richardson gang' . . . This was characteristic of many of the entries. Most were speculation, unsupported by facts. There was no insight into my character, personality or motives, other than that my crimes

revealed me as a violent professional thief-cum-robber. . . . I expected to learn something about myself, but what I learned was that they had no insight at all. . . . their analysis was either pedantic or tautologous or just plain wrong. . . . It made a lot of confetti and that was about all it was worth. . . . A few of the cons were outraged that priests had taken part in the assessment process. Under the seal of confessional . . . some of them had told some clerics things in confidence, and they had written them up for any nosy screw to browse through.[37]

It is difficult to know what weight should be attached to prisoners' views of the contents of their files. Although their comments should not be accepted uncritically, equally they should not simply be dismissed as of no value. A lifer has just one occasion on which he has the right to formally state his case for release, to the member of the local review committee who interviews him. He must therefore rely on the fairness of those who are charged with reviewing his case.

Delay in outcome of reviews

Those involved in looking after prisoners are well aware of the tensions created amongst inmates who are awaiting the result of their reviews. Naturally, the longer the period of waiting, the greater the tension is likely to be. Not only may this cause problems for the individual reviewees but it may also have an adverse effect on other prisoners and on staff. In its Report for 1985/86 the Prison Department stated that by the end of 1985 the average time between consideration by the LRC and the Parole Board was ten and a half months.[38] This was said to be caused by an increase in the lifer population and the need for additional staff in P2 Division to cope with the volume of cases. Not surprisingly, the announcement of the ten and a half month period attracted adverse comments from various bodies, including the Board of Visitors and Her Majesty's Chief Inspector of Prisons. The Parole Board, in its 1986 Report, reveals that, '. . . following an increase in the complement of the Life Sentence Section at the end of 1985, the average time taken between consideration by the L.R.C. and consideration by the Board had been reduced to below eight months by the end of 1986 (para. 15).

Flexibility in Security Categorisation

The 'Revised Strategy' envisages a gradual progression towards release so that as he moves through the system a lifer should be subjected to an increasingly less secure environment. Yet, Peter Timms, a former governor of Maidstone prison, has argued that a more creative approach was adopted in the early 1950s.[39] Although he considers that the present policy towards lifers works reasonably well, he feels that there should be greater flexibility in security classification so that suitable prisoners may be transferred to open prisons more quickly. The current 'stepping stone' principle whereby prisoners move in stages from closed to open conditions has tended to lengthen some sentences unnecessarily. He also seems to favour the facility, in appropriate cases, for allowing lifers to work outside the prison boundaries in the relatively early stages of their sentence.

Influential support was given to Timm's calls for greater flexibility in security categorisation and the need to guard against unnecessarily lengthening sentences in the report of the Control Review Committee (CRC) published in July 1984.[40] The CRC expressed its concern that security categorisation was insufficiently objective, resulting in a tendency to over-categorise and thereby delay progress towards lower security establishments. A more objectively based security categorisation system was thus recommended (see paras. 80–85). Whilst accepting that career plans are a useful tool in sending the prisoner the right signals about the connection between the behaviour and the course of his imprisonment, the CRC added:

> We would like to see a move towards individual programmes for prisoners, incorporating more diverse activity than at present and geared towards the abilities and needs of the inmate himself. (para. 96)

The provision of incentives was recognised as a particularly invaluable mechanism for control, and the impact of the relative discomfort of life in a Category C prison, in the opinion of inmates, when compared to that in a Category B establishment, did not escape the CRC's attention. Although it may be argued that, regardless of the comparative comfort involved, a move to a semi-open prison is an important step towards release, it was felt that,

> the style in which lower category prisoners are presently run is more appropriate to a short-term population, and that more attention may need to be given to developing the handling of long-term prisoners, well into their sentences, in ways that recognise their experience in the higher security prisons from which they

have come. This may mean developing separate long-term segments of Category C and D prisons where, for example, the rules governing personal possessions might be more liberal. (para. 102)

Issues of this sort are important if a policy is to be pursued of making security downgrading and progression through the system 'a consistent and psychologically credible process' (para. 103).

The Prison Department appears to be beginning to tackle the question of providing adequate incentives in lower security establishments. The present Home Secretary has authorised additional privileges in open prisons so as to assist prisoners to strengthen and retain their contacts with family and friends. Since April 1986 there has been no limit to the number of letters which prisoners may send and receive; there are earlier and more frequent opportunities for home leave, and payphones to which prisoners have access are being installed. The Prison Department has declined to extend these privileges to Category C prisons thus far. Instead, it intends to evaluate the impact of these changes in open establishments before proceeding any further.

The call for small units

In his discussions with the Parliamentary All-Party Penal Affairs Group, John McCarthy, a former governor of Wormwood Scrubs, maintained that lifers should be held in smaller units than they are at present (paras. 67 and 68). In order to treat them as human beings, to enhance their feelings of worth and to give them a vested interest in the stability of the unit of which they were a part, lifers should be actively involved in the operation of their unit. McCarthy argued that self-contained domestic units accommodating up to 35 or 40 lifers were essential – the prisoners would still go to workshops and join in other activities where they would meet other categories of inmates. But he felt that if the units exceeded 40, then 'inmates culture' would build up and prisoners would spend less time communicating with staff and with each other. These small units would assist in the development of group processes and would generate a regime which increased self-respect by enabling prisoners to exercise more responsibility for their decisions. Admittedly, the operation of smaller units would be more costly in terms of the staff involved. McCarthy claimed that existing wings at lifer main centres and some dispersal persons could be converted into the sort of units he advocates.

This proposal is supported by Gordon Fowler, a former Chief

Inspector of Prisons and Deputy Director-General of the Prison Service. In addition to the benefits that would accrue to lifers, the work of prison staff would be much more rewarding. There is a vital need for staff to be involved in the community life of the wing, and real security and control can only be achieved by knowing what is going to happen, before it does happen. In other words, a good relationship must be formed between staff and prisoners. In support of the McCarthy proposal, the Parliamentary All-Party Penal Affairs Group recommended that small units housing up to 40 prisoners, who need not be exclusively lifers but may also include other long-term prisoners, should be set up on an experimental basis, and thereafter be closely monitored and evaluated (paras. 72 and 73).

The Need for Hope

Not surprisingly, concern has been expressed about the position of prisoners who serve particularly lengthy periods of detention. The difficulties in fostering a sense of purpose and direction in such people are all too obvious. The Parliamentary All-Party Penal Affairs Group recommended that if an earlier review date has not been fixed then all prisoners should be reviewed after they have spent ten years in custody with subsequent reviews at least every five years (para. 81). The knowledge that his case was being considered by the Parole Board, a group of people who were essentially not part of the prison system, would be a valuable psychological asset to the prisoner, and he would also know that he was not being overlooked. Furthermore, such a system would help to engender a sense of hope for the future which would in turn assist in motivating the prisoner to adopt a constructive and positive approach to his sentence. Elsewhere, it has been argued that a period of five years is too long. Peter Timms suggested that a more reasonable period which prisoners could manage would be three years. He felt that not only is it more realistic to assume that a lifer could think and plan in intervals of three years, but it would also ensure that any changes or developments in him would not be overlooked.

It has sometimes been maintained that in what might be described as 'hopeless' cases – that is, where it is clear that the prisoner has a lengthy period of detention ahead of him – it would be cruel to raise his hopes and expectations by regular reviews and then to dash them by continually refusing to set a provisional release date. The PAPPAG, however, felt that even in these cases it would be even more damaging to the prisoner to deprive him of even the faintest glimmer of hope. He should be given regular reviews, but he should also have the right to opt out insofar as the reviews were concerned with deciding whether he should be given a release date (para. 88). This led the Group to propose that a system of review be adopted consisting of two separate parts – one which examines his conditions and career plan, and the other relating to whether he is suitable for release

Problems of Long-Term Imprisonment

There is now a gradually increasing body of evidence about the impact of long sentences on prisoners, some of which appears to be slightly conflicting. Roger Sapsford's study based on 60 lifers in a northern prison who were at various stages of their sentence led him to conclude that there was no evidence of a syndrome of 'institutionalisation' or 'deterioration' of the sort that has been reported in studies concerning mental hospital patients. But he did find some effects of long-term detention – such as an increase in introversion, a tendency to talk about the past rather than the future, a decrease in 'future time perspective', an increased tendency to be perceived by staff as 'institutionalised', and a very marked decline in family relationships.[41] Additionally, those who had served 12 years or more showed less interest in self-improvement and keeping their minds active, a greater alignment with staff, but also a seemingly higher level of anxiety. In their account of the visits they made over four years to the maximum-security block of Durham prison, Cohen and Taylor (1981) talked of the 'obsessive concern' which long-term prisoners have about signs of deterioration:

These men felt that all around them were examples of people who had turned into cabbages because they had not been sufficiently vigilant. Every day they encountered an old sex offender who spent hours merely cleaning and filling the teapot, a mindless activity which the old man appeared to be contended with. And this was their problem: at what price would they achieve peace of mind and contentment? Would they start behaving like the old man, as a way of banishing the ghosts of time, the fear of deterioration, and not knowing what was happening to them? In other words, would the cumulative result of years of working at something which looked like adaptation, in fact really be a process of learning how to deteriorate? (p. 115)[42]

Coker's (1985) study of lifers who had served an average of nine years imprisonment before being released on licence indicated that 'they had not been seriously damaged or incapacitated by their experiences. This conclusion is supported by other studies that, although men may fear it, they do not deteriorate, though their contacts with the outside world may atrophy through enforced neglect' (p. 229).

James Orr, a former Director of Prison Medical Services, described the direct effects of long-term imprisonment on the physical health of prisoners as not apparently deleterious, but the impact on his mental health is 'another matter'.[43] Even then,

> most prove remarkably resilient and only very few exhibit deleterious mental changes during the course of their serving their sentences. . . . In those prisoners who are susceptible overt mental changes can be expected to appear at around the 4 to 6 years stage of a long sentence. These changes are usually impermanent and reversible and take the form on an increased tendency to apathy (the longer a person is in prison, the less likely is he to understand his offence and accept his guilt), withdrawal and regression (typically his personality becomes increasingly rigid and he becomes childishly concerned about his personal possessions) and finally confusion. (p. 3)

However, a small number of prisoners show such abnormality that they become psychotic. In order to soften the effects of long-term imprisonment, Orr suggested that a prisoner be given as wide a choice of courses of action as possible and he should be given the opportunity to make decisions for himself. His mind should be stimulated by meeting different people and visiting different places; contacts with relatives and friends should be maximised and informal.

After spending 18 months working with lifers in an attempt to examine the relationship between this category of prisoners and the probation service, a group of probation officers reported that 'the predominant problem identified by lifers was one of isolation'.[44] The prisoners identified three forms of isolation:

(i) Physical isolation from people outside – long periods without visits, feeling alienated from one's family, 'no fellowship' with 'ordinary' people and being separated from 'every good thing in the world'.

(ii) Powerlessness – nams – nam set a provisional release date. The decisions for himself, feeling that he was being kept in the dark about his future, frequently resulting in a lack of reality and a notion of what is important.

(iii) Emotional – many lifers talked of self-imposed isolation which they had adopted as a form of psychological survival in the early part of their sentence. In some cases, the sense of isolation became so acute that the lifers felt unable to initiate communication themselves, and they became increasingly overlooked. There was also a feeling of being beyond help, so that prison and probation staff found it difficult to 'reach' them. Some experienced this most keenly in the first 18 months, several felt it most acutely between the second and fifth years, and 60 per cent said it applied for most of the time.

The lifers and those working with them offered practical suggestions to alleviate these problems. Firstly, they felt that group work would be invaluable in providing an opportunity to identify and share common difficulties and to break down some of the barriers which the lifers had created around themselves. Secondly, most lifers talked of the need for someone to listen to and understand them. No specific person could be identified to fulfill this role, but whoever it is should encourage open communication, permit the prisoner to discuss his problems and simply let him talk. Not surprisingly, the third point was the importance of contacts with the outside world. Lifers see themselves as having very low status when viewed by outsiders. Thus regular visits by members of the family and probation officers, or by a prison visitor were seen as very significant. There is a crucial need to tackle the lifer's lack of confidence of being accepted by 'normal' outsiders. Finally, although they appreciated the inevitable limitations on the extent to which they can determine their own future, lifers are concerned to be actively involved in planning. They welcome the opportunities they have to make a personal contribution to reviews, and felt there is scope for extending their involvement.

The Report of the Control Review Committee and Problem Prisoners

The Control Review Committee was set up by the then Home Secretary in September 1983 against a background of prison disturbances and riots, especially in the dispersal system. It concluded that:

There will inevitably be control problems if long-term prisoners are held in a system that gives inconsistent messages about the course of their sentences or the consequences of their actions, and if prison managers' only recourse in the face of disruption is to switch prisoners between normal location and the segregation unit, and between one prison and another. (para. 133)

Moreover, the CRC felt that notwithstanding the various reforms they recommended there would continue to be some long-term prisoners – namely, those serving at least five years – who would pose a serious threat to the stability of life in the prisons. Such prisoners should be held in some sort of small specialised unit (see in particular paras. 51 to 56).

There are three basic assumptions underlying this recommendation. Firstly, at any given time there exists an identifiable group of long-term prisoners who present serious control problems. Secondly, the best way of managing these inmates is to move them to small special units. Thirdly, these units will be effective in reducing the number of serious control problems in long-term prisons. Following the publication of the CRC's report in 1984, the then Home Secretary established the Research and Advisory Group on the Long-Term Prison System (RAG) whose terms of reference were:

> To provide the Prison Department ... with a source of advice on the research needs arising from the report of the Control Review Committee ... and, in particular, to advise on the planning. co-ordination and evaluation of the proposed long-term prisoner units.

The RAG report was published in 1987.[45]

As to the identification of 'problem prisoners'. the RAG found that there was much disagreement between different sources within the prison system about which prisoners could be described as 'difficult'. They felt that this 'emphasises the fact that prisoners may behave very differently in different environments and at different points in their sentence' (para. 35). The success of small units in managing difficult prisoners was regarded as one which can be tested and evaluated by empirical research. Whilst accepting that a short period of segregation may not be harmful or purely negative, the RAG warned against long periods of segregation because that would actually reduce the likelihood that the prisoner concerned will subsequently be willing or able to cope with normal prison life (para. 38). Small units would though, fulfill the basic need to remove difficult prisoners from long-term prisons. Provided there is a sufficiently high ratio of staff (including specialists) to prisoners, the staff/inmate relationship should improve. In addition, staff should be able to monitor and influence prisoner/prisoner relationships to a greater extent than in a large wing (para. 39). The contribution of small units to the reduction of control problems was also seen as empirically testable, and the RAG proposed that an attempt should be made to evaluate the effect of small units – both on the level of control incidents in long-term prisons, and on the degree to which staff and inmates in such prisons feel safe and confident (para. 40).

The RAG went on to identify certain general principles which should underpin the special unit strategy. These may be summarised as follows:

   (i) The regime brief of each unit should be laid down centrally, in line with a centrally-planned strategy for the development of a system of special units.

   (ii) Although the regimes of the units should be complementary, they should not be related in any simplistic progressive manner so that one might then be perceived as the 'end of the road' or as a 'unit of last resort'.

   (iii) They should not be a punitive in purpose – they ought not to be regarded as a further form of punishment. Conditions in units should, as far as possible, resemble those in normal long-term prisons, with prisoners entitled to the same privileges as those allowed in the dispersal system.

   (iv) Units will extend the options available for managing persistently difficult prisoners – that is in addition to segregation units and prison hospital.

   (v) A prisoner should be able to choose whether or not to take part in any of the activities provided in the units – though if he opts not to participate at all he may have to remain in his cell.

   (vi) Since a fundamental aspect of the special unit strategy is to try to create situations in which prisoners can take stock of their behaviour and be encouraged to find ways of modifying it, there must be a high degree of staff involvement with them. The interpersonal skills of staff, especially uniform staff, will be critical, and a 'personal officer' scheme – whereby an officer is to work closely with a prisoner – is likely to be a means of encouraging a good staff/inmate relationship. Appropriate staff training in this respect is important.

(vii) It is impossible to specify how long prisoners should remain in the units. Relevant factors include the extent to which the units can effect changes in prisoners' attitudes, social skills and conduct, and how the prisoner is likely to behave on return to normal conditions.

(viii) The Prison Service should be completely open about these units and how they operate. The should also be accountable and thus be made the object of special care by governors and Regional Directors, and should receive attention from Boards of Visitors, and ultimately HM Inspectorate of Prisons.

In consequence of the recommendations made by the RAG, the Prison Department has identified five sites as being suitable for the special unit strategy. These have been welcomed by the RAG, although details about the nature of the regimes and specialist facilities at two of them have yet to be determined.

NOTES

1.   Murder (Abolition of Death Penalty) Act 1965.
2.   S.1(2) Murder (Abolition of Death Penalty) Act 1965.
3.   S.53(1) Children and Young Persons Act 1933.
4.   S.53(2) Children and Young Persons Act 1933.
5.   S.8(1) Criminal Justice Act 1982.
6.   S.8(2) Criminal Justice Act 1982.
7.   S.12(7) Criminal Justice Act 1982.
8.   These figures were provided by the Statistics Division of the Prison Department.
9.   For further information about the possible causes of this trend see, for example, Mike Maguire, 'Lifers, Tariff and Dangerousness', April 1987, *Prison Service Journal*, pp. 13–18.
10. Whilst at the hostel prisoners should obtain employment so that they can get back into the routine of normal life – getting up in the morning and going to work on time and so on. This also gives them the chance to organise the financial side of their lives and perhaps to save some money.
11. Following the Mountbatten Report which was presented in December 1966, prisoners are divided into four categories according to the degree of security deemed necessary for their containment, and they are allocated to prisons with the appropriate security arrangements: see *Home Office Report of the Inquiry into Prison Escapes and*

Security, Cmnd. 3175, 1966. London H.M.S.O. Classification as follows:

Category A: Prisoners whose escape would be highly dangerous to the public or the police or the security of the State, no matter how unlikely that escape might be.

Category B: Prisoners for whom the very highest conditions of security are not necessary but for whom escape must be made very difficult.

Category C: Prisoners who can be trusted in open conditions, but who do not have the ability or the resources to make a determined escape attempt.

Category D: Prisoners who can be trusted in open conditions.

12. House of Commons Debates, Vol.49. Written Answers to Questions 30 November 1983, col.514.
13. Or two years in the case of young offenders.
14. *The Times*, 4 March 1987; *Independent* 3 March 1987. 131, S.J.326.
15. House of Commons Debates, Vol,120. Written Answers to Questions. 23 July 1987, cols.346–8.
16. Strictly speaking, the ruling in the Handscomb case only applied to discretionary life sentences, but the Home Secretary made it clear that the revised procedures will also affect mandatory sentences.
17. [1985] A.C.318.
18. Unless the governor considers that it would be inappropriate to do so – for example, the prisoner's mental state indicates that he would be unable to cope with the decision at this stage.
19. See the Home Secretary's Statement of 1 March 1985.
20. See footnote 12.
21. Career plans are not prepared in respect of Category A prisoners.
22. Prison Department Circular 2/1989 para. 33.
23. Report on the Parole Board, 1986 (1987), London H.M.S.O. para. 28.
24. This comment was made by Lord Windlesham at a seminar entitled 'Release on Licence' held at All Souls College, University of Oxford, on 8 May 1986.
25. D. Smith (ed.), *Life-Sentence Prisoners*, Home Office Research Study No.51. 1979. London: H.M.S.O. at p.9.
26. Roger Sapsford, *Life-Sentence Prisoners*, 1983, Milton Keynes Open University Press. p.16.
27. M.Fitzgerald and J. Sim, *British Prisons*, 1982. Oxford, Basil Blackwell.
28. The same possibility exists in respect of vocational training courses.
29. John Staples, *The Management of Life Sentence Prisoners*, April 1981, Prison Service Journal, 4 at p. 6.
30. Maguire M., Pinter, F. and Collis C., 'Dangerousness and the Tariff' (1984), *British Journal of Criminology* 24 (3), pp. 250–68.
31. The Home Secretary may take the view that there are special mitigating or humanitarian reasons for doing so, or he may be prompted to intervene if the lifer has responded exceptionally well to prison training.
32. Parliamentary All-Party Penal Affairs Group, *Life-sentence Prisoners*, 1986, Chichester: Barry Rose – especially para. 77.

33.   That is, The Directorate of the Prison Medical Service.
34.   J. B. Coker and J. P. Martin, *Licensed to Live*, 1985, Oxford, Basil Blackwell.
35.   See, for example, Home Office. *Review of Parole in England and Wales* (1981), London HMSO; and Gordon B. Trasler, *The Use of Documentation in Making the Parole Decision* (1978), unpublished lecture, Department of Psychology, University of Southampton.
36.   V. O'Leary and D. Glaser, 'The Assessment of Risk in Parole Decision Making' in D. J. West (ed.), *The Future of Parole: Commentaries on Systems in Britain and U.S.A.* (1972) London: Duckworth.
37.   John McVicar, *McVicar by Himself* (1979) London: Hutchinson, at pp. 48, 49.
38.   Report of the work of the Prison Department, 1985/86. Cm.11, London: H.M.S.O. para. 111.
39.   See his comments to the Parliamentary All-Party Penal Affairs Group in their report on Life-sentence Prisoners, 1986, para. 66.
40.   Home Office, *Managing the Long-Term Prison System*, The Report of the Control Review Committee, 1984, London: H.M.S.O.-42.
41.   See Roger Sapsford, *Life-Sentence Prisoners*, 1983. Milton Keynes: Open University Press; and 'Life-Sentence Prisoners: Psychological Changes During Sentence', 1978, *British Journal of Criminology*, vol.18, pp. 128–45.
42.   Stan Cohen and Laurie Taylor, *Psychological Survival. The Experience of Long-Term Imprisonment*, 1981. Harmondsworth: Penguin.
43.   J. H. Orr, 'Medical Aspects of the Treatment and Management of Prisoners Serving Sentences of Life Imprisonment', *Prison Medical Journal*, Spring 1981, pp. 2-6.
44.   Tony Raban, Barrie Crook, June Wright and Jo Thompson, *Work With Life-Sentence Prisoners at Nottingham Prison*, October 1983.
45.   Home Office, *Special Units for Long-Term Prisoners: Regimes, Management and Research.* A Report by the Research and Advisory Group on the Long-Term Prison System, 1987. London: H.M.S.O.

6 Methodology

Against the background of a steadily expanding population of life-sentence prisoners and an increase in the average amount of time being spent in detention, an investigation was undertaken into the way in which a particular group of lifers had been dealt with by the penal process.

THE INTERVIEWS

An approach was made to the Home Office and permission was formally obtained to undertake the research,[1] and it was decided to collect comparative data from two sources. Firstly, a random sample of people who had been convicted of murder and who had been given a provisional date for release on licence would be interviewed. Through members of staff at the appropriate prisons an invitation was made to those who were eligible to participate in the study. It was felt that such prisoners were, hopefully, in the latter stages of their detention and were thus in a position to look back over the time they had spent in custody. (Their release dates were only provisional, so that there was always the possibility that they might in fact be kept in prison beyond those dates). Whilst not everything they said can be assumed to be absolutely accurate, and many of their comments were in the nature of personal views and opinions, the fact that they had provisional release dates should lend a certain degree of objectivity to the information obtained. In addition, one of the obvious dangers to be avoided was the possibility that prisoners might think that whether or not they agreed to take part in the study and, if they did, what replies they gave, might affect their sentence. In other words, their decision to participate, and the nature of it, might increase or decrease the time they would spend in custody. That the prisoners to whom the invitation was made might regard the research with some suspicion could not be avoided, but the requirement that they must have a provisional release date was intended to minimise the extent to which they might feel they were in an invidious position.

In the event a total of 82 lifers[2] were interviewed, and with one exception they were detained either in an open prison, or in a prison hostel on the Pre-Release Employment Scheme, at the time of the

177

interview. The one exception was a young man who was in a Category B non-dispersal prison and was shortly afterwards transferred to a hostel. It was considered inappropriate to require him to spend part of his detention in an open prison because of his epilepsy. The staff of the various establishments kindly provided facilities for the interviews to be conducted in a suitable environment. At the open prisons – namely, Ashwell,[3] Ford, Leyhill and Sudbury – and in most prison hostels, the interviews were held in a separate room with only the researcher and lifer present. In the hostel at Bristol prison, most of the interviews took place in the prisoners' own rooms.

At any one time, there was of course only a limited number of prisoners convicted of murder who had a provisional release date. This effectively prolonged the completion of the fieldwork since, having interviewed those who were eligible and willing to participate in the study, I then had to wait until the next 'batch' became available. In the event, the interviews were conducted from September 1985 to May 1987.

One of the primary objectives of the interviews was to obtain descriptive information about the sentence which each prisoner had served, and about his of her feelings during the years spent in custody. Since it was likely that the prisoners' responses would be very varied, and it was hoped that they should feel able to express themselves as freely as possible, it was felt inappropriate to use a prepared questionnaire. At the same time, however, there were of course certain areas of discussion which were common to all interviews.

Each lifer was asked to relate what had happened to him or her from the moment that the life sentence had been imposed. What prisons had he been in, and in what order? In each case, he was asked to describe what life had been like, for instance, what had he done to pass the time during the day? This required an explanation of the routine to which he had been subjected, and the different sorts of work and recreational activities he had pursued. It also gave the prisoner the opportunity to describe the nature of the regime in the prison or at least in that part of it in which he had been accommodated. Was it fairly relaxed and informal, or was it more formal and structured? Given that the 'ideal path' through the custodial part of a life sentence, as envisaged by the Revised Strategy, is that prisoners should be detained in a gradually more liberal environment, one obvious issue to be examined was the extent to which the lifers were aware and appreciative of any diminution of restrictions which were placed upon them. Moreover, what sort of problems (if any) did they experience as they moved into less restrictive environments? Was it simply a pleasure, for example, to be able to see open countryside instead of prison walls, or did they find it difficult to get used to the increased physical freedom?

It is hoped that a large number of those sentenced to life imprisonment will be released on parole by the Home Secretary, subject to the conditions stipulated in the life licence. It is, therefore necessary to have regard to the need to prepare such individuals, as far as possible, so that on their release they are able to re-establish themselves and settle back into a life outside prison. This process of resettlement raises a number of issues – the need for a minimum level of financial security (which usually means obtaining employment), and the ability to organise oneself to carry out basic tasks such as going to work, doing the shopping and paying bills. Attention also has to be focused on the ways in which the lifer gets on with those around him, not simply with work-mates, and colleagues, but on a broader social level. The crimes which led to life sentences being imposed may well have been committed, at least partly, as the result of the individual's inability to cope with very difficult circumstances. In such cases, those who advise the Home Secretary must be satisfied that the prisoner is able to deal with difficult or stressful situations before release can be recommended with any confidence.[4]

With such considerations in mind, the lifers in this study were invited to talk about various issues which might have particular relevance to their release. For example, they were asked whether, at any stage of their imprisonment, they had pursued any educational and/or vocational courses. The acquisition of skills and qualifications might be a very significant factor in their search for employment when released. Indeed, it may well be thought that a criminal record which included a life sentence is likely to be a considerable handicap in this respect, thus emphasising the need to counteract this problem by being able to persuade potential employers of one's suitability for the job. At the same time, there may be other reasons for undertaking courses whilst in prison, the most obvious one being that they occupy the prisoner's mind and so help pass the time.

The great majority, if not all, lifers, will be required to spend some time at a prison hostel before being released – this is usually a period of six months, though sometimes it is nine months. This is regarded as an important stage of the sentence because it provides what is arguably the clearest evidence of how well the prisoner is likely to settle back into 'normal Life'. He is required to get a job and is left to organise himself so that he arrives at and leaves his place of work at the appropriate times. A proportion of his wages must be paid for his board and lodging at the hostel. Although the lifer is required to be in the hostel at specified times, he is also given a certain amount of freedom to come and go as he pleases. He thus has the chance to try to establish some sort of social life and to re-acclimatise to life in general. But what do prisoners themselves think about the time spent in hostels? Do they feel it serves the purposes envisaged by the penal system, either for themselves or for other prisoners?

As well as looking at what the lifers did during the couse of their detention, the research sought to obtain some idea about their relationships with other prisoners and with prison staff. To some extent, the nature of the prison may dictate that a life-sentence prisoner can only mix with other lifers or those serving lengthy sentences – as at Kingston Prison. At other establishments though, such as Category C and D prisons, there will be the opportunity for lifers to associate with both long-and short-term prisoners. It may be that, given the choice, lifers prefer to mix only with other lifers because they feel they are in a rather unique situation serving an indeterminate sentence and that only they can properly understand the problems which they face. Conversely, if they have already spent some time solely in the company of other lifers, they may find it refreshing to talk to short-term prisoners.

One of the concerns of prison staff here is that the way in which lifers relate to other prisoners may provide a useful indication of how well they might cope if released on licence and especially how they might respond to certain pressures and stresses. It is well known, for example, by prison staff that some short-term prisoners are rather 'boisterous' – they breach prison disciplinary rules, for which they may, at worst forfeit some remission of their sentence. Even so, they know that they will be released by a particular date at the latest. It is equally well-known that many of these determinate sentence prisoners spend much of their time talking about their release, which may only be a matter of months or weeks in the future. It is precisely these sorts of factors which may influence a lifer not to mix with short-term prisoners. If a lifer gets caught up in some sort of boisterous behaviour, he has a lot more to lose. Even those who have a provisional release date may find that their date is put back for a considerable time, measurable perhaps in years rather than months. In addition, lifers may find it very frustrating to hear other prisoners constantly talking about release, especially if they do not have a provisional release date and cannot, as yet, see any 'light at the end of the tunnel'.

The relationship between prisoners and staff is another important consideration. That staff must submit reports on prisoners' progress clearly requires the relationship between them to be sufficiently close so that meaningful and reliable observations can be made. Not only must staff get to know prisoners, but the latter should be encouraged to put a minimum level of confidence in the staff so that more than merely superficial assessments can be attempted. If prisoners do not reveal anything about themselves or their problems and their fears, it will be extremely difficult, if not impossible, to make any worthwhile comments. In addition, prison staff may be able to offer assistance to prisoners in dealing with personal and/or domestic problems. Failure to resolve such problems may have an adverse effect on the prisoner's progress. Thus, it was felt necessary to ask the lifers in the survey to talk about their attitudes towards and relationships with members of prison staff.

If prisoners are to be assisted in their preparations for release, they must obviously be able to think about the future and the specific issues which affect them. In some instances, these preparations may be quite complicated and require a considerable period of time to complete. But at what stage can prisoners serving life sentences begin to think about their future and plan accordingly? In the early part of the sentence in particular, they may be suffering from some form of shock at having been given life imprisonment. Yet before there can be any thoughts about his future and what he is going to do when released, a lifer must understand the nature and implications of his sentence. To some extent, this may depend on whether he has had any previous experience of the criminal justice system, especially of imprisonment. Even if he has such experience, the enormity of the offence and the sentence may inhibit him to the point where he cannot perceive that he has any future. Some lifers may, at least early on in their detention, believe that they will inevitably spend the rest of their natural lives in prison. Others may be aware of the likelihood that they will be released eventually, but have no idea when that is likely to occur. This state of affairs may exist not only in the days and weeks immediately after sentence has been passed, but may continue for a matter of years. Indeed, a lifer may be well into the middle or latter stages of his detention before he forms any idea of how long he thinks he will serve in prison. Even then he may be unable to make any confident prediction. Such uncertainty and indeterminacy may make it difficult not only for the lifer to make constructive plans for the future but also for those who are encouraging him to do so.

Each of the 82 lifers in this study was asked if he could recall at what stage he was able to think of the future for himself and begin to make arrangements for his release. Did this tend to occur once he reached a certain stage in his progress through the system, perhaps when he was moved to a semi-open or open establishment, or was it only when he actually received a provisional release date?

The question of the extent to which prisoners adopt what might be regarded as a 'constructive approach' to their sentence and plan for their future is clearly dependent on a variety of factors. Amongst these is the nature of their relationship with prison staff, who may or may not be able to support and encourage prisoners in this respect. Furthermore, in view of the Revised Strategy's aim of accommodating lifers in more liberal regimes as soon as possible and giving them the opportunity to be more responsible for their behaviour, it is important to have some idea of the extent to which lifers feel they have any influence over their sentence. The dangers are all too obvious. If lifers think that they have no influence over how long they are likely to serve in prison, motivating them to take a constructive attitude to their sentence is likely to be extremely difficult. How far do they think that good or bad behaviour is likely to affect their release? Do they take the view that their crime merits a particular sentence and nothing which they might do can make any difference?

In the previous chapter, reference was made to the fears of institutionalisation which might follow from long-term imprisonment. It is perhaps inevitable, for example, that those who are detained for such lengthy periods should be concerned that they might feel cut off from the outside world. This in turn may make the task of preparing lifers for release even more difficult. One of the ways in which the penal system seeks to avert such dangers is through prison visits and/ or correspondence with lifers, which may help them to maintain contact with what is happening outside prison. They may also be valuable in that they provide moral support; the lifer feels that despite the offence someone still cares about him, and he still has some value or worth as a human being. Conversely, visits and/or letters may have quite traumatic effects, for they emphasise to the lifer what he has to forego. Understandably, people tend to become emotional, especially during prison visits, and this may cause the lifer considerable mental anguish. Thus, he may conclude that he can better cope with his predicament by deliberately cutting himself off and not having contact with anyone outside prison.

Another factor in the process of readjustment is the extent to which prisoners feel they are being assisted by being allowed out of prison for short periods. The opportunity to go shopping for a day or to spend a weekend at home with the family will usually only be given to prisoners whilst they are in open conditions. Bearing in mind the length of time for which many of them will have been detained, it may be assumed that prisoners will find it very strange when they first go out into the community. Prices of goods will have increased since they were sentenced. (In some cases, prisoners may have been sentenced before decimalisation occurred in February 1971). There might be difficulties in getting used to the traffic – simple tasks such as crossing the road may be quite problematic. On a different level, lifers may be very self-conscious of being life-sentence prisoners and be troubled by the feeling that people are looking at them (which may of course be quite untrue). These are the sorts of issues which might be expected to affect prisoners when they are first allowed out of the institution.

In addition to talking about the sentence, the lifers were asked to discuss the offence which led to them being given life imprisonment. Naturally, it is helpful to be able to examine the sentence in the light of what it was that justified the imposition of such punishment. It may be that certain types of murderers tend to be dealt with in a particular way by the penal process – their progress through the prison system may follow similar paths. Their thoughts and attitudes towards their sentence may bear some relationship to the nature of their murder.

At the same time, it was interesting to note how lifers assessed what they had been convicted of doing. Did they think they had been rightly convicted of murder?; did they admit killing but claim some justification so that they ought to have been convicted of the slightly lesser crime of manslaughter?; or did they deny killing at all? One of the many concerns of prison staff is to assist the prisoner in coming to terms with what he did. Those who do commit such a serious offence as murder may find it very hard to accept responsibility for the enormity and heinousness of their behaviour. It is often felt that only by admitting responsibility and acquiring proper insight into the circumstances which surrounded the crime can the prisoner make the appropriate adjustments so that such behaviour is extremely unlikely to be repeated. Failure to accept full liability may also be regarded as a sign of potential dangerousness, and release from detention may thus be delayed.

The difficulty here is in knowing where the empirical truth of the matter lies. The Confidential Memorandum will provide the 'official version' of the offence, but that is based upon what happened in court, and there can be no guarantee that 'the truth, the whole truth and nothing but the truth' was discovered thereby. But the decision of the court must inevitably form the basis of assessment of what the prisoner did, at least in the absence of any further conflicting information. The possibility ought not be overlooked, however, that prison staff may, having read accounts of the offence, conclude that the court's decision was rather harsh and thus may not seek to persuade the prisoner to admit that what happened is entirely in accordance with the 'official version'.

Following on from this, and bearing in mind the desire to encourage prisoners to adopt a constructive approach to their sentence, the lifers in the study were asked to say how they felt about being officially labelled as 'murderers'. The obvious concern is that those who feel that they have been wrongly labelled will be alienated from the penal system and this may make it more difficult to motivate them to adopt the desired attitude towards their sentence. Furthermore, even if the prisoner accepts that he did commit a murder, the fact that he has been formally labelled as a 'murderer' may well present considerable problems for him on release. Thus, the lifers were invited to comment on whether, for example, they felt they would suffer social embarrassment because of their conviction, or how much more difficult it would be for them to obtain employment.

They were also asked to indicate whether they felt they had spent the right amount of time in prison, or too long or too short a period. More than anyone else they were in a position to be able to look back at the offences they had committed (or were convicted of), and to assess the ways in which they had been punished. Some may have felt that even though they had done something very wrong they had nonetheless been detained for too long. This may not simply be as a result of comparing the crime and the punishment: it may have been because they felt that the length of their detention had created its own special problems which made their resettlement unduly difficult. Some may have thought that they had not been punished severely enough in view of the fact they they had taken the life of another. Others may have found it impossible to say – how can you put a figure on the loss of life? In any event, the lifer's attitude towards his sentence may have a bearing on the likelihood of him successfully re-establishing himself outside prison. If he has 'a chip on his shoulder' because he thinks he has been treated unjustly, he may be more likely to get into trouble and thus be recalled and put back into prison.

Finally, the 82 lifers were asked whether they felt that prison had changed them in any way. They may have thought they had changed, but was this brought about by their detention or by some other cause? It may have been that imprisonment had given them the opportunity to take stock of their lives and to make some adjustments. They may have matured simply with the passing of the years – in other words, maturation would have occurred in or out of prison. The offence itself and their understanding of how and why it happened may have 'left its mark' on them. Whatever the answer, it was important to obtain some evidence about the extent to which their detention may have had a rehabilitative or other effect on them.

PRISON RECORDS

One of the aims of the research was to provide information which might be of use in the implementation of the current policy of the Prison Department in the management of life-sentence prisoners. There is no single source from which all the relevant information can be extracted. The interviews with the 82 lifers provided an invaluable contribution, but it would be dangerous to base recommendations and conclusions solely on their responses. This is not to suggest that what they said is unreliable because of their status as life-sentence prisoners or as convicted murderers. It is simply an acknowledgement of the fact that no single group of people can provide a comprehensive picture of how the system works.

In recognition of this, and in an attempt to broaden the basis of the information obtained, an examination was made of the contents of the prison records of the lifers who were interviewed. These records contained copies of the reports which had been prepared on the prisoners as they progressed through their sentence, including the F-75 reports. They also included the Confidential Memorandum prepared by P2, or P4 Division. Thus, it was possible to record details of what had been reported by prison governors, uniform staff, psychologists, consultant psychiatrists, medical officers, chaplains, education officers and probation officers about each of the 82 lifers.[5] This information provided useful material which could be compared

– and possibly contrasted – with the responses of the prisoners during their interviews. It also permitted an investigation into the extent to which those who submit reports on lifers agree with one another about the prisoner's attitude towards his sentence and the progress that is being made.

Notes were also made, largely from the Confidential Memorandum, about the offence of which the prisoner had been convicted. This data provided relevant background material in that it constituted the official version of what the individual had done to justify the imposition of a life sentence. Not only is this useful in itself, but it helped to explain the attitudes and approaches adopted by staff towards the prisoners. Those who have killed in the heat of a quarrel may, for example, react to their sentence quite differently from those who have killed in the furtherance of gain. So-called 'domestic murderers' may be felt to represent no real security risk and may safely be moved very early in their sentence to a relatively liberal regime. Conversely, the man who killed whilst carrying out a robbery may be regarded as a danger to the public and thus require Category 'A' or 'B' status for quite some time. In these instances, there may be a greater need to adopt a gradual process of release and to carefully test the prisoner when he is in semi-open conditions to see how he responds to being given more responsibility for himself. Clearly, these considerations may have implications for the type of policy that is appropriate to the management of lifers.

A 'MANAGEMENT PERSPECTIVE'

There is within the staff of the prison service a significant amount of practical experience of dealing with and 'looking after' life-sentence prisoners. In the course of their employment as uniform prison officers, or as governor grade staff, or, for example, as psychologists or psychiatrists working in penal establishments, various individuals have encountered lifers and have first-hand knowledge of the problems that might arise during the custodial part of the sentence. Any investigation of the way in which the penal system responds to such prisoners ought therefore to take account of this experience. So, in acknowledging this, and as a further attempt to widen the basis of the research, a sample of people were invited to express their views and opinions both on the way in which the system has operated hitherto and on specific reforms which they would like to see implemented in the future. These discussions were held between February and June 1987.

Naturally, one of the objectives here was to obtain responses from individuals who, between them, have worked in the full range of penal institutions, not only in prisons of varying security categorisation, but also in those accommodating male and female prisoners, and young persons. These people were invited to make whatever comments they felt appropriate, both critical and laudatory. Given that career plans arc intended as a means of underlining a sense of purpose and direction for lifers and thus providing some structure to the sentence, staff working in prisons were asked to make specific observations about them. How frequently did the prison files contain such a plan, and how helpful did they find them? Did they think that career plans should be retained, or perhaps amended in some way? Here again, it was felt that the nature of the discussions did not lend themselves to the use of prepared questionnaires; they were unnecessary and they might have inhibited the free flow expression.

NOTES

1. The Home Office also provided a research grant of £7000 over a three-year period to fund the project.
2. Eleven of these 82 cases were also in the sample of 250 murders in the first part of the research.
3. Since the fieldwork was undertaken, HM Prison Ashwell has been reclassified as a Category C establishment.
4. This is, of course, in addition to the question of whether the prisoner has served a sufficient term of imprisonment so as to meet the requirements of retribution and deterrence.
5. In all but one of the 82 cases, prison records were examined at the prison where the interviews were conducted. In one case, however, the record was not available at the prison and the appropriate information was taken from the file at P2 Division.

7 An Analysis of the Interviews and Prison Records

INTRODUCTION

One of the prime concerns of this chapter is to provide a largely numerical analysis of the interviews I had with the 82 lifers who had been convicted of murder and had reached a stage at which they had been given a provisional release date. Before they decided whether or not they wished to participate in the study, it was emphasised to them that their decision would have no effect on their sentence. I explained the nature of the research, its aims and objectives, and the various sources from which information was to be collected. Perhaps not surprisingly, when they realised that I had been given permission by the Home Office to carry out the project, some of my potential interviewees seemed a little uneasy. They appeared to be suspicious about the degree of my independence from the Home Office and/or the extent to which my work might be used in a way which would prejudice the interests of lifers. Eight people declined to participate in the study.

LENGTH OF DETENTION

The management of life-sentence prisoners must take account of a wide variety of factors, one of the most basic of which is the length of time prisoners are likely to have to spend in detention. The population of lifers has been steadily rising and at the same time the average length of imprisonment has increased, from eight or nine years in the early 1970s, to about ten and a half years by the mid-1980s. Simple logic might suggest that the longer a person is deprived of his freedom, the more likely it is that he will present his custodians with control or security problems. Table 7.1 reveals the amount of time which the lifers in the sample will have served assuming their provisional release dates are adhered to. The figures represent the period between the date on which sentence was passed and their

TABLE 7.1   *Time Served in Custody Since Sentence Passed*

Number of years	Relative Frequency	Cumulative Frequency
6 or 7 years	7 (8.5%)	7 (8.5%)
8 or 9 years	21 (25.6%)	28 (34.1%)
10 or 11 years	28 (34.1%)	56 (68.2%)
12 to 14 years	14 (17.1%)	70 (85.3%)
15 to 19 years	8 (9.8%)	78 (95.1%)
20 to 24 years	4 (4.9%)	82 (100.0%)
Totals	82 (100.0%)	

assumed release on licence; time spent in custody on remand awaiting trial is not included.

On average, these lifers will have spent 11 years and 4 months in prison since their date of sentence, but that conceals a considerable variation in individual cases. The shortest period of detention was six years six months, whereas the longest was 24 years 10 months. These statistics clearly confirm the trend whereby lifers are being detained for longer periods. Admittedly, the figures relate solely to convicted murderers, but it is unlikely that the inclusion of lifers convicted of other offences would radically alter the picture.

NUMBER OF PRISONS SERVED IN

A prisoner who is detained for a considerable time is likely to serve his sentence in a number of different establishments. The length of time spent in any one prison should take into account on the one hand the need for the inmate to settle into the regime and for staff to have sufficient opportunity to be able to make informed comments on his progress, and on the other hand the desire to avoid the danger that if he stays there for too long he will be subsumed in its routine and will cease to show his true character. In some instances, a prisoner may be transferred to another institution simply to change his environment, without reducing his security categorisation, and this may undermine his sense of 'progressing' through the system.

Table 7.2 shows the number of prisons in which the lifers I talked to had been detained. The figures do not include instances where only a short time was spent in a prison, for example whilst en route from one institution to another, or for the purpose of accumulated visits.

TABLE 7.2 *Number of Penal Establishments in which Lifers Served*

No. of prisons	Relative Frequency	Cumulative Frequency
3	2 (2.4%)	2 (2.4%)
4	10 (12.2%)	12 (14.6%)
5	14 (17.1%)	26 (31.7%)
6	19 (23.2%)	45 (54.9%)
7	20 (24.4%)	65 (79.3%)
8	9 (11.0%)	74 (90.3%)
9	2 (2.4%)	76 (92.7%)
10	1 (1.2%)	77 (93.9%)
11	1 (1.2%)	78 (95.1%)
12	2 (2.4%)	80 (97.5%)
15	1 (1.2%)	81 (98.7%)
16	1 (1.2%)	82 (99.9%)
Totals	82 (99.9%)	

However, they do take account of transfers to a prison hostel as the final stage before release on licence.

Four-fifths of those in the sample were detained in not more than seven establishments, but there must be concern for the other 20 per cent insofar as they might fall foul of the dangers identified above. It is also worth noting that 37 of the 82 lifers were detained in more than one prison of the same security categorisation, though in three of these cases the transfer was from a dispersal (highest security) to a non-dispersal Category B establishment.

As to the idea of progressing to conditions of increased liberty within the confines of the institution, it was interesting to discover that eight lifers had at some stage been moved back to a higher security prison. Four of these were moved from an open prison and the other four from a hostel. All of them were transferred to a closed prison. One lifer was moved out of a hostel on two separate occasions – firstly because he simply could not settle at the hostel, and subsequently because he had a fight with his room-mate. Another was considered to have been transferred to open conditions too quickly and seemed unable to cope with the sudden increase in freedom and responsibility. The other six were moved back because they took unfair advantage of a more liberal environment and were judged to have breached prison regulations.

TIME IN OPEN AND SEMI-OPEN PRISONS

Emphasis is placed by P2 Division on the need to transfer lifers to semi-open conditions as soon as it is felt safe to do so, in order that staff can begin to test their suitability for release. This process can be continued and developed in open prisons where the physical signs of the prison boundaries are even less overt and prisoners have greater freedom of movement. Moreover, after transfer to a Category D establishment, lifers may be allowed to travel outside the prison, for example on a shopping trip, or on home leave, and obviously their conduct at these times is carefully monitored. It cannot be denied that it is impossible to subject a prisoner to precisely the same conditions that exist in the normal world whilst he is in a penal establishment, but all the lifers I interviewed accepted that it was necessary for them to be tested as to their suitability for release.

Table 7.3 provides an indication of the numbers of those in the sample who experienced semi-open and/or open conditions.

TABLE 7.3   *Extent of Detention in Category C and/or D Prisons*

	Relative Frequency
Served in Cat. C and D	48 (58.5%)
Cat. C but not Cat. D	2 (2.4%)
Cat. D but not Cat. C	28 (34.1%)
Served in neither	4 (4.9%)
Totals	82 (99.9%)

The discovery that almost two-fifths of those in the sample had not been in semi-open prison was quite surprising. It might be supposed that this was caused by the fact that many lifers had been sentenced some years ago when less importance was attached to the time served in Category C conditions. But the figures in Table 7.4 do not support this. It is clear that although the numbers sentenced in earlier years were very small, a significant proportion of those sentenced more recently had not been sent to a semi-open establishment.

In all but one of the cases in the sample, viz. case 39 (referred to below), the lifer was to be released from a hostel. Thus, in varying degrees, the majority had experienced a programme of gradual

TABLE 7.4   *Cases Where Category C Was Omitted According to Year of Sentence*

Year of Sentence	Number who Omitted Cat. C	Total Sample
1963	0	1
1965	1	2
1967	1	1
1969	1	3
1970	0	1
1971	1	1
1972	1	3
1973	0	3
1974	1	6
1975	1	8
1976	3	10
1977	7	17
1978	6	11
1979	3	6
1980	5	8
1981	1	1
Totals	32	82

adjustment to freedom and self-responsibility, but at the same time less than three out of five sampled both open and semi-open institutions. That four lifers served no time at all in Category C or D conditions seems quite remarkable. Briefly, these cases were as follows:

Case 19 This lifer had been sentenced in 1969 and had spent much of his detention in closed institutions. There was a broad basis of agreement amongst prison staff that there was a great danger that if detained for much longer he would become so institutionalised that the chances of successful release and re-establishment in the community would be severely prejudiced. He had had strong and sustained support from family and it was felt appropriate to release him through the PRES, so he was transferred from a Category B prison directly to a hostel for the final nine months of his detention. Though the trial judge had recommended he serve at least 20 years, he was to be released just over 18 years after he had been sentenced, and he had spent about seven and a half months in custody on remand.

Case 39 At the time of the offence this young man was only 14 years old, and was still just 21 when I interviewed him. He had made a good deal of progress during his detention, and had been transferred to a youth custody centre after his 19th birthday. It was decided that, in view of his progress and of the nature of the offence, he should be released six and a half years after sentence had been passed, and yet there was no suitable Category C or D establishment where he could be accommodated in the latter stages of his detention. Thus he remained at the YCC, but on terms and conditions which closely resembled those applicable to PRES.

Case 40 Here the lifer had been sentenced in 1965 and was first released on licence in 1977. But his licence had been revoked and he had been recalled to prison on four occasions, mainly for breaches of the licence conditions. There was never any suggestion that he was unable to cope with freedom. His recalls to prison were in response to what was regarded as 'bloody-mindedness' on his part. Thus, there was no need to release him gradually through semi-open and open prisons. He had served sufficient time in custody to meet the requirements of retribution and deterrence, and it simply remained for him to adopt a more co-operative approach to the conditions of his licence.

Case 45 The essential point in this case was that the lifer concerned suffered from quite a severe form of epilepsy which made him very accident-prone. Throughout his detention it had been impossible to allow him to work in many of the workshops because of the very real danger that he would have a fit and be seriously injured. For his own safety, therefore, it was felt that he ought not to be kept in semi-open or open conditions where there would be less immediate supervision of him. He was to be transferred directly from a Category B prison to a hostel and released from there.

A transfer from secure to open conditions may not be thought to be in the prisoner's interests because of the perceived inability to cope with the sudden increase in freedom and responsibility. Nevertheless, the great majority of the lifers in the sample who were moved from a Category B to a Category D prison did not appear to have suffered any major difficulties in this respect. Whilst they were very aware of the increased opportunity to walk about the prison and to see clearly beyond its boundaries, they felt they had adjusted to the new environment satisfactorily. Staff usually confirmed these sentiments generally in their reports, although they sometimes put a little more emphasis on problems of adjustment. Only two of the 28 showed any real cause for concern, and both of them had been transferred to open conditions at a relatively early stage in their sentence. Immaturity was felt to be the crux of the problem, and they were each found to have breached prison regulations, which resulted in one of them being sent back to a closed institution. Grounds clearly existed for criticising their transfers to Category D prisons, but the difficulties arose because they were moved out of a secure regime too quickly rather than as a result of a sudden change in the nature of their environment.

As well as noting the numbers of lifers who served in Category C and/or D prisons, it is interesting to consider the aggregate amount of time spent in such establishments. The average length of detention in both regimes was just over three years and one month. The most that any of those in the sample spent in semi-open and open conditions was six years and ten months. This was a case of a young man who was due to serve about 14 years in total. He had appeared to be progressing well, but had been sent back from a Category D prison to a closed establishment for fighting with another prisoner, so that he ultimately served time in two semi-open and two open prisons. At the other extreme, the least amount of time spent in these conditions was four months, by a young lifer who was expected to serve about eight years in detention. Three more were kept in Category C and D conditions for only five months, two of whom were in their mid-20s and were to be released after just over eight years, and the third was in his mid 60s and was expected to spend a little more than ten years in prison.

Obviously, it is desirable to test a prisoner's suitability for release whilst he is in an environment which most closely resembles that which exists outside prison. Conditions in a semi-open prison are clearly more liberal than those in closed institutions, but they inevitably provide less opportunity for prisoners to make decisions for themselves than those in open prisons. It was, at first sight, rather surprising to find that two prisoners were transferred directly from semi-open conditions to a hostel. Again, there is a theoretical danger that such a transfer will involve too dramatic an increase in the level of freedom for the lifer and this might then delay his release. The two cases were briefly as follows:

Case 41 This man was still only in his mid-30s when I interviewed him. He had been sentenced in 1969, and whilst he was in a semi-open prison it was recommended that he should be released as soon as possible to prevent damage to his mental health from prolonged detention. He was given a provisional release date of October 1985 (that is, roughly 21 months after the recommendation was made). But the reports in his file indicated that no suitable accommodation could be found for him, and so he remained at the semi-open prison. Thus, in order to prevent any further delay in his release, he was moved directly to a hostel for the final stages of his detention.

Case 42 This lifer was in his mid-50s when sentenced. His offence was regarded as a prime example of a 'domestic' murder and he was originally given a provisional release date which would have meant that he would have served about eight years in detention. In view of his behaviour in prison and his advancing years, it was felt unnecessary for him to spend time in open conditions and he was transferred directly from a Category C prison to a hostel. But he was sent back from the hostel to a closed institution after complaints about his conduct. He then spent 18 months in semi-open conditions and was again moved directly to a hostel, where I interviewed him. There had never been any suggestion that he was unable to readjust to life outside prison. He could cope with freedom, but he had been called back from his first move to a hostel because he appeared to have abused his freedom by misbehaviour.

A SENSE OF FREEDOM

The downgrading of a prisoner's security categorisation from A to B to C to D carries with it the clear implication that there should be a corresponding diminution in the level of supervision and control of his conduct. It may be surmised that the impact of this would be most evident to the prisoner when he is transferred from a Category B prison, the perimeters of which consist of brick or concrete walls, to a Category C establishment which is bordered by a fence through which the outside world is much more visible. Semi-open prisons provide a greater sense of space, yet it would be too simplistic to assume that as a prisoner progresses through the security categorisations he will necessarily feel 'freer'. The lifers I interviewed were naturally aware of their increased freedom to move around the prison, but they repeatedly made the point that their sense of freedom was dictated very much by the nature of the regime operated by the staff. Ironically, perhaps, many seemed to feel less restricted or constrained whilst in a Category B establishment than in a semi-open prison.

Prisoners in the sample frequently spoke of the relaxed, informal and very 'human' atmosphere in Kingston Prison which accommodates lifers and a few long-term inmates, and they often contrasted this with what seemed to be the relatively strict regimes in semi-open prisons. One relevant feature of this was the way in which prison regulations were interpreted, and especially what 'perks and privileges' were permitted. Most were very critical of the fact that on the one hand a transfer to a Category C prison was encouraging because it seemed to be a step towards release, but on the other hand their perks and privileges had simultaneously been reduced. For example, a lifer may no longer be allowed to keep a budgerigar, or to have his own bedspread, or to wear his own shoes. The essence of the complaints was not simply that their existence was being made more uncomfortable, but that some staff adopted a 'bloody-minded' attitude and their sense of progress was being undermined.

It also became very apparent from my conversations with lifers that whilst they welcomed the reduction in overt signs of containment and security as they moved to semi-open and open establishments, they always retained a very keen sense of 'being in prison'. The boundaries of an open prison are the least visible of all, and yet they were very clearly defined in the minds of the prisoner. The essence of imprisonment is the knowledge and awareness of the loss of liberty, and not simply the physical negation of a person's freedom.

The Revised Strategy envisages that since lifers will spend lengthy periods in detention they will need various types of assistance if they are to be successfully re-established in the community. Understandably, the nature and extent of this assistance may vary considerably from case to case, but it is assumed that the vast majority will require a process of 'acclimatisation' to freedom. In some instances this may have to be a gradual process, especially if a lengthy period has been spent in closed conditions. Nonetheless, 44 of the lifers in the study (53.7 per cent), felt that either they had not needed this assistance, so that they could have been released directly from a closed prison, or that the prison authorities had exaggerated the amount of assistance they required.

This is not to suggest that these lifers totally dismissed the help that was offered to them. During shopping trips out of prison, whilst on home leave, and when working in the community, they were aware of changes that had taken place since they had been sentenced. Prices had increased, new coins had been introduced, fashions had altered, new models of vehicles had been produced and the volume of traffic had increased. But many lifers did not regard these changes as problematic for, although it was good to experience them first-hand, they had been aware of them through reading newspapers, watching television and visits from family and friends. The opportunities to get out of the prison were welcomed as part of the process of re-familiarising themselves with normal life. Some treated them as crucial, whilst others looked upon them as useful.

There were frequent comments made by staff in their reports that lifers would require support and assistance in coping with the need to make their own decisions, and to assume responsibility for their behaviour. For example, the view was sometimes expressed that a particular lifer would initially have difficulty in getting used to the fact that he could walk around the prison. Having become so accustomed to being told where to go and when to do so, it would take a little time to adjust to the fact that these were things for him to determine for himself. In the more extreme cases the process of adjustment would have to be very gradual if release was to be successful. Some lifers, however, did not agree with this, and where this was so staff invariably indicated that the prisoner did not fully appreciate the difficulties that would be encountered.

ASSOCIATES IN DETENTION

One of the unique characteristics of a life sentence is that until a provisional release date is given the prisoner faces an indeterminate period of detention. He may know what the average length of time is, the 'going rate', or his lawyers, the police, prison staff or other prisoners may have indicated how long they think he will serve. But there is an inescapable uncertainty for him. Indeed, a number of those I talked to said that they found it impossible, and sometimes dangerous, to put any reliance on a projected release date. Sometimes they felt that lawyers or police officers would be unduly optimistic, in their efforts to soften the impact of the sentence. Prison staff either could not be trusted or were insufficiently aware of the thoughts of those in P2 Division who advise the Home Secretary. Fellow prisoners could not be regarded as reliable sources or indicators.

Furthermore, even when a provisional release date had been given there was always the possibility that it might be revoked. Many lifers told me that it was not simply a question of trying to keep out of trouble and not breach prison regulations. They were afraid that mere suspicion that they were 'up to no good' would be sufficient to delay their release, not just for a few months, but more likely for a few years. Some said they had encountered staff, albeit relatively few, who deliberately sought to provoke prisoners so that they might be convicted of disciplinary offences and their detention prolonged.

In view of these fears and of the innate uncertainty of the sentence, it might well be thought that lifers would only choose to mix with others in the same predicament who shared their anxieties and concerns. Table 7.5 shows the sort of inmates with whom the lifers in the sample associated.

TABLE 7.5   *Lifers Associates During Detention*

	Relative Frequency
Mixed only with lifers or long-term prisoners	27 (32.9%)
Mixed only with short-term prisoners	1 (1.2%)
Mixed equally with both	47 (57.3%)
Mixed with neither	7 (8.5%)
Totals	82 (99.9%)

The discovery that nearly a third mixed only with other lifers or long-term prisoners (that is, seven years or more), was surprising insofar as one might have expected a higher proportion to have behaved in this way. Their reasons for limiting their associates were not simply those stated above. They and others highlighted what were keenly felt to be aggravating characteristics of many short-term prisoners, such as their tendency to talk constantly about release, a topic which many lifers purposely tried to put out of their minds in order to cope with the indeterminacy of their sentence. Some short-termers would moan about the fact that they still had another X weeks or Y months to serve, and many lifers understandably found this extremely unsettling. In comparison their problems were much greater, and they could get through their detention better by avoiding short-termers.

The other main factor which persuaded many lifers to seek their own company was that short-term prisoners were often young, immature and disruptive. I was frequently told, by prisoners and staff, that lifers strive to get through their sentence as quietly as possible. The last thing they want is 'a lot of young tearaways' making a lot of noise and flouting prison regulations. In the earlier phases of detention lifers are unlikely to encounter prisoners serving short sentences, but once they are transferred to semi-open and open prisons integration is inevitable. The nub of the issue, as many lifers see it, is that if a short-term prisoner misbehaves he can only lose part of his remission or parole, but he still has a date by which he must be released. The lifer, though, is in a much more precarious position, for if his conduct is called into question he runs the risk of having his detention prolonged, probably for a matter of years.

Notwithstanding these fears, nearly three out of every five of those I interviewed said that they had voluntarily associated with short-term prisoners, usually as well as other lifers and long-termers. In most cases their feelings about mixing with short-or long-term prisoners were fairly evenly balanced. Only three lifers said they had really enjoyed spending their time with short-termers. The majority agreed that short-termers could pose the sort of problems described above, but felt that there were important reasons for not avoiding them. Lifers often seemed to be subsumed by prison life, apparently oblivious to what was happening in the world outside, whereas short-termers were not. Talking to and working with prisoners who had only recently come into prison and who were relatively soon to be released was seen as a means of keeping in touch with the 'real world' and avoiding institutionalisation. In crude terms, mixing with short-term prisoners was looked on as an aid to successful release.

One lifer told me that he had associated only with short-term prisoners. He was a young man, still in his mid-20s when I interviewed him, and he had purposely not spent his time with other lifers because he felt that he would tire of their friendship. He stressed that he was anxious to get back to a 'normal' life, and not think about or be reminded of his time in prison. Short-termers were obviously in a different category to himself and they tended to talk about what was going on outside the prison. So he was quite happy to mix with them, for he would never get to know any of them very well and yet they helped him to retain a degree of contact and familiarity with the real world.

There were no apparent common characteristics amongst those who chose not to associate with other prisoners, such as their age, background circumstances, or the nature of the offence. They simply wanted to serve their time in detention quietly and resume their lives in the community with as few reminders as possible of their sentence.

COURSES

As expected, the lifers in the sample described how they had spent periods of their detention carrying out a variety of tedious jobs. The only apparent benefit of this was that the work was done – mail-bags were produced, typewriters repaired, electrical circuits and so on. Fortunately, however, many penal institutions offer educational and/ or vocational training courses for prisoners. The nature and range of these courses varies from one establishment to another, although it is generally true to say that those which accommodate longer-term prisoners provide a wider choice of facilities.

One of the fundamental objectives of the penal system is that prisoners, especially those serving long periods of detention, should be encouraged to use their sentence constructively so that they are unlikely to re-offend when released and be better able to re-establish themselves in the community. These objectives should not be dismissed as naive and unrealistic. When they begin their detention, prisoners invariably face a range of problems. Many are worried about what is happening to their families and close friends outside, but a large number also have personal difficulties which they may be able to combat given the appropriate opportunity and support. For example, some simply cannot read and write, some do not have basic numeracy skills, and others have no obvious trade or profession. Naturally, it is not being suggested that by tackling these issues a successful release can be assured, but the prospects of doing so should be distinctly improved.

The lifers I interviewed mentioned two principal reasons for pursuing educational and/or vocational training courses: (i) they were a means of enhancing their chances of obtaining employment on release, and (ii) they were simply a way of passing the time. Table 7.6 provides a breakdown of the relevant statistics.

Where lifers undertook courses for more than one reason the figures in Table 7.6 reflect the dominant purpose. More than half of those in the sample pursued courses solely or primarily to maximise their job prospects, whereas just under a third treated them as a means of passing the time.

TABLE 7.6 *Nature and Purpose of Educational and/or Vocational Training Courses During Detention*

	Relative Frequency
Educational course – for job	5 (6.1%)
Educational course – to pass time	5 (6.1%)
Vocational course – for job	10 (12.2%)
Vocational course – to pass time	9 (11.0%)
Both courses – for job	28 (34.1%)
Both courses – to pass time	11 (13.4%)
No courses	14 (17.1%)
Totals	82 (100.0%)

Many lifers expressed reservations about the provision of these courses. Firstly, some establishments offered only a limited number of them so that it was quite possible that the particular course which a prisoner wanted to pursue was not available. The preferred course might be available at another prison, even of the appropriate security categorisation, but transfers are disruptive and the benefits gained from being able to do the chosen course have to be set against other considerations such as the existence of a suitable vacancy and difficulties which potential visitors would have in travelling to the prison. The second main criticism was that transfers to other institutions could have an inhibitive effect. They often either prevented a prisoner from completing a course (in that it was not available at his new prison), or, where the prisoner was expecting to be transferred in the near future, it was thought inappropriate to begin a course for fear that he might be unable to continue it after the move. On balance though, most of the lifers appeared to regard courses as useful and worthwhile. A few commented that they had welcomed the fact that some of their tutors were not members of the prison staff and thus not part of the prison culture. Contact with these tutors was another means of retaining a sense of awareness of life outside the institution.

THE PRE-RELEASE EMPLOYMENT SCHEME (PRES)

The current policy is that the vast majority of lifers will be released via the PRES, which in practice means that usually the final six months of detention will be spent at a prison hostel. In a few cases, the period may be nine months. As stated earlier in the chapter, all but one of those I interviewed were treated in this way, and even the one exception was accommodated in circumstances which resembled those on the PRES.

Staff in prisons and those in P2 Division look upon this phase of the sentence as being especially significant. It enables the prisoner to live a life which most closely approximates to that which he would pursue if released. It seeks to create the experience of release without the complete freedom that would be associated with that release, and thus provides invaluable information about how well the individual is likely to cope in the community. In this respect, it is the most testing time of the sentence. But it ought not to be seen solely as an aid to prison staff and P2 Division, for it attempts to give lifers the opportunity to get back into the routine of going to work outside the prison, and perhaps to re-learn how to organise their lives. Although their jobs are unlikely to be well-remunerated, they will hopefully be able to save some money to help them to get established when finally released. Regulations require prisoners to return to the hostel by a stipulated time at the end of the day, but they will have the chance to go out in the evenings and at weekends so that they can resume some sort of social life and spend time with family and friends.

During my talks with them I invited the 82 lifers to air their views on the utility of the PRES, and an analysis of their responses is provided in Table 7.7.

Before making any comments about these figures, it should be noted that at the time I spoke to them only 22 (that is 26.8 per cent) of the lifers had any direct personal experience of the PRES and living in a prison hostel. But this does not mean that the views

TABLE 7.7 *Lifers' Views on the Value of the Pre-release Employment Scheme*

	Relative Frequency	
Useful simply to get back to normal routine:	2	(2.4%)
Useful simply to save money:	3	(3.7%)
Useful on both counts:	41	(50.0%)
Useful for other lifers but not for self:	32	(39.0%)
Not at all useful to anyone:	4	(4.9%)
Totals	82	(100.0%)

expressed by those who lacked such experience should automatically be disregarded. All but one of them had been in an open prison, where the regime was relatively liberal, staff were generally in the background, and prisoners were responsible for organising their own lives. Most had been out of the prison, on shopping trips and home visits, and many had regularly worked in the community or attended courses at colleges nearby. Thus, they had experienced a lifestyle which was not dissimilar to that on the PRES, and they had been appraised, especially by prison staff, of what life was like at a hostel. In the circumstances, it would be wrong to assume that their comments were based on ignorance and therefore unworthy of consideration. Moreover, the research offered an insight into the frame of mind in which they approached the PRES, and insofar as this reflects the attitude of lifers in general it might facilitate our assessment of the potential utility of the Scheme. Finally, there were no obvious comparisons to be drawn between the opinions of those who had personally experienced life at a hostel and those who had not; there was a range of responses from both groups.

Although the vast majority of lifers in the sample viewed the time spent on the PRES as potentially valuable, only 56.1 per cent felt that they had derived, or would gain any personal benefit from it. The 39 per cent who said it might be useful to some lifers other than themselves argued that the crucial issue was the extent to which prisoners were able to rely on support from their families and friends. They stressed that they did not seek to underestimate the difficulties that beset lifers on release; rather they felt that the support they had received was the most important factor in enabling them to maintain an appreciation of what was happening in the world outside and of what would be required of them after release. Any benefits that might be derived from the Scheme could be acquired from having the backing of family and friends.

As some remarked in the course of our conversations, it is easy to overestimate the utility of the Scheme. Only modest amounts of money could be saved, and the establishment of a social life could be severely prejudiced if and when it became apparent that the individual was living in a prison hostel! As for getting used to the routine of getting up and going to work, they argued that they had already gone a long way towards this whilst in an open prison. Of those who expressed these views, more than a third (11 out of 32) were living in a hostel at the time and were therefore talking from personal experience. Furthermore, only 7 (of the 32) had previously served a custodial sentence and so might be thought to have had the advantage of first-hand knowledge of the problems of resettlement.

The four lifers who looked upon the PRES as a complete waste of time all had previous convictions but had not necessarily been deprived of their liberty. They maintained that it is impracticable to show prisoners what life is like outside the institution and simultaneously subject them to prison discipline and regulations. They shared the opinions described in the preceding paragraph, that the Scheme can realistically provide only minimal benefits to prisoners. Being in a hostel was essentially no different from being in any other type of penal establishment, though none of the four had any personal experience of the Scheme. Staff reports on each of them suggested that it would be valuable for them to sample life on the PRES, both for the potential benefits which the prisoners might derive and so that staff could further assess their suitability for release.

A SENSE OF THE FUTURE

It is implicit in the desire for lifers to adopt a constructive attitude towards their detention that they should be encouraged to have a sense of direction and purpose. They need to acquire a sense of the future as it relates to them. Assuming of course, that they are not likely to spend the rest of their natural lives in prison, they should appreciate that they will be released, albeit not in the immediate future, and that they will face many problems when it happens. Not only must they solve those which existed before they were sentenced, but they will have to tackle difficulties which arise from the stigma of being labelled 'a murderer' (or some other serious offender), and from long-term detention. It is part of the responsibility of prison staff, probation officers, psychologists and the like to assist them in this task, so as to maximise their chances of a successful release.

In the early stages of detention in particular, a lifer may find it very hard to come to terms with the enormity of the offence and he may be deeply shocked at being given a life sentence. Indeed, he may not even understand the meaning of the sentence. Although staff may explain it to him, he may not be in a fit state to comprehend what is being said. Feelings of shock and numbness may endure for months or perhaps even longer, and until they subside it is highly unlikely that any progress can be made. Moreover, those who have not previously experienced loss of liberty must become accustomed to a completely strange lifestyle and environment. In such circumstances, the concept of 'the future' may be meaningless.

Even when prison life is more familiar, when the individual has realised what has happened and he has settled down, the anticipated length of his detention may be so intimidating that the only way he feels he can survive, (that is, retain some sense of sanity and reality), is to live simply from day to day. Either he finds it impossible to think of the future, or he consciously decides not to do so. At best, it is something which he might be able to contemplate a few years hence. Each of the lifers I interviewed was asked at what stage in his detention was he first able to think meaningfully about the future and make plans, albeit very tentatively, about release. Table 7.8 shows the range of their answers.

TABLE 7.8   *Stage at which Lifers Could Start to Consider the Future*

	Relative Frequency
Main centre	20 (24.4%)
Category B prison	17 (20.7%)
Category C prison	10 (12.2%)
Category D prison	5 (6.1%)
When given release date	29 (35.4%)
Hostel	1 (1.2%)
Totals	82 (100.0%)

That more than a third said that it was only when given a provisional release date that they felt able to look to their future and life outside prison was not surprising. Some were in a semi-open prison when they received this information, though more were in an open establishment. They had adopted the view that notwithstanding predictions as to the length of their detention, the situation had always been so uncertain that it was pointless, and perhaps dangerous, to start thinking about what they might do when released. They had never been able to have sufficient confidence in what other people had said, and there was the fear that their hopes would be dashed. Some said that although staff and fellow lifers had made encouraging remarks to them, they were only too aware of what they regarded as incomprehensible decisions about the release of other prisoners, and of disappointments which they had themselves suffered during their sentence. Nothing could be taken for granted: until they got their provisional date, it was not safe to contemplate the future.

It was interesting to find that transfer from a closed (Category B) prison to a semi-open or open establishment only rarely sparked off thoughts about the years ahead. Presumably, this reflects the general feeling amongst lifers that although they may be moving in the right direction, their situation is still very precarious. On the other hand, it was encouraging to see that a sizeable proportion of the sample were able to look to the future in the comparatively early years of their sentence. Apart from the 20 lifers who were at a main centre at the time, 17 were in Category B prisons. It is often assumed that prisoners in the middle phase of their detention will have recovered from any initial shock and settled into the sentence but be unable to 'see any light at the end of the tunnel'. They are sometimes said to be suffering from 'mid-term depression', so that there is little likelihood that they can be motivated to contemplate the years ahead. It is important to note, therefore, that six of the 17 lifers had in fact served less than three years since the date of their sentence. Thus, 26 lifers (almost a third of the sample) began to think about their future roughly within the first three years.

As to the remaining 11 lifers, a variety of factors seemed to have been instrumental in bringing about their thoughts for the future. For two of them it was being transferred out of the dispersal system, albeit to another Category B prison. Another was in a non-dispersal prison and was told that he was being moved to open conditions. A fourth was told of the date of his first LRC review. Two others simply felt that they had matured as individuals after about five years in detention. The remaining five said that it was the more relaxed, 'human' regime and the opportunity to take advantage of a range of facilities within the prison which had led them to start considering the future.

There were no obvious characteristics which had any significance in determining whether a lifer was likely to be able to plan for the future at a particular stage in his sentence. The only possible exception to this was his previous experience of custody. Table 7.9 provides the relevant statistics.

Two points should be borne in mind when looking at these figures. Firstly, of the total sample, 26.8 per cent had prior experience of a custodial penalty. Secondly, since there were only a small number of lifers who said it was when they reached open conditions that they

TABLE 7.9 *Stage at which Lifers Could Begin to Consider the Future by Previous Experience of Custody*

	Proportion who had served a custodial sentence
Main centre	50%
Category B	11.8%
Category C	20.0%
Category D	40.0%
Release date	20.7%
Hostel	0.0%

could begin to think of the future, the fact that two of them had previously been deprived of their liberty clearly cannot be treated as significant.

CONTROL OVER LENGTH OF DETENTION

The tariff which, following the adjustments made by the Prison Department in the light of the Divisional Court's judgment in the Handscomb case, is now determined within a few months of the date of sentence for most murderers, indicates the length of time which it is felt should be spent in custody to meet the needs of retribution and deterrence. Since release will only be sanctioned when the prisoner is no longer regarded as a threat to the safety of the public, the tariff date represents the earliest possible point at which release will take place. One of the immediate potential problems that is likely to ensue from this is that a lifer may feel that regardless of how well he conducts himself in prison and of the use he makes of his detention, he must necessarily spend a minimum time in custody. This is obviously not conducive to the creation of a positive and constructive approach by the lifer to his sentence. Whilst it is only right to acknowledge that the tariff date may be brought forward where the Home Secretary is satisfied that exceptional progress has been made during detention, it remains to be seen how frequently this occurs.

The apparent dominance of the tariff and the inability of lifers to influence the time they spend in detention was emphasised by Maguire *et al.* (1984), and the responses I received generally reinforced this belief. More than three-quarters (63 out of 82) said that they had always felt that good behaviour and a positive attitude to the sentence could never bring their release on licence any nearer, though bad conduct might well prolong their detention. Twelve others said that behaviour in prison was simply immaterial. They had heard of cases where prisoners had behaved impeccably, of whom staff had talked in glowing terms, and yet their applications for parole were repeatedly rejected. Conversely, other prisoners had breached regulations and made no apparent efforts to improve themselves, only to be released after what seemed to be a relatively short term of imprisonment. The sole factor appeared to be the nature and gravity of the offence. If it was not regarded as particularly heinous, or if there were mitigating circumstances, then release would probably come at an earlier stage than in other cases.

Only seven of those I interviewed expressed any optimistic remarks on this issue. In each case they said they had always hoped that they could lower the tariff by their attitude and conduct in prison, but they had never felt confident about it. There were no obvious common characteristics of these cases.

VISITS AND LETTERS

The extent to which prisoners receive visits from family and friends and correspond with people outside the prison may also play a part in their attitude towards their sentence and how they prepare for release. This is especially true of those who are detained for lengthy periods. Receiving visitors and letters are obvious ways in which prisoners can keep in touch with what is happening in the world outside. In addition, they provide a means of communication through which prisoners can alleviate worries about their families, and so on which might undermine their progress. At the same time, visitors and correspondents may benefit from having the opportunity to keep in contact with prisoners and to encourage them through their detention.

No less than 75 lifers in the sample indicated that visits and letters had had these beneficial effects and that they had enabled them to retain a sense of worth. The fact that, although they had been convicted of what are widely regarded as particularly serious crimes, someone still cared for them sufficiently to come and talk or to write to them, helped them to preserve some self-respect. Three lifers felt that they had not benefitted personally from visits or letters, but that their families had. To them, their loss of liberty was more harrowing for their loved ones than themselves. The remaining four lifers had attached no importance to visits and letters at all. In each case, relationships with people outside prison had broken down at a very early stage of the sentence, but the lifers did not treat this as problematic.

There is, however, a potentially unfortunate aspect about visits and letters which was embodied in the remarks of several lifers who said that they were also a 'wind up'. In other words, prisoners would look forward, often with great anticipation, to seeing their families, only to find that the visits served to emphasise the impact of their segregation – it reminded them very forcefully of what they were missing, bringing the rigour of their punishment more sharply into focus. Letters could produce similar reactions, albeit less dramatically. Some lifers commented that the end of a visit was a particularly difficult experience – emotions heightened and everyone became upset. There was though, an ironic side to visits and letters. On the one hand, prisoners are usually anxious to know what is happening to their families and friends, but when they learn of the problems people are having to deal with they are likely to feel very frustrated at their inability to help. Notwithstanding these frustrations, the vast majority of lifers said that on balance visits and letters had been important to them.

LIFERS' ATTITUDES TOWARDS CONVICTION FOR MURDER

The likelihood that a prisoner will adopt a constructive attitude towards his sentence is a complex question raising a variety of issues, one of which is the extent to which he accepts that his conviction was deserved. It is, of course, quite understandable that a person charged with such a serious crime might deny liability, either wholly or in part. Sixty of the lifers in this part of the study had pleaded not guilty.

However, where long after the trial and when the shock of being given a life sentence has passed a prisoner still feels that his conviction was not justified, it is quite likely that staff will have difficulty in persuading him to take a positive approach to his detention. His sense of injustice may have an unsettling and nagging effect on his mind. Seven lifers told me they bore no responsibility at all for the victim's death. Of these, four accepted they were not entirely unconnected with the incident but claimed that their involvement was only very peripheral and that someone else had independently carried out the fatal assault. Another 52 admitted they were responsible, either alone or with others, for killing the victim but remained convinced that they ought to have been convicted of the lesser crime of manslaughter. In 35 of these cases it was argued that the main reason why they had not murdered their victims was that they had not acted with 'malice aforethought'. The others said they had been provoked to kill.

The fact that only 22 thought they had rightly been convicted of murder may be a cause for concern. It should not be dismissed as a sign of an understandable reluctance to be thought of, or to think of oneself as, a murderer. All 82 lifers accepted that their convictions would never be altered. The claims of those who thought their convictions unjust were not based simply on their own personal opinion of what ought to be regarded as murder. Rather they felt that the true nature of the case had not been accurately portrayed and assessed by the legal process. That such a sizeable proportion should approach a life sentence in that frame of mind is not encouraging.

One lifer declined to discuss the offence. The rest were very conscious of two particular problems that would follow from being formally labelled as a 'murderer'. Firstly, there is the mixture of fear and contempt that many people might have of them. Secondly, their chances of securing employment may well be prejudiced, especially when they are called on to describe their previous work record. At the same time, it is only right to point out that several interviewees said that their experience of work outside prison and of mixing in the community had shown that ostracization was not inevitable. People who knew that they had been convicted of murder nonetheless accepted them for what they are, and many of the people they would meet were unlikely to be aware of their conviction.

LIFERS' ATTITUDES TOWARDS THE LENGTH OF THEIR DETENTION

It would be unwise automatically to discount lifers' views about how long they should be kept in prison on the ground that their opinions will be biased and thus unworthy of serious consideration. In a sense they are in the best possible position to assess the gravity of their offence, and their feelings about the correctness of the term of their detention may affect the use they make of it and perhaps the ease with which they re-establish themselves on release. If a lifer reaches the point where he feels he has been detained for too long, not only might he become unsettled, but more importantly he is likely to lose motivation.

Almost two-thirds of those I talked to expressed the opinion that they had been imprisoned for too long. Their comments were based mainly on their perception of the heinousness of the offence (which sometimes varied from the court's view), and the progress which they felt they had made during detention. In general, it was suggested that they had been detained for two to three years more than necessary. In a few instances these opinions were supported by comments made in their prison records by staff who had recommended release earlier than was authorised by the Home Secretary. Naturally, all the lifers prefaced their remarks by acknowledging the extreme difficulty of trying to measure the loss of life against the loss of liberty, but only nine felt unable to give some sort of answer. Eighteen thought that they had been punished correctly, and one said that he was to be released sooner than he deserved. He was to be kept in prison for just over 12 years for his part in a robbery which had 'gone wrong' and the victim had been fatally stabbed. At the same time, he could not indicate how long he thought he ought to have spent in prison.

It is worth stressing that the lifers did not focus their attention solely on the seriousness of the offence. Regardless of their views of their conviction, they were conscious of the fact that the offence had highlighted a problem which needed to be addressed, and their opinions about the appropriate length of detention took account of this.

LIFERS' VIEWS ABOUT THE EFFECTS OF IMPRISONMENT

One of the major concerns about long-term imprisonment which criminologists have begun to investigate in recent years is the fear that prisoners might become 'institutionalised'. In simple terms, this implies that a person who is subjected for a lengthy period to a regime which gives him only a very limited opportunity to make decisions for himself may become incapable of successfully pursuing an independent lifestyle outside the institution. Certainly, those lifers I spoke to were very alert to this danger, as were prison staff. However, more than three-quarters of the sample maintained that imprisonment had had no apparent effects on them. They may have 'mellowed' over the years, but that was simply the result of getting older and would have happened in any event. Eighteen said that prison had helped them to mature; they had met people who had to cope with greater problems than their own and this enabled them to see their own predicament in a broader perspective. They had learned to be more tolerant and how to react in difficult or stressful situations. One young man though, found it impossible to say whether, on balance, the impact of imprisonment had been good or bad. He had matured and learned to understand and control his emotions, but the pettiness and bloody-mindedness (as he saw it) of prison regulations had led him on occasions to be devious, and his encounters with staff and other prisoners had made him very cautious of his fellow man. Hopefully, these less desirable characteristics would disappear in time.

A GENERAL COMMENT

Finally, there were one or two underlying features of my conversations with these lifers which have only been hinted at so far. There was an overwhelming lack of trust and confidence in the efficiency and reliability of the penal system, and universal criticism of the delay in being given the answers to parole applications. Having to wait inordinate lengths of time, measurable sometimes in years rather than months, caused considerable distress not only for the lifers but also for their families and friends. The fact that they were not officially given any explanation or reason for applications being rejected and had to rely on the occasional hint from a member of staff merely served to aggravate matters.

Only very rarely did any of them feel able to have confidence in prison staff. A governor or uniform officer might make encouraging remarks, that the prisoner was well thought of and that his reports were very supportive, but all too often these proved to be misleading. The obvious explanations were that either the member of staff had deliberately raised false hopes or he was out of touch with the views of P2 Division. Not surprisingly, lifers tended to mix with staff only superficially, and sometimes not at all.

The significance of these points is that they were symptomatic of a general feeling of helplessness and isolation. Naturally, some lifers felt less helpless and isolated than others, but most seemed to feel that decisions were taken about them by people in London with whom they could not effectively communicate and they simply had to accept what was determined for them. This sense of 'anomie' appears to have undermined the attainment of a constructive attitude to the sentence which the Revised Strategy seeks to achieve. Lifers tended not to feel sufficiently secure in the belief that making the appropriate effort would be to their advantage.

LIFERS' RECORDS

During the main part of their detention lifers' cases will be reviewed every 12 months or perhaps more frequently, in the early stages in particular, so that their progress can be regularly monitored and any developments can be taken on board. Major reviews will be undertaken for the preparation of F75 reports and subsequently when cases are considered by the LRC and the Parole Board. Reports are usually produced by the same cross-section of staff – the governor, an assistant or deputy governor, possibly two probation officers (one based in the prison and one in the place where the lifer intends to settle on release), the chaplain, a psychologist, psychiatrist and/or medical officer, and sundry uniform staff such as the prisoner's case officer (if he has one), an education and/or works officer, and a senior or principal officer.

Reading through them, it became clear that the reports invariably concentrated on specific issues, such as the way in which lifers talk about the offence, their general demeanour during the discussion, and the extent to which their accounts reflect the 'official version', how far they understand and have come to terms with a life sentence, what remorse they show, and the apparent sincerity of any remorse, how and with whom they spend their time, whether they seem to be looking ahead and trying to plan constructively, their attitude towards staff and acceptance of authority, the way they react to problems, and how much contact they have with the outside world.

Predictably, the emphasis which staff place on these issues tends to vary according to the stage which has been reached in the sentence. In the early years, attention is more likely to be focused on the reaction to and understanding of the sentence. When he has settled down the lifer will probably be encouraged to talk about the crime and to set about ensuring that it will not be repeated. Later on, the prime concern will be how well release preparations are proceeding, and the lifer's appreciation of the difficulties he will face. One quite distinctive characteristic of the reports was that many of those drafted by uniform officers were very brief, frequently only five or six lines long, so that they gave an extremely bare outline of the prisoner's conduct. In contrast, reports by other staff tended to be much fuller and sought to offer some analysis of the lifer's behaviour and attitude as well as a description of it.

It may be, as Coker (1985) remarked, that changes of environment and personnel, caused by moving lifers from one prison to another, ensure that reports are not as subjective as might initially be feared. But the results of this study confirm the point acknowledged by Coker (1985) that observations made by staff early in the sentence tend to be repeated by colleagues so that, once acquired, labels usually stick. This was particularly true when a lifer was seen as subversive or as a potential danger to society and, as Maguire *et al.* (1984) indicated, such a label would not be lost until perhaps nine or ten years had been served.

It was encouraging to find that report-writers generally agreed with one another about the progress that was being made, and many of the lifers' remarks about their attitudes towards their sentence mirrored those of the staff. Not surprisingly though, there were occasions where differences of opinion were expressed. On one level, the tone and emphasis in a report might vary with that of another. A medical officer described the man in Case 26 as 'aggressive and homicidal', whereas the assistant governor noted that he had at odd times shown signs of aggression, but produced a more supportive report which stressed how his attitude to authority had mellowed. The wing manager in Case 46 praised the lifer's 'first class attitude' towards the offence and sentence, and yet the governor was generally more critical, and highlighted the apparent lack of remorse. Another wing manager, in Case 72, talked of the lifer as 'deeply devious', in contrast to the governor, who was more struck by the prisoner's recent maturation.

Of more concern though, was the discovery that there were instances where writers' opinions seemed to be in direct conflict with each other. For example, in reports made in Case 22 about four months after the trial a uniform officer confidently asserted that the lifer had not yet come to terms with his indeterminate sentence. But the chaplain was equally sure that although he had initially been taken aback the prisoner now fully understood his predicament and had settled down. In Case 48 the medical officer criticised what he saw as the lifer's lack of remorse, whereas the governor and the probation officer took the opposite view.

In addition, the study provided examples where the recommendations of report-writers were either rejected entirely or only partially implemented. In Case 17 the lifer was required to spend the last few months of his detention in a hostel on the PRES in spite of an assistant governor's view that it would be quite inappropriate to adopt such a course. Some three years after she had been sentenced, the lifer in Case 25 was recommended to be transferred to an open prison by a psychotherapist. She was eventually moved to such a prison, more than six years after the recommendation was made! The probation officer in Case 49 strongly favoured a period on the PRES, yet the LRC rejected the proposal. In the event, the probation officer's suggestion was acted upon.

There was also a group of cases in which members of staff indicated that the lifer should serve a shorter period of detention than that which he in fact served. In Case 5 the wing manager suggested a maximum of eight years, but release was only permitted after nine years. In Case 6 the assistant governor recommended seven years at most, but the provisional release date required more than eight and a half years. In Case 23 a governor thought that release could properly be granted after about ten and a half years had been served, but the lifer was due to be detained for a further two and a half years.

It was acknowledged earlier that when reviewing cases the principal concern of report-writers is the safety of the public, but it is recognised that other issues may also have a very real impact on the timing of release. In Case 52, for example, an assistant governor and a medical officer supported the lifer's parole application, whilst at the same time admitting that the sexual characteristics of the offence would probably prolong his detention. It seems that the recommendations of the trial judge are likely to weigh very heavily when parole is considered. In Case 75 an assistant governor said that the prisoner could safely be released after about nine years, but he accepted that the trial judge's opinion (of 12 years) would take precedence. As it transpired, he was correct; the provisional release date was 11 and a half years after the date of sentence. In Case 76 a governor supported release at the 12-year mark, though the trial judge had recommended 15 years. In fact, almost 17 years was to be served.

The main area of disagreement between report-writers and the lifers I interviewed centred on the ways in which prisoners should be tested as to their suitability for release. Many lifers argued that the sorts of tests they are subjected to in semi-open and open prisons (arising from their enforced association with short-term prisoners), were unrealistic and thus an unreliable means of assessing the risk they posed to the public. Staff, on the other hand, saw the way in which lifers reacted to these difficulties as a useful indication of how well they would cope with problems and pressures that would inevitably befall them on release.

A degree of disagreement amongst report-writers and between staff and prisoners is to be expected. Yet the fact that these disagreements occur illustrates that reviewing a person's progress through detention, and assessing the level of risk to the public that his release would pose, are highly complex processes which cannot be pursued in a wholly scientific manner.

8 A Sample of the Interviews With Lifers

In order to give a more comprehensive account of the interviews I had with lifers, and not rely solely on an essential statistical analysis, this chapter provides summaries of 30 cases, demonstrating the range of responses I received. Unfortunately, it is not possible to record the confidential remarks in prison files because of the risk that individuals could discover what had been written about them. The summaries reflect the course which the interviews took and some of the expressions that were used. Naturally, they should be read in conjunction with the previous chapter, to illustrate the data that is shown there. They are intended not as definitive explanations of the interviews, but as a means of enabling the reader to appreciate the diversity of the views and opinions. Many of the responses were repeated over and over again, and I have tried to show this in the summaries, if only to demonstrate the frequency with which the comments were made.

Case No. 6

This man had served just over seven years of his sentence at the time of the interview. He spent the first month at his local prison where he was accommodated in the main wing. He spent the first week working in the mailbag shop and thereafter worked in the laundry. He said he was watched closely by prison staff although their attitude towards him was quite friendly.

He was then moved to a Main Centre prison where he stayed for the next three years or so, and he spent all of the time working in the tailors shop. During the evenings he attended classes in 'O' level Maths and English. After he had been there for about 12 months there were disturbances as a result of which the security tightened up quite considerably and he was kept in his cell for longer periods. He felt unjustly punished in that he was being prejudiced as a result of what other prisoners had done. At the same time he felt that the attitude of staff towards prisoners was generally quite good and all the prisoners on his wing were serving life sentences and they got on quite well together.

He was then transferred to a Category B prison where he spent the next three and a half years. For the first 12 months he spent his working time assembling childrens' typewriters, and thereafter he worked in prison reception, in the tailors shop, and assembling electrical switches. He described the atmosphere in the prison as being very friendly both amongst staff and other prisoners. He felt that prisoners were left to organise themselves to a much greater extent which he regarded as a good thing. He attended classes in Maths and English, Poetry and Woodwork.

He was then moved to an open prison and had been there for about ten months at the time of the interview. There he had worked in the textile shop sewing 'T' shirts and had also done a four months electronics course which he felt was helpful. He was one of the first two life sentence prisoners to be accommodated at this prison and the staff were rather wary of him. Initially they watched him very closely although this had eased off gradually. Relationships with other inmates were reasonably good and he did not think that the life-sentence prisoners tended to associate only with each other. He said he was looking forward to going to prison hostel where he would have more freedom and he would have the chance to re-establish a normal life-style. He felt it was necessary for prisoners to take the initiative to learn to organise their own lives and to prepare for release and to prevent themselves from vegetating or becoming institutionalised. He still felt that he had wrongly been convicted of murder and ought to have been convicted of manslaughter instead.

Case No. 7

Here a young offender, only 17 years of age when he committed his offence, had served about eight and a half years in prison at the time of the interview. Immediately after sentence he had been taken back to the prison where he had been held on remand, but this time kept in the hospital wing for about a month. He was put in a single cell and, although there was officially no work for prisoners to do there, he got out of his cell by volunteering to clean the landing. If he had chosen to do so, he could have spent most of the time (that is 21–22 hours in the day) in his cell, either sleeping or reading. Most of the staff were pleasant to him, as were the other prisoners. In view of his youth people generally adopted a sympathetic approach to him. He was then moved to the main wing of the prison where there was little for him to do but wait to be sent to another prison. At this time he was not allowed out of his cell, even to do any cleaning. He was kept in a single cell and was allowed about half an hour's exercise in the morning and another half hour in the afternoon, otherwise he was locked up. The staff on the main wing he described as 'impersonal', probably because there were more staff and more inmates in that part of the prison.

He was then sent to a prison for young offenders and spent over three years there. He took the opportunity to catch up on some education, studying for 'O' levels, and his main hobby there was power-lifting. He spent most of the mornings and afternoons working in various machine shops. He said his power-weight training was something which occupied his mind and helped to pass the time. He also studied for 'A' level examinations although he was moved to another prison before he completed the course. He felt that he did not get on very well with the other prisoners there: he felt more mature than most of them and described himself as a loner. He also did not spend very much time talking with staff. He said they would try to engage him in conversation in order to bring him out of his shell, but he felt it was the wrong environment for him to do so, particularly when the other prisoners were young offenders. Later on, when he was in prison with adult offenders, he felt able to talk more. He argued that had he been sent to an adult prison at an earlier stage he would have grown up more quickly.

He then went to a Category B prison for about two years. There he continued his academic education and also worked in the typewriter assembly shop. He gave up power-lifting and took up running instead. He said he appreciated the greater freedom and the quieter atmosphere. He became aware of being observed all the time, and thought this was rather insidious and he always felt tense and very watchful. He described life there as like being in a goldfish bowl and felt unable to act naturally. The other prisoners there were on the whole fairly quiet. He felt that he had benefitted in that he had come to realise that there were other people who were certainly as intelligent as he was if not more so and as a result he lost some of his arrogance. In general, he felt that the people there were more friendly, more human, and the attitude of the prisoners towards the staff more mature. Everybody realised they had got to live together and get on with one another, and there was no point in causing trouble.

From there he was moved to an open prison and had been there for about two and a half years at the time of the interview. He did not like having to live in a dormitory when he first got there. This was an unpleasant experience having had a single cell during the previous time that he had been in prison. After six or seven months he was given a room to himself and that, he felt, was a big improvement. He spent much of his time working in the stores and unloading lorries that were bringing goods into the prison. Lifers were a distinct group from the other prisoners, although he also mixed with short-term offenders who behaved maturely and sensibly. He got on reasonably well with most of the staff, and said he was less aware of being observed. The greater freedom of the open prison was a welcome change, and he had appreciated the gradual increase in freedom as he had gone through the system.

At the time of the interview he was shortly to move to a prison hostel and said he was very much looking forward to it. It represented a chance to get back to a more normal life-style. He had been out of prison on a few occasions and enjoyed them very much. There were certain things that had come as a bit of a surprise for him – for example, the noise of the traffic when he visited the town centre – but he felt he could adjust fairly quickly to the world outside.

Case No. 8

This man was aged 17 when he was convicted and sentenced to life imprisonment and had been in prison for about ten years at the time he was interviewed. From the court he was taken to a local prison and was accommodated on the main wing, and he was locked up in his cell by himself for most of the day. Apart from his half hour's exercise in the morning and another half hour in the afternoon, he spent most of the time reading. This continued for about four or five months. The prison staff left him alone and he did not mix with the other prisoners.

At the end of the four or five months he was moved to a prison for young offenders and spent about 16 months there. During the weekdays he worked in the mornings and afternoons in the laundry and was allowed two hours association in the evenings which he spent mainly playing snooker and darts. He also attended educational classes in reading and writing. He described the staff there as being a little more friendly, more human. For example, they would help him if he wanted to write a letter, but again they left it to the prisoners to decide whether they wanted to talk or whether they did not. He tended to mix with a small group of prisoners and this was true throughout his time in prison.

From there he moved to a top security adult prison where he was accommodated for nearly three years. There he had more freedom to move about the wing in which he lived. Prisoners were allowed to organise things more; for example, they could do their own cooking. He continued his education (reading and writing) working on that full-time, and then went to work in the tailors shop. Life was easier there because all the other prisoners were either serving long, fixed-term sentences or (like him) were doing life sentences and he felt it less upsetting not to see short-term prisoners coming and going. He spent some of his spare time working out in the gym and he also did a cookery course. The staff did not bother him and he did not bother them.

He was then transferred to a Category B prison where he was kept for the next three years or so. In some ways he found that at the Category B prison he had less individual freedom; for example, he was not able to cook his own food and was locked up in his cell frequently. He tended to keep himself to himself, not bothering too much with the staff and mixing only with a small group of prisoners.

From there he moved to a semi-open prison and stayed there for just under two years. This he described as being better than the previous prison because it was much cleaner, although he added that he did not have as much freedom as he had been given in the top security prison. He had been in an open prison for about eight months at the time he was interviewed. Since arriving there he spent most of his time either bricklaying or pursuing his education. He was accommodated in a dormitory and he found that this was difficult to get used to primarily because of the noise, having spent the previous nine years or so in a single cell where he had got used to a certain amount of peace and quiet. He felt he had more individual freedom at the open prison than previously and described the attitude of the staff as being 'not strict', although he did say that they tended to treat prisoners 'like kids'. This was possibly because there were so many short-term prisoners at the institution and they tended to behave rather immaturely. He felt that the visits that he had had from his family and the letters he had received were very important to him. They gave him some contact with the outside world and it was very reassuring to know that people still cared for him.

He looked forward to going to hostel in a few weeks time because that would be a further stage towards his release. He had a job to go to and would be living with his family. He spent a lot of time thinking about the future and consciously tried not to dwell on the past.

Although he had been in prison for about ten years he felt that he had, as he put it, 'learnt his lesson' after about five years. He attributed his crime largely to the immaturity of youth and he had since 'grown up', though this was something that would have happened naturally and was not a result of his imprisonment. As his release from custody got nearer, time seemed to pass increasingly slowly. He said that although he had been in prison for ten years or so, he had found that on his trips out of prison that things had not really changed that much. He admitted that he found that life in the towns and cities was much busier and noisier than he had been used to, but this was not something which caused him any anxiety.

Case No. 11

This man had been sentenced about 12 and a half years before the interview. He had pleaded guilty, and said the sentence had not come as a shock to him. From the court he was taken to a top security prison and spent the first couple of nights in the hospital wing. He was locked up and left alone, and he had not needed any medication. He was then taken to one of the main wings where he spent the next ten or 11 months. Initially, he worked in the sewing machine shop and then took up studying English and Spanish. These activities occupied him for about four hours a day. He mixed with other prisoners quite readily, and had never had any trouble getting on with other prisoners at any stage of his sentence.

He was transferred to a dispersal prison where he was detained for almost six years. There he had done a number of courses including a City and Guilds Engineering course. He also worked in the weaving shop, in the laundry, and in the stores. He had enjoyed quite a lot of freedom there, and described his time as 'great – as far as prisons go'. First name terms were used and, although initially he had been rather taken aback by this, he gradually realised that was how things were at the prison and accepted it. He was very aware that in a dispersal prison he was being watched all the time. The surveillance was very visible and his reaction was simply to try to ignore it.

From there he went to a semi-open prison which he described as 'terrible, unbelievable', because of the pettiness of the regime. Rules and regulations were strictly applied. Although there were short-term prisoners there, he tended to mix with the long-term and life-sentence prisoners because the short-termers were usually 'whinging away about their wives and one thing or another – you don't get that with long termers ... they don't want to listen to other peoples' problems, they have got enough of their own'.

He spent just under three years at the semi-open prison and then moved to an open establishment. Throughout his time in prison he had had visits from his family and they had kept him informed about what was going on in his home town. He was also going out to a local college three times a week and felt that he had been able to keep in touch with the world outside. He enjoyed his time in the open prison, and particularly appreciated working outdoors on the estates. He also liked the fact that in the open prison he had to think for himself and organise his own life. He said that he had no real difficulties in adjusting to the greater individual freedom and increased personal responsibility that accompanied his move there. This was helped by the knowledge that he was getting much closer to his release. Again he had disliked the fact that during his first three months at the open prison he had been accommodated in a dormitory. On the whole he felt the staff were better at the open prison than in the semi-open establishment, mainly because they tended to leave prisoners alone. He felt that one of the things that had happened to him as a result of his imprisonment was that he was much more cautious about the people he mixed with and his choice of friends. He had found no difficulties when going out of prison to attend the local college, and got on well with other students on the catering course. During his trips out of prison, whether for a day or a few days, he was able to 'switch off' and forget the prison completely until he had to come back again. One of the things that had particularly struck him when he first went out of prison was the extent to which prices had increased.

As for going to the hostel he felt that that was going to be the hardest part of the sentence. He said 'I've got to start learning to work – you see in prison you don't really work – you do a day's work from 8.00 to 11.30 in the morning and from 1.00 until 4.30 in the afternoon and I've done a day's work, but it isn't like working outside. That six months (in the hostel) is going to have to get me used to working in the community and all sorts of problems are going to crop up'. However, he went on to say that he had received letters from friends who had already been in a prison hostel and they had reassured him that he would be able to cope quite adequately. Overall he was looking forward to the time he would spend in hostel with a positive attitude. He regarded prison visits as vitally important because they gave him both moral support and enabled him to keep in touch with what was going on in the outside world. He said it was a pleasant change to be able to hold a normal conversation with someone and not talk about what was going on in prison.

Case No. 15

Immediately after sentence this prisoner was taken back to the remand centre where he had been held prior to his trial and he was put in a strip cell for the first three days and was given sleeping tablets. For the next four months he was kept in a hospital ward with about 25 other prisoners. Apart from one hour's exercise a day, he spent his time watching television and reading. He felt that many of the other people in the hospital ward were criminally insane.

From there he was transferred to a local prison where he spent the first two weeks in a hospital cell, locked up all the time apart from one hour's exercise. He was then moved on to the main wing for three or four months where the regime was fairly strict. He spent a couple of hours in the morning and the afternoon sewing mailbags. Meals were eaten in cells and there was no association. At the same time, other prisoners and prison staff were reasonably friendly.

His next move was to a top security prison where he was kept for about three years. This was more pleasant for there was association each evening and sporting activities at weekends. He worked mainly in the engineers shop in the mornings and afternoons and spent some of his spare time making models. He described the attitude of staff in general as co-operative, with one or two of them being quite friendly. Meals were again eaten in cells.

He then moved to a Category B non-dispersal prison which was more relaxed. There was less tension there and less overt signs of security. He spent most of his working time in the plastics shop. He tended to mix more with other prisoners there, and spent some of his spare time in the gym and running, and also attended some Maths classes. The staff were more friendly and less visible than in the top security prison.

He then spent two and a half years in another Category B non-dispersal prison but which accommodated only life-sentence prisoners. This was much better again because the atmosphere was very easy. He hardly ever saw the staff but when he did they were very helpful, and it was in this prison that he had begun to lose his suspicion about the motives of staff. He spent most of his working time in the typewriter shop and again pursued hobbies such as model-making, and also spent some time running and exercising in the gymnasium.

From there he had gone to an open prison and had been at the open prison for just over two years at the time of the interview. He was critical of the accommodation in that he had had to spend some time initially in a dormitory. Most of his work was on the estates in the prison. He said he mixed well with the other prisoners, both long- and short-term offenders. Like many of those I interviewed, he was critical of the time it had taken for him to get his release date: he had waited 14 months since making his application. He said the staff were 'OK', although they tended to keep a low profile. He was due to go to hostel in a few months' time, but he saw this largely as a waste of time. The one concern he had about release was the difficulty in getting a job, and he had lost touch with most of his family whilst in prison. He had received very few letters, and his last visit had been ten years prior to the interview. He felt that his time in prison had made him a steadier and more thoughtful person. He did not just 'live for today' as he had when he was younger, but was now more careful in the way in which he planned life for the future.

Case No. 16

At the time he was interviewed in the prison hostel, this man had served just over 17 years in prison. When sentence had been passed on him, the judge had recommended that he should be detained for a minimum of 20 years. During the first part of his prison sentence he was a Category A prisoner. He had been acutely aware of the fact that he was treated as someone whose every movement had to be monitored and carefully watched, and he was escorted whenever he moved to different parts of the prison. He was not physically segregated from other prisoners although it appears that because of his security categorisation he did not have the opportunity to associate to any great extent with other inmates. Communication with staff was at an absolute minimum. There was no social discourse between them.

He spent about 12 months in each of his first two prisons and in both cases his main job was as a cleaner. In the second prison, work was not compulsory and if he chose to do so he could simply stay in his cell. The staff in the second prison were less aloof. His third establishment, where he spent four years, was a dispersal prison and for part of the time there at least he had a little more physical freedom. The work that he was given to do was of an extremely mundane and unstimulating nature. Again, he had very little contact with staff.

He then moved to another top security prison for five years. He would have liked to have stopped longer simply because of the convenience of visits for him there. He did a number of jobs which were again of a very routine nature. Partly as a means of stimulating his mind and also in an attempt to improve his general education, he studied for an open university degree which he later achieved with honours. Although prison staff tended to keep their distance from him, he communicated and mixed quite readily with other prisoners.

The trial judge had recommended a minimum of 20 years imprisonment, but he had always hoped that he would be released before then. He was pleased therefore that his next move was to a non-dispersal Category B prison where he spent about two years. He saw this as a positive move towards eventual release. At the same time, he was slightly sad to leave the previous prison where he had been given quite a considerable degree of freedom within his wing and life had been reasonably calm. At this new prison he not only found himself with other prisoners serving long sentences, but he encountered many who were serving much shorter terms. He did not find this problematic, for as he said, he was free to associate with whom he chose. He continued with his open university course. Then he was moved to a semi-open prison where he spent three years or so. Although he was given more physical freedom, he was still very aware of being constantly observed and having his behaviour analysed. Here his case was reviewed and he described the two years that he waited for an answer to this review as being a particularly testing time. He said the attitude of the staff towards prisoners was 'very prepy'.

From there he was moved directly to a prison hostel where he was to spend nine months. He said that in many respects living in a hostel was the same as being in any other penal establishment. His plans for release were proceeding satisfactorily and he settled into his job.

His gradual down-grading in security categorisation during the course of his sentence was obviously appreciated, particularly when he ceased to be a Category A prisoner. There was genuine regret for his involvement in the crime that led to the life sentence being imposed upon him and also at the fact that he had also spent such a long time in penal institutions.

Case No. 18

At the time of the interview this man had served just over ten years in prison. After sentence he had been taken back to his local prison and spent the first three or four days in a single room in the hospital wing. Apart from three or four hours' association and exercise he was locked in his room. From there he was moved to an ordinary wing where he spent the following two months or so. For about six hours a day in the morning and the afternoon he worked in the mailbag shop, although meals had to be eaten in cells. At that stage he chose not to associate with other prisoners. He felt very aware that most of the other prisoners at this particular institution were serving relatively short sentences (that is, no more than four years) and as a lifer he was something of a celebrity. The staff generally left him alone.

He moved to a maximum security prison and was kept there for about three and a half years. He was accommodated on the long-term wing where he made a couple of good friends and one or two acquaintances. He worked in the sewing-machine repair shop, in the engineering shop, and started a cabinet-making course, although this was then stopped by the prison staff. The staff tended to be rather distant although he did get some constructive advice from one or two of them. He chose to eat his meals in his cell. After he had been in the prison for about two years or so there were some riots and after that he worked as a cleaner.

He was then transferred to a Category B dispersal prison for three years. This he described as 'very good' with first name terms being used by both staff and inmates. Initially he had been very anti-social but, as he put it, the staff 'didn't bite'. He was also initially rather wary of other prisoners, and tended to keep away from them because he did not want to be dragged into things. But he gradually relaxed and grew to like the prison and began to show some trust in other people. Most of the staff, he said, were genuinely good. He appreciated the freedom that was given to prisoners within the confines of the institution. Cells were open all day and prisoners even had their own key to their cells, although locks were ultimately controlled by computer, under the operation of the staff. He had taken an engineering course which he completed successfully, and also worked in the engineering shop. He did various evening classes in Maths, Geometry and Graphic Communication. The staff were polite but did not try to get prisoners to talk. They were 'fairly human' and would try to help prisoners if assistance was sought.

From there he went to an open prison where he spent two years or so, but he had not liked his stay there. He admitted that he had not wanted to leave the dispersal prison and had approached the open prison in a very negative frame of mind. He was critical of having to sleep in the dormitory with a lot of other prisoners. In particular, he said there were many short-term prisoners who were used by prison staff as 'grasses' in that they would tell tales on other inmates, and he was also critical of the fact that short-termers could be petty. After six months in the open prison he was pleased to be given his own room. Not surprisingly, he only associated with other life-sentence prisoners. One of the things he particularly appreciated about the open prison was walking in the rain! That was something he really enjoyed simply because he could not have done it in other prisons. At the same time he added that the prison staff tended to be rather distant. On his shopping trips he said that one of the things that really struck him was the great mass of colours in peoples' clothing. Whilst at the open prison he had been under more tension because it would have been so easy to 'slip' and be put back into a closed institution. He talked about the re-settlement scheme he had been part of at the open prison and this had meant that he had been working in a local hospital for sub-normal individuals. He had felt very sorry for patients there and finally asked to be taken off the resettlement programme.

During his time in prison he had had visits from members of his family but these tended to put him in a rather depressed mood. In particular, family visits provided him with too many reminders of life outside. At the time of the interview he was in a prison hostel and had been there for about five months. He described this as being something of an anti-climax. He was pleased to be there, but not elated. He worked as an engineer, turning and milling, but although in many respects he was living a normal life he said he was still subject to the prison regime and part of the prison system. He felt that, for example, the rule whereby he had to be back at the prison hostel by 10.45 each evening was unnecessary, for people would not stay out too long anyway because they had to get up and go to work the following day. This he felt was typical of the pettiness of the system. Other prisoners and staff at the hostel were polite. He said he did not really feel properly free whilst at the hostel, and was a little apprehensive about having to look after himself for the first time after so many years.

Case No. 19

At the time of passing sentence the judge recommended that this man be kept in prison for at least 20 years. When interviewed, he had served more than 17 years of his sentence. He spent the first three months in a hospital wing in a local prison where he was confined to a single cell. He tended to keep himself to himself although he did pass some of the time talking to staff. He described these three months as particularly boring.

He then spent the next few months at a top security prison where he worked in the wrought iron shop. The wing in which he was accommodated was one where all the prisoners were serving lengthy sentences and he readily associated with them. The staff, he said, tended to leave prisoners alone.

A further nine months were spent in another top security prison which he described as being very enclosed. The only work available was either in the sewing-machine shop or cleaning. There was association until about 9 o'clock in the evening and he spent most of his spare time either in some sport activity or reading. Again, he said, the staff tended to leave prisoners alone.

He then spent about 15 months in what is now a local prison and his clearest memories of that time are that he read a good deal and spent a lot of time making toys, basketware and pursuing sports. Following that he spent another 15 months in a top security prison working mainly in the paint-spraying shop and he said at that time he mixed well with the other prisoners.

The ensuing three years were served in another maximum security establishment where he remembered the large windows and the absence of bars, although he said the cells were very small. For some of the time there he worked as a storeman, and spent many hours in the gymnasium. The attitude of the staff was quite friendly, many of them referred to prisoners by their first names.

He was then transferred to a Category B prison for about two and a half years which he appreciated because it was closer to his home, thereby facilitating visits from his family. He had a variety of jobs, such as making plastic bags and shopping bags, doing demolition work around the prison, and working as a cleaner.

A further seven months or so were served in another local prison, where he worked mainly in the laundry and on the gardens. In this prison there was quite a mixture of prisoners in that some of them were doing quite short sentences and some were relatively young, and he mixed easily with all of them. What mattered was not the length of the sentence that the person was serving but whether he got on with him and liked him as an individual.

He then moved to another Category B prison for about four or five months, again with a mixture of short- and long-term sentence prisoners. There he spent most of his time making key rings, working in the gardens and as a cleaner.

A further nine months was spent at a top security prison – a time which he described as being not very happy for him. One of the main reasons was that it was too far away for his family to visit him. He spent a few months in a Category B prison and then a further six or seven months in a top security prison.

He was moved again to another top security prison for 14 months, working as a storeman, and in the tea room, and as a window-cleaner.

Three years were then spent in a Category B non-dispersal prison where he worked in the education department, and from there he moved to a prison hostel where he had been for about seven months when he was interviewed. He seemed quite content to be at the hostel. Part of this was no doubt because he was able to see his family a good deal and that was something which had always been very important to him. He had obtained a job working in the local community which he seemed to find very rewarding. Before being sentenced he had expected to be given a sentence of roughly ten years, so that he regarded the sentence he received as unduly harsh. However, he had been helped through his sentence quite considerably by the support he had received from his wife and family. Despite having spent so much time in prison he was determined to look to the future and not dwell on the past. He described prison as being like a garage, but one where the cars could never be repaired properly, they could never be restored to perfect running order.

Case No. 20

This man had been sentenced relatively recently, for at the time of the interview he had served less than seven years imprisonment. After sentence was passed he was taken back to a Category B prison where, for the first few hours, he was put in a strip cell in a hospital wing, and was then moved to an ordinary cell for two or three days. There he was left by himself. He then spent four or five weeks on one of the wings sewing mailbags. The staff were friendly and the other prisoners were polite, and he had appreciated some good advice from one of the prison doctors.

He was then moved to a top security prison where he stayed for over four years and four months. He did not enjoy the first four or five months there because he spent most of his time locked up in his cell. This was the result of riots that had taken place at the prison just before his arrival. His only regular time out of the cell in those early months was for one hour's exercise a day. Thereafter things gradually got better. He attended education classes in English but eventually gave them up. He then worked in the machine shop sewing buttons. He ate his meals in his cell and tended to mix only with a small group of prisoners. He found the staff at this prison a rather mixed bunch, some were quite good but others made no attempt to get to know prisoners.

He was then transferred to a non-dispersal Category B prison where all the prisoners were serving life sentences. This he described as a good prison where the atmosphere was much more relaxed. Cells were opened up at 7 o'clock in the morning and locked again at 9.15 at night. He was able to use the gymnasium seven days a week and there were cooking facilities and good educational courses. Most of the staff were quite friendly and were on first-name terms with the prisoners. He worked in the typewriter shop and also briefly as a cleaner in the hospital.

From there he moved to an open prison where he had been for about two months at the time of the interview. He had found no problems in adjusting to the greater freedom, and he had found little change in the outside world on the shopping visits he had had thus far. It was slightly strange at first, having to sleep in a dormitory, but he gradually adjusted.

Some of the short-term prisoners were rather selfish in that they did not respect the rights of privacy of other inmates. The staff were generally good, quite friendly and polite. He was undertaking a bricklayers course and other aspects of construction work. He was due to go to a prison hostel in about six months time and he was looking forward to this because he thought it would be more relaxed than being in a prison as such and would give him the opportunity to earn some money. He had no real fears for the future. He had received much support from friends and family outside and had been offered a job on his release. Visits had been very important to him in relieving the pressures of prison and they had particularly been helpful in keeping contact with his family.

Case No. 21

This lifer had served about seven years at the time of the interview and had been only 17 years of age at the time of his offence. He spent the first week of his sentence in a hospital wing where he generally kept himself to himself. He had not wanted any sympathy and was content for the staff to leave him to his own devices. After that week he was moved to another prison and he spent the first week in this second prison in a single cell in the hospital wing, where again he spent most of the time by himself (although he was allowed to exercise with other prisoners). He was then put on an ordinary wing where he shared a cell with another young offender. During the mornings he spent some time cleaning the landing, but he was locked up for much of the afternoons. He then got a job as a tea orderly and was thus able to spend much more time out of his cell. He knew a number of other prisoners and they tended to look up to him as a young man serving an indefinite sentence. They also showed some sympathy for him. The staff (initially) tended to leave prisoners alone until they got to know one another. After about eight months he was transferred to another establishment where he spent about three years. There were no real problems during his time there. He worked as a cleaner and also cut hair for the other prisoners. He did a number of educational courses and took advantage of the good sports facilities. He got on well with other prisoners, and the staff again tended to leave prisoners alone until they became familiar with one another.

Then he was moved to a semi-open prison and was unhappy about the loss of privileges he suffered as a result. There was much less opportunity to associate with other prisoners and he was locked up in his cell when he was not at work. He also found the food particularly unpleasant. He spent a short time working in the weavers shop which he found exceptionally noisy, and then he began to attend education classes full-time. Initially he shared a cell with another prisoner but eventually he was moved to a single cell. He mixed with all sorts of other prisoners regardless of the length of their sentence. Staff were very mixed – some quite approachable and helpful, others much less so. After three years at the semi-open prison he then went to an open establishment. At first he was kept in a dormitory but was then moved to a single cell which he found much better. Like many other prisoners I interviewed he had not been happy spending time in the dormitory where the general noise tended to keep him awake until the early hours. Some prisoners had no respect for the rights and wishes of others. He worked all day in the kitchens, although he spent some days out of the prison as part of his pre-release programme. Days shopping in the nearby town and going home on leave had been very helpful and had presented no problems. He had been aware that people were rushing around, but nothing more than that.

He had had regular visits from his family and they had been very supportive. At the time of the interview he had arranged where he would live when released and where he would work.

He had expected to be convicted of manslaughter and still did not really believe that he was guilty of murder, although he accepted full responsibility for his victim's death. He said that he would never forget the crime or the sentence.

Case No. 23

Twelve years in prison had been served by this young man at the time of the interview. He was only 17 years of age when sentenced and the trial judge had suggested that he should be detained for at least 15 years. It seems that the prisoner had not fully appreciated this at the time and had expected to do about ten years. After sentence was passed he returned to the prison where he had been kept on remand, but was put into an ordinary wing. He was very quickly moved to a local prison where he spent about eight weeks. He was in a single cell and was locked up most of the time, although he was allowed out for exercise and to watch television. He was then moved to a third prison for a few months where he spent part of the time in a single cell but at other times he shared with another young offender. He worked in the laundry and also did full-time educational classes. Staff and prisoners were generally quite talkative.

From there he was transferred to a young persons' prison where he stayed for about three and a third years. Again, he attended full-time education classes although he also worked assembling car seats. He mixed with a variety of other prisoners and he felt that the staff were rather mixed – some were very helpful, but others much less so. In view of the fact that he knew that a lengthy sentence lay ahead of him he felt rather unsettled. He was then moved to a Category B adult prison where he spent about two and a half years. He found this was a more relaxed prison, and he did a course in radio and television engineering and took advantage of the sports facilities. Some of the older lifers helped him to accept his sentence and to make use of it.

He was then transferred to a semi-open prison and appreciated the greater degree of freedom that was afforded to him. He described the atmosphere as being very relaxed and easy-going. He did another course in radio and television engineering and enjoyed various group discussions which lifers indulged in. In the course of these he met people from outside the prison and found this a very beneficial experience.

After two and a half years there he was moved to an open prison where he spent about 15 months. The first 12 months of the time at the open prison were quite satisfactory but then he was put into a room which he shared with another prisoner and the two of them did not get on with one another. He was moved into another double room but again the same problem arose. He got involved in a fight with his room-mate and as a result he was transferred to a closed prison. Quite understandably he was very worried about his predicament at this stage, having been sent back to a much more secure establishment, and he was quite aware that this would inevitably delay his ultimate release. He spent about three months there, and although he did some part-time education classes he spent most of his time locked up in his cell. He was then moved to another semi-open prison which he regarded as a step in the right direction. He undertook education classes in both academic and vocational subjects. There were a number of short-term prisoners there and some of them created disturbances, but he felt that they tended to respect his status as a lifer and they caused him no particular difficulties.

From there he was moved to another open prison and had been there for about seven months when I interviewed him. He worked as a storeman and had started attending evening classes, though these had been discontinued. In his spare time he played various sports and also practised his violin. Staff were not very visible though they would provide help and assistance if required. He was due to be transferred to a hostel in about 11 months time and he said he looked forward to this because it was a further step towards release. He had spent a morning out of the prison on a shopping trip in a nearby town and the one thing that he had noticed was the increase in prices. Otherwise he had encountered no problems or difficulties. He had decided that on his release he would return to his parents and, although he had not been offered a job, he hoped to take advantage of the courses he had undertaken in radio and television engineering. He said that the 13 years he was to serve in prison was obviously a very long time, particularly for a person of his relatively young years, but he fully accepted responsibility for having taken someone else's life. He felt that any sentence should take into account not only the need to safeguard the public, but also society's view of the gravity of the offence.

Case No. 24

My interview with the prisoner took place in a prison hostel and by that time he had served about 21 years in prison. After sentence was passed he was placed in the hospital wing of a top security prison where he stayed for about 12 months. Fortunately, he worked quite long hours as a hospital orderly. He then spent the next eight or nine years on one of the wings in the prison. There he worked in the book-binding shop and as the officers' orderly. He described the atmosphere in the wing as being relaxed and the staff were said to be quite approachable. On the whole, he tended to keep himself to himself although the other prisoners were reasonably friendly and he passed some of his spare time with one or two of them. After he had served about nine years of his sentence he was downgraded to Category B prisoner.

He was then moved to a non-dispersal Category B prison where he spent the next three and a half years. He worked in the kitchen from quite early in the morning until late at night time. Again, some of the staff were quite approachable and helpful, and he associated with one or two of the other prisoners. From there he moved to another non-dispersal Category B prison for a further three and a half years or so. His time was spent once more working in the kitchens and for very long hours. The staff were more interested in cooking and in people who worked in the kitchens, and he felt that they tried to be more helpful towards the prisoners.

He was then moved to a semi-open prison for nearly four years. The routine was very much as it had been at his previous two prisons although he took a break from working in the kitchens by undertaking an industrial cleaning course. He was, of course, aware of the greater physical freedom at a semi-open prison but still regarded himself very much as being in detention. From there he was transferred to an open prison for two years which he described simply as 'another prison without a wall'. Initially he worked on the market garden, but then spent about 14 months as a farm labourer. Fortunately, he was accommodated in his own room at the open prison and therefore incurred none of the difficulties associated with life in dormitories. He had appreciated the time he had spent outside of the prison, such as shopping trips, going home on leave and going out in the evenings and weekends playing in bowls teams and gardening for an elderly lady. Although staff were generally invisible, he was nonetheless very aware of being watched by them and felt that he was on trial. This caused him some tension but he simply got used to it. He was then moved to a hostel and had been there for about five months when I interviewed him. His work was quite some distance away from the hostel, in a hospital laundry, and he had found the job through an employment agency. He was due to be released some four months later. He planned to get married and thought he had a job arranged on his release.

Although he had spent a very lengthy time in prison he said that the sentence had gone quite quickly and he felt this was largely due to the fact that the jobs that he had carried out in prison always meant that he had been working for long hours. He felt that had he pleaded guilty he would have spent less time in prison. The one benefit that he felt that he had acquired during his sentence was that he was able to control his temper much better and could walk away from potential trouble.

Case No. 25

The one female lifer I spoke to had served about 12 years in prison. At the time sentence was passed she said she felt under considerable pressure and needed medication to help her cope. Initially she was placed in a single cell and left by herself. Gradually she began to mix with a small circle of other prisoners. She was soon moved to a closed prison where she spent about nine and a half years. She admitted being 'a little terror', breaking windows and cutting herself, which she described as a cry for help. She also admitted that she was very anti-authority, particularly when she learned how long she would have to wait before being released on parole. She did not feel able to relate to anybody and thought that no-one understood how she felt and the predicament that she was in. For most of the time she shared a dormitory with five other prisoners, although she did have a single room for about two years. This was regarded as a lifer's privilege. She worked as a sewing machinist and also spent about five years in the kitchen. Staff would talk to her if she wanted them to, especially if she needed their help. Generally, like most prisoners, she distrusted them.

She found it particularly hard knowing that her son was growing up outside prison without her. This was something that she had only begun to accept during the last four years or so. Most of her friends in prison tended to be serving shorter sentences, in the region of two or three years, and through them she was able to keep in touch with what was happening outside prison. At first, she did jobs simply as a means of earning money, although she usually came to enjoy them.

She was then moved to an open prison and had been there for more than two and a half years when I spoke to her. Initially she hated it. It was strange and she had no friends there. She could see freedom but somehow could not touch it. She began to settle down after three or four months, but described the visible freedom in an open prison as a 'wind-up'. At first sight it appears very different but prisoners are still very aware of the prison boundaries and regulations. There seemed to be fewer staff than in her previous prison and she did not think they had been of any help to her. She was due to be transferred to a hostel where she would have to stay for about 12 months. She did not believe that the time in hostel would be particularly useful because many of the people there did not have the ability to cope with their problems. On the other hand, she appreciated that the system should try gradually to prepare prisoners for their release. She was getting used to being responsible for herself and taking her own decisions. She felt she had a reasonable prospect of getting a job.

She thought that after about five years no further benefit could be derived from being in prison and that the time that she spent thereafter had been unproductive. To keep someone in prison solely on the ground of retribution was unjust and pointed to the inconsistency (as she saw it) in the amount of time that prisoners spend in custody. Some seem to spend longer than those who have committed what she regards as more serious offences. At the same time she acknowledged that prison had helped her. She had seen the extent to which other people had suffered and that had enabled her to appreciate her own comparative good fortune.

Case No. 33

After sentence this man was taken back to the local prison where he had been kept on remand, and he refused to be detained in the hospital wing and instead spent the first night of his sentence sharing a cell with two other prisoners. After that he was given a cell by himself. For the first three weeks he was locked up for 23 hours a day. The staff were rather remote and not sympathetic; they tended to 'cold-shoulder' him. After those three weeks he was moved to an ordinary wing and again shared a cell with two other prisoners for about four weeks. He appreciated the opportunity to talk to other people at that time. He worked in the mornings and afternoons sewing mailbags. There was very little chance to associate with other prisoners, though when he was able to do so they were very interested in his case. Yet he found it very hard to talk about his sentence, and preferred to be left to think things out for himself.

He was then transferred to a top security prison for about six months, where he was accommodated in a wing with other long-term prisoners. Within the wing there was a considerable amount of individual freedom and staff generally left prisoners alone. He got on with the other prisoners quite well. He was very aware that the atmosphere in the wing gradually became more and more tense, which inmates regarded as a consequence of an over-authoritarian attitude being taken by staff. For example, the number of strip searches noticeably increased. In addition, the prisoners felt they were not being given a proper opportunity to air their grievances. The situation gradually became more acute and eventually there were disturbances in the wing. He was then moved to another top security prison where he spent about two and a quarter years. This, he said, was a time of survival. The atmosphere was very tense. He described a number of the prisoners as being very violent towards each other, and as a result he mixed much less with other inmates. He was also rather critical of the staff in that they made no real effort to get to know prisoners. They seemed to make no attempt to differentiate between prisoners. He started an open university course on two days a week which he said gave him a goal to achieve and helped to occupy his thoughts. He said the staff viewed education rather suspiciously in that they regarded it an an undeserved privilege for prisoners and gave them a rather 'cushy' existence.

He was then transferred to a Category B prison for adult lifers and was detained there for just over four years. He regarded this as a very constructive part of his sentence. The atmosphere was much more relaxed and staff were more caring and 'human'. He felt he was able to use his time constructively and had the opportunity to make decisions and assume responsibility for himself. He continued to work towards his open university degree, though he also worked in the typewriter assembly shop. At the same time he said that three years was about the maximum amount of time that anybody should spend in one prison and so he was quite glad to get a transfer to another institution.

He was then moved to an open prison and had been there for about three months at the time I spoke to him. He found life in a dormitory with more than 20 other prisoners was 'terrible' because he had no peace and no privacy. He did not mind being accommodated with short-term offenders mainly because he, like them, had a release date, but he added that they could be very petty in their attitude. He had not found the transition from closed to open conditions particularly difficult. He had been out of the prison on a day's shopping trip and had not incurred any problems and had not felt strange or conspicuous. When we spoke he had obtained an ordinary degree through the open university and was studying for honours. He was due to be transferred to a prison hostel in about nine months time where he would spend the last six months of his sentence. He felt that he could have been released without this final stage, although he appreciated that he would have the opportunity to save some money.

He said he had always been conscious of the danger of becoming institutionalised and was aware of the need that prisoners must learn to cope for themselves. He also felt that visits and letters had been important in providing moral support, in giving him a sense of being cared for by his family and friends, and enabling him to maintain contact with the outside world. When asked to talk about the sentence in general, he said that he had expected and possibly wanted to be condemned and to be punished and rejected by other people because of what he had done. This he said would provide a process of purging his guilt. Indeed he felt that this was very necessary in order for him to be fully rehabilitated. Not surprisingly, he highlighted the problem of uncertainty which follows an indeterminate sentence. This was particularly acute at the start of the sentence and he had found it very difficult to know how he could help himself. It seemed to him that the staff in the prisons did not fully appreciate the plans that were being made for prisoners by those in the Home Office headquarters. He said that he had always felt a total lack of control over his own fate.

Case No. 34

This man was in his mid 30s when he was sentenced, and he spent the first two days of his sentence in a single cell in the hospital wing lying on his bed. He had one brief visit from an assistant governor. After those two days he was moved to another wing of the prison, which was a top security establishment, and he spent about ten weeks there. He was locked up for all but one hour of the day and was left alone. He was then moved to another wing which accommodated long-term offenders and spent about two and a half years there. He was put in a single cell and at first he did not mix with the other lifers because he could not relate to them. He worked as a cleaner which he described as very undemanding. He also did a six month cabinet-making course although he did not manage to complete it because of a work-to-rule by the staff. Staff did not like the idea that educational facilities were provided for prisoners. He was critical of the fact that they tended to have very little detailed knowledge about prisoners and many of them adopted a petty-minded and sarcastic attitude towards inmates which served only to confirm the 'them and us' syndrome. For about 18 months he was given no work to do and spent much of his time making matchstick models. There were disturbances in the prison as a result of which the regime and atmosphere became much more strict and tense.

He was then transferred to a lifer-only Category B prison and spent about two and a half years there. He regarded this as a good move for him because it suggested that he was being viewed favourably as a candidate for an early release. It was hard for him to accept the use of first name terms between staff and inmates. He said that during this time he began to realise that he had to try to create the 'right image'. His case was reviewed whilst he was in this prison, having served only about five years of his sentence, and he regarded this as almost too good to be true. He was then moved to an open prison where he spent about seven months. Again, he regarded this as a good move in that it indicated that he was on the way towards a speedy release. On the other hand, he was very critical of being accommodated in a dormitory where a lot of short-term offenders tended to be very disruptive He was particularly critical of prisoners who deliberately tried to 'wind-up' those serving long sentences. He felt staff were antagonistic towards lifers because lifers showed the short-term prisoners that they could and should stand up for their rights even though they were in prison. But he was suspected of being involved in physical violence towards another prisoner and consequently he was transferred to a closed institution.

He strongly denied any involvement in the assault on another prisoner at the open prison, but he spent the next four months in a closed establishment and he was then moved to a Category B prison where he had been detained earlier in his sentence. Not surprisingly, he felt much antipathy for the penal system and there was a mutual feeling of distrust between himself and the staff. After two years he was then transferred to another open prison and had been there for about five months when I spoke to him. He was due to spend a further four months there before being transferred to a hostel.

He felt that personally he did not need to be subjected to a gradual process of readjustment and resettlement, though he admitted that he felt rather frightened about release. This, he said, was derived from what he knew of the world outside and he wondered whether 'a decent person' could survive.

Visits and letters had been important to him at the start of his sentence, in that they helped him to get used to being in prison and having to stay there for a lengthy period, but they had become much less useful in the later stages of his sentence. He said that having to wait for visits from friends and relatives was very stressful. The biggest problem he had incurred during his sentence was that of finding ways of passing the time.

He felt he ought to have been acquitted on the ground that he had only killed in self-defence. Before he was moved back from open to closed conditions he had expected to do about eight and a half years. (He was likely to serve just over ten years in prison). He was critical of the lack of detailed knowledge which prison staff had about inmates and he felt that this was something that needed to be remedied if a genuine and serious attempt was to be made by the prison system to successfully rehabilitate and resettle lifers.

Case No. 36

This prisoner was only aged 17 at the time he was sentenced. He spent the first weekend of his sentence in a hospital wing where he said there was nothing to do but read. He was allowed one hour's exercise and was able to chat and play chess with about a dozen other prisoners. In general, staff tended to leave prisoners alone though occasionally they would talk. He then spent a week in an ordinary wing, where he was accommodated in a single cell and was allowed to work sewing mailbags. The sentence had not come as a great shock to him, for he had expected to be detained indefinitely and consciously decided to shut himself off from the outside world.

He was quickly transferred to a local prison where he spent the next 12 months. He described life there as being very noisy and spent much of his time reading and studying. He shared a cell with another young prisoner, and although he got on quite well with his room-mate he said that many young prisoners tended to be rather head-strong and thoughtless in their behaviour. He was then moved to a young persons' prison for three years where he appreciated the fact that he had his own room. He continued to study and also worked in one of the workshops constructing wall ties. He found the staff very helpful, particularly in so far as they assisted him to talk about and resolve his problems.

He was then moved to a Category B adult prison for about three years. Initially, he was very suspicious of the use of first-name terms and he was struck by the amount of physical freedom and openness that existed within the prison. Both staff and inmates were generally very friendly. Most of the day was spent in one of the workshops, assembling circuit boards, or in the electronics design shop, and he also spent about two months as a cleaner. He enjoyed the more relaxed and informal atmosphere at the prison. From there he was transferred to a semi-open prison where he was kept for about 21 months. He felt the atmosphere there was very tense because of the existence of rival groups of prisoners. He was then moved to an open prison but only spent ten days there. He had an argument with some other inmates and it was suggested that he should be transferred to another open institution where he had been for about two months when I spoke to him. He found this second open prison much more relaxed. The fact that prisoners were made to think for themselves was very good and he thought that the emphasis was rightly placed on the need for prisoners to make decisions for themselves and to assume responsibility for their own behaviour. Although there was no fence around the prison, there was still a barrier in his mind and being in a open prison required great powers of self-control. Despite being a little apprehensive about meeting new people, he was looking forward to being released. He was due to spend six months at the open prison and then move to a hostel for the final six months of his sentence.

He regarded letters and visits as very important in that they had helped to keep him going during his sentence and to maintain contact with the world outside. He also appreciated the fact that by visiting him and writing to him people had shown that they still cared for him as an individual.

At the start of his sentence he had been told he would serve about eight years in prison, although he thought it would be perhaps nearer ten years. (He was due to serve just over ten years). He said there was a danger in keeping people in prison for too long. If this happened, imprisonment ceased to be a punishment for the offender because he could just shut himself off from everything and could subsume himself in the prison environment.

Case No. 39

This was a case of a young man who was only 15-years-old when sentenced. From the court he was taken back to the remand centre where he had been detained whilst awaiting trial and he remained there for the first four and a half months of his sentence. The indeterminate sentence was not a shock to him: he had expected it to be passed and thought that he would be kept in prison for about eight years. He made a deliberate decision not to think about the sentence but to try to take things day by day. Initially, he was put into a hospital ward where most of the other detainees had been charged with murder. He spent most of the time either cleaning the ward or playing cards, and he said most of the staff left prisoners alone although one or two of them would try to engage them in conversation. He also read, watched television and did matchstick modelling. He spent his final month at the remand centre on an ordinary wing where he shared a cell with one other prisoner. He spent two or three hours a day in educational classes and was allowed about two hours an evening in association.

He was then transferred to a youth treatment centre where he spent about three and a half years. He described the facilities there as being very good and commented on the fact that the inmates wore their own civilian clothes rather than uniform. The atmosphere and the regime were very informal: staff referred to inmates by first names. There was a total of only about 30 inmates, ten in each of three houses. Of those 30 three were serving indeterminate sentences. He said that it was more like a home than a prison, and he was put in a single room. Schooling was compulsory and he attended classes for three hours a day, five days a week. He also attended group meetings which gradually became more frequent, although he said he found the discussions useless. He did not appear to have been very impressed by staff; they were pre-occupied with getting the residents to admit to non-existent problems. The staff were very keen to talk to residents, particularly on a one-to-one basis, though he felt they over-did this. He mixed with all sorts of residents, male and female, regardless of what they had done. Whilst at this youth treatment centre he changed a lot, by which he meant that he learned to stand up for himself verbally and to speak his thoughts. He said he also learned to express his feelings.

He was then transferred to a youth custody centre and he had been there for about two and three-quarter years at the time I spoke to him. During the first two weeks there he was given an induction course to explain the nature of prison life, and he was accommodated in his own cell. He spent about five months working in the sewing-machine repair shop and about a month in the stores, and had then spent about 18 or 19 months working in the kitchen. He added that he had decided to make catering and management his career and had taken classes to help him achieve this. After his two weeks induction he was moved to another wing, where he said the staff were generally very good in that they treated inmates as people and not as offenders. Although he was the only lifer at the YCC, he had never been 'wound up' by the other prisoners. When I spoke to him he was due to be released directly from the YCC in three days time.

He said that visits were helpful provided they did not take place too frequently. He thought that about one every three months was right. His main reason for this was that to make them frequent would make unfair demands on his visitors. On the other hand, he said he had written or received thousands of letters whilst in prison and regarded these as really important for they had helped him stay in touch with life outside prison. For the final eight months of his sentence a situation had been created so that his lifestyle closely mirrored that which he would have experienced had he been accommodated in a prison hostel. This meant that he was allowed to go out of the prison in order to pursue community work during the daytime, which mainly involved gardening, painting and decorating. He had been on home leave on two occasions – experiences which he felt were very beneficial in developing his relationship with his family and getting used to being treated as a civilian.

Case No. 40

This man had served more than 21 years in prison when I spoke to him. After sentence had been passed he was taken back to a Category B prison where he had been kept on remand and he spent the first night in a single cell in a hospital wing. The following day he was moved to the main wing of the prison where he remained for about six months or so. He spent most of the mornings and afternoons working in the tailors shop and was allowed to associate with other prisoners during the evenings. He said he mixed with all sorts of inmates, though none were serving life sentences. He described the staff as 'a mixed bag', but none of them made any real attempt to get to know the prisoners. He had expected a life sentence to be passed and thought that he would do about nine years or so. From the outset he had taken the view that his behaviour in prison could not really affect or influence the length of his detention.

He was then moved to another Category B prison where he was detained for about nine years. The routine there was very much the same as it had been at the first prison. He worked in the blacksmiths shop and played football at the weekends. The longer-term prisoners were gradually given more privileges as time passed and after about 18 months the amount of time they were allowed to associate also increased. Life seemed to become reasonably informal and relaxed. People referred to one another by their first names.

He was then moved to a dispersal prison where he stayed for about two and three-quarter years. As this was a maximum security establishment, this did not appear to him to be a good move for him. He had, however, been assured that he was not regarded as a security risk and the move was simply one of convenience. After about one and three-quarter years at the dispersal prison he was given a release date, so his situation looked quite optimistic. He worked in the engineering shop operating presses and he said the atmosphere was generally quite relaxed. Again people were on first-name terms with one another. He was allowed to wear his own clothes and prison staff tended to leave the inmates alone. He was then moved to a prison hostel with a view to spending his last six months there.

When he had served just under 12 years, he was released on life licence, but he did not keep his appointments with his supervision officer in the probation service and so his licence was revoked and he was recalled to a Category B prison. He had been out on licence for about 13 and a half months. After about four months he was re-released on licence, but again his licence was revoked and he was recalled to a Category B prison after he failed to keep in regular contact with his probation officer. This time he had been out on licence for ten months. He stayed in prison for about nine months before being released for a third time.

Four months later his licence was revoked yet again because he ignored the conditions stated in the licence. He was released for a fourth time after about 16 months but was then found to be involved in various fraud offences for which he was later convicted, having been on life licence this time for about three years, his licence was revoked for a fourth time. After spending another two and three-quarter years in prison he had been moved to the hostel and had been there for about a month when I interviewed him. He was due to be released in a further five months time.

He was very critical of what he regarded as the petty-minded attitude that the authorities adopted towards him. He felt that they were being unrealistic in the demands that they were making of him and the sort of conditions that they stipulated in respect of him.

Case No. 41

At the time of the interview this man had been in prison for about 17 and a half years. From the court he was taken back to the local prison where he had been on remand and he was put into a single cell on a special wing for remand prisoners and stayed for the first two months of his sentence. For a few hours in the morning and in the afternoon he sewed mailbags, but otherwise spent most of the time in his cell. There was little contact with other prisoners and the staff were very matter-of-fact – they made no attempt to talk to or get to know the prisoners. He was then transferred to a Category B prison for about 18 months. As a Category A prisoner he was put into a single cell and was not allowed to associate for the first four months there with other prisoners. Only when he came off the Category A list was he allowed to associate. His work consisted of sewing patches. He said the staff interviewed him on various occasions but generally left him alone. In the early stages he was still very shocked at having been given a life sentence and he did not believe that he deserved to be convicted of murder. His solicitors told him that he would probably serve about ten years in prison, but he tried not to think about the long-term future.

He was then transferred to a top security prison where he spent about ten years. This, he said, was better than his previous establishment. All the prisoners there were serving long sentences (by which he meant four years or more), and they got to know each other quite well, though he added that he made acquaintances there rather than friends. The food was better and the prison staff were quite informal and relaxed in the way they spoke to prisoners. He worked in the sewing-machine shop and in the heavy fabric shop and had a much greater degree of freedom to walk around the prison than previously. He also spent some time working in the engineers shop and as a cleaner. From there he spent the next two and a half years in a Category B prison where the regime was more formal, though the accommodation was better furnished. Again he worked in a sewing-machine shop.

The following three years or so were spent in a semi-open prison and he immediately noticed that the atmosphere was much less formal and more relaxed. Prisoners were accommodated in units rather than cells and it was nice to be able to get out into the fresh air. There was greater physical freedom to move about the prison, and whilst there he was given a provisional release date. He was told that he would serve the last six months of his sentence on the PRES, but unfortunately there were no vacancies at the specified hostel.

As a result of the difficulties in finding a vacancy his release date was effectively delayed for about six months. He eventually moved to the hostel and had been there for about eight months when I spoke to him. He had got a job as a labourer and said that he very much enjoyed the increased freedom he was given. Nonetheless, he felt that he could have been released directly from the open prison and did not feel that he would have incurred any great problems in readjustment.

He said that because of geographical problems it had been difficult for his family to visit him whilst he had been in prison. He had kept in touch with them through writing letters although after a time he felt there was little that he could usefully say. By the time he is released he will have served about 18 years. He felt no bitterness, and there was little point in arguing that he ought to have served less time in prison. He had stopped thinking about the world outside after about six months of his sentence and not surprisingly he had got very accustomed to the prison environment.

Case No. 42

This man was in his mid-50s at the time he received his life sentence. He was taken back to the prison where he had been kept on remand and spent the first day in a hospital ward where he was left alone. Then he was moved to one of the ordinary wings in the prison and shared a cell with another prisoner. During some week-days he spent the mornings and afternoons plaiting rope. The staff left him alone but he was able to talk to other prisoners whilst he was working. Basically though, he described himself as 'a bit of a loner'. Although he had expected to be given a life sentence he still felt very depressed and had no idea how long he would serve in prison. After about six months he was transferred to a top security prison where he stayed for about two and a half years. There he said he had a greater degree of freedom to move about the prison and was given more recreational facilities. He attended leather and woodwork classes, largely in order to give him something to do, and he spent most of his working time as a cleaner in the workshops. He was accommodated in a single cell and he ate his meals there. The staff and other prisoners were quite friendly, and he tended to mix with other lifers whom he felt were likely to be in the prison for longer than other inmates.

From there he was moved directly to a semi-open prison for about three and a half years. Indeed, after he had spent a total of six and a half years in prison he was given a provisional release date which meant that he would have been released on life licence after about eight years detention. He described life in the semi-open prison as a little better than in the top security establishment and by this he seemed to have meant that it was easier for his family to visit him. As might be expected, he commented on the greater physical freedom to walk around a semi-open prison but said that in one sense this was tempered by the fact that staff seemed to adopt a stricter attitude towards prisoners. Whilst there he worked with civilians carrying out maintenance to the prison.

He was then moved to a prison hostel but after he had been there for about three months a complaint was made about him to his probation officer, as a result of which he was brought back to a closed prison and was kept there for about six months.

At the end of that time he was then transferred to another semi-open prison for about 18 months and he described his experience there as 'unbelievable'. He talked of the young offenders there who were very disruptive and badly behaved, many of whom he thought were drug addicts. Nonetheless, he said the staff were very good and he appreciated their caring and informal attitude towards him. He was then moved again to a hostel and had been there for about three weeks when I spoke to him. He was due to be released about six months later, by which time he would have served just over ten years. He did not feel that he needed a gradual process of readjustment by being moved to a semi-open prison and the hostel. At his age he felt that he could have been released directly from a closed institution. In view of the geographical location of his family it had been very difficult for him to receive visits from them and he felt that inadequate arrangements had been made by the authorities in this respect.

He fully appreciated that he had done something very wrong and that he needed to be punished as a result. However, he stressed that he regarded the length of time which prisoners had to wait for the results of their parole applications as scandalous. He thought that five or six years in prison would have been adequate to meet the requirements of retribution and deterrence. He was also critical of the fact that the authorities seemed to be unaware of the financial difficulties of some prisoners and this was something in need of urgent attention.

Case No. 43

I spoke to this man just two or three days before he was due to be released from a prison hostel. After sentence had been imposed he was taken back to the remand centre where he had been awaiting trial and he was placed in the hospital wing. He had expected to be given a life sentence, but still felt very depressed for about the first 12 to 18 months. He shared a dormitory in the hospital wing with about 22 other prisoners. Fortunately, there were a number of people there with whom he was on friendly terms and that helped him pass the first two weeks of his sentence. He was then moved on to a young prisoners' wing where he shared a cell with another prisoner. Unfortunately, there was no work for him to do and apart from an occasional hour's exercise or work in the gym he spent most of the time locked up in his cell.

After about two weeks on that wing he was transferred to another prison for about 18 months and again shared a cell on a wing with other young offenders. He was able to mix with other young lifers and they worked in the morning and afternoon in the prison laundry. He described the staff on his landing as being quite friendly and he made some friends amongst the other prisoners. At that stage he thought he would serve about seven to eight years, although that seemed to be a very long time. From there he was moved to a top security prison for about two years, where he was able to enjoy more association with other prisoners. He undertook an engineering course during the day-time and also spent about eight months attending various educational classes. He worked for about 12 months in the engineering machine shop operating a capstan lathe. He described the staff as being 'OK'. He said they regarded him as being rather cheeky. He thought there were a lot of 'bad' offenders there. For most of the time he was kept in a single cell.

He was then moved to a dispersal prison for about two years and described his time there as very good. There were lots of facilities, both vocational and recreational, and the atmosphere was very relaxed. Staff referred to prisoners by their first names which he found rather strange at first but soon got used to it and did not regard it suspiciously. He felt safer there than at his previous prison. He was unable to work for some months as the result of an accident playing football but spent about 12 months as a cleaner and about nine months in a weaving shop.

He was then transferred to a semi-open prison for about three years where he said he felt lost for the first couple of weeks. The regime was strange to him and he knew very few people there. He spent about four months on a painting and decorating course which he described as 'a failure' because he felt that he had been given inadequate instruction by the tutors. He worked as a cleaner for about 18 months and in the woodwork shop, making tables and chairs for about 12 months. He said the staff left prisoners alone. Most of the other inmates were serving short sentences which he did not find at all problematic. In fact he said he had got used to being with short-term prisoners because each year he spent about four weeks at a prison where there were many such inmates whilst he was having what are called accumulated visits.

He was then transferred to an open prison for about two years and he knew that this was the last stage before spending time in a prison hostel. He said it used to be the case that prisoners would only spend about six or eight months in an open prison before being released but the procedure changed and much longer periods were spent in open conditions. The increased freedom that he was given was very welcome and he had no problems in coping with it. He worked for the first four weeks or so on the gardens and then spent 12 months working in the laundry. Life in the dormitories was 'horrible', in that there was no space and no privacy, and he was very glad to be given his own room after about four months. He described staff as being quite satisfactory and added that they kept a low profile. He had been allowed out of the prison on various occasions and it felt very good to get away from the institution. He noticed that life seemed to move at a very quick pace compared to what he remembered and he was very aware of the increased prices, but he felt no real problems in being outside the prison.

He was then moved to a hostel and had been there for about six months. Naturally, he appreciated the greater freedom of the hostel and described his time there as being generally good, although he was very conscious of having to be back at the hostel at 10.30 each night. He regarded his time there as being profitable, both to save money and to further adapt himself gradually to the idea of being released. Not surprisingly, he said he really wanted to forget about the past and preferred not to spend a great deal of time explaining what happened to him, though he accepted that this would be necessary to some extent and that he would be embarrassed by it.

It had been difficult for his family to visit him regularly, hence he had been granted accumulated visits each year, though he had appreciated regular correspondence with them. Throughout his time in prison he had been treated satisfactorily but he thought he ought to have served about eight years. He felt that having spent that amount of time in prison he had sufficiently matured as an individual and had served long enough in view of the nature of his offence. (He was due to serve about 11 and a half years). He said he was very sensitive at being known as 'a murderer' and found this very depressing. He regarded his crime as being a very stupid and foolish episode which was largely a result of his immaturity. Although he appreciated the need to release prisoners, who had served lengthy periods of detention, very gradually and slowly, he had been aware of the pressure that is created whilst in an open prison and in a hostel, as a result of being so near and yet so far from freedom. He said he had never felt that his behaviour could decrease the amount of time he would spend in detention, but was always aware that if he misbehaved, he could increase his length of imprisonment.

Case No. 44

This man had served about 14 and a half years when I spoke to him. After sentence was passed, he was taken back to a top security prison and was placed in a single cell on an ordinary wing. (He was not put in a hospital wing). Having been given a life sentence, he was automatically classified as a Category A prisoner but this was for the first six weeks only. He was left alone for the first 24 hours or so but thereafter was put to work in a textile shop making wigwams. He described this as being particularly boring though he did it for about 12 to 18 months. The staff left him alone and he did not seek their company. He mixed with a few other prisoners who tended to be serving life sentences because he felt that they could relate to one another. He described his reaction to the life sentence by saying that 'something just dies in you', 'the world stops'. He expected to serve about 12 years, which had been intimated to him by his solicitor.

He was then moved to a Category B prison for about six years, though he said he never tired of it. He was put in a single cell which became his home, and he felt that in a sense some degree of institutionalisation was inevitable. He was on a wing with other long-term prisoners and the staff were easy-going. During that time he said he was a bit of a recluse. His father died and he became rather anti-authority. For a number of years he pursued a City and Guilds Letter-Press Printing Course by evening classes. He also worked in the tailors shop, the sewing machine shop, and as a storeman. He then spent two years in another Category B prison, but said that he had not appreciated the group therapy sessions and the importance that was placed on what he described as 'self-exposure'. He did not think that group work fundamentally changed peoples' characters or personalities but he criticised the constant observation that prisoners were subjected to, for the degree of mental strain that it caused. Nonetheless, he said that as a result of his time at this prison he felt that he was more tolerant and more willing and able to listen to other people and to take steps to prevent himself from losing his temper.

He was then transferred to a Category B prison which catered only for lifers and spent 18 months to two years there. This he described as the best prison he had been in, in that life was reasonably quiet and relaxed. He was treated with a certain amount of trust and the staff regarded prisoners as human beings rather than just numbers. From there he was moved directly to an open prison for about three years. He criticised the physical conditions of the open prison, although at the same time he appreciated the very good educational facilities that were offered there. Like most prisoners he found having to share a dormitory rather difficult, and preferred the privacy of his own room. He said that lifers always have their own hobbies and tended to be regarded as loners. He found the absence of any prison walls there a rather frightening experience, although he felt that he suffered at least partially from agoraphobia. He was fully aware of the need for him to undergo a very gradual process of readjustment to ultimate freedom. He described the staff at the open prison as being quite good in that they left prisoners alone and regarded them with some respect.

From there he was moved to the hostel and had been there for about five months when I talked to him. He saw this as a very necessary stage in order for prisoners to be able to stand totally on their own feet and organise their own lives. He said the pace of life was much quicker than it had been before he was sentenced and he needed the opportunity to save some money. Although it had been very difficult for his family to visit him, he felt that visits were an important means of keeping in contact with the outside world. They also helped prisoners to develop new ideas and adopt a fresh outlook which was necessary to counteract the inevitable institutionalisation of imprisonment.

Although he had been in prison for quite a long time, he said he had been able to think about the future right from the early stages of his sentence. At the same time, during the sentence he had become disheartened and depressed, particularly when refused his parole applications and on those occasions he had deliberately tried to stop thinking about the future.

He had reservations about the way in which the review process was carried out by the prison authorities. In particular, he felt that those who were making reports on him and other inmates did not spend sufficient time getting to know them so as to be able to make meaningful, constructive comments. He also felt that it was necessary for the essence of the reports to be disclosed to prisoners so that they might be reassured and encouraged, and the relationship with staff could be improved. He was also critical of the fact that, as he saw it, prisoners are forced to play a game to present what is perceived to be the right image. He said that if the authorities wanted prisoners to be honest with them, then they must be equally honest with inmates. As he put it, 'Never try to con a con'.

He accepted the murder conviction and thought that the sentence he had received was about right, although he added that the authorities should never over-punish a person. The great majority of prisoners will be released and he felt that there was a danger that if they were detained for too long the chances of a successful release would be adversely prejudiced. Although he appreciated the time spent in the hostel, he said that the PRES was still essentially parental and supportive and he felt that there ought to be yet another stage between the hostel and release which would give prisoners a greater degree of independence but fall short of complete freedom. He felt that one of the important aspects for him was to learn how to be a human being again. Prison, he said, makes you a number. It dehumanises you and so the system must try to rehumanise inmates before they are finally given their freedom. He was also very critical of the pettiness that exists within prisons, especially in the way in which the prison regulations are enforced by staff. In addition, he emphasised the need not to punish prisoners' families, by, for example, making it difficult or impossible for them to visit inmates.

Case No. 45

My interview with this prisoner was rather unusual in that it took place whilst he was still in a Category B prison. In view of his epilepsy and the problems that resulted from this, it was felt appropriate that he should not have to spend time in a semi-open or open prison but should be transferred directly to a prison hostel from where he would ultimately be released. When we spoke he had served about ten and a half years of his sentence. He had been only 15 years old at the time of the crime and 16 when he was ordered to be detained during Her Majesty's pleasure. From the court he was taken back to the remand centre and was put in an ordinary wing and spent the first two months in a single cell locked up for most of the time. He had little or no contact with anyone else. His epilepsy was to be a constant inhibiting factor in that he was not able to work in the ordinary workshops.

He was then moved to a young persons' prison for about four years. Initially, he shared a cell with another inmate but was then given a single cell, although later he again had to share with someone else. He had been prepared for a heavy sentence but nonetheless felt very distressed and depressed. In those early months he had no real idea how long he would serve. A probation officer had indicated that about five years would be appropriate but he did not really put any great stress on this. Although he spent some time cleaning, he passed much of his time on full-time education classes. He said the staff were very mixed. Some were quite pleasant, some were rather aloof, and others deliberately tried to make life difficult for prisoners. As far as other inmates were concerned, he tended to mix mainly with those serving long sentences.

He was then transferred to a Category B prison for adults and had been there for about six years and throughout that time he was accommodated in a single cell. He had attended some education classes but had ceased to do so simply because he lost interest. Apart from that, he had worked as a cleaner and in the print shop, wrapping parcels, but had to be taken off that through lack of supervision. He felt he always had to try to make some constructive use of his sentence though during the times when he was depressed this was very difficult. Again, staff at his prison were very mixed. Many were quite friendly, but one or two could be rather difficult. He was on a wing with long-term offenders with whom he naturally felt he had quite a lot in common. He had regular visits from his family and friends which he regarded as quite important. He did not treat them as a 'wind-up' but found it was very reassuring to keep in touch with what was happening in the world outside and to feel wanted and cared for by other people. He felt that letters were also important for the same reasons.

He had received his release date only two or three months before I spoke to him. He had been on trips out of the prison on about three occasions and felt that this was a very important part of his release programme. Although he appreciated that he had got to serve the last nine months of his sentence in a prison hostel, he felt he would have been able to establish himself successfully if released directly from the closed prison because of the support he was getting from his family and friends.

He thought he ought to have been convicted of manslaughter rather than murder, and yet he felt that his sentence of what was to be just over 12 years in detention was not unduly harsh. He did add, though, that he felt that the life licence served no useful purpose. He regarded the penal system as very inconsistent in the length of sentences that it imposed on criminals bearing in mind the nature of their offences. At the same time, prison had helped him mature more quickly than he would otherwise have done and he felt that he had a much better understanding of the problems of other people.

Case No. 46

When we spoke, this prisoner had served about eight years in prison and was due to be released about a fortnight later. After sentence was passed he was taken back to the local prison where he was kept on remand and he was placed in the hospital wing, where he stayed for about two weeks. He described the other people in the wing as being very strange, 'real loonies'. Not surprisingly, he spent most of his time by himself and just a few hours cleaning the ward. The staff left him alone and made no attempt to talk to him or discuss any of his problems. Then he was moved to a single cell on an ordinary wing for about a month and spent the final two weeks before he was transferred sharing with short-term prisoners. He worked in the mornings and afternoons in the texile shop, making nurses' and cowboy outfits, and was allowed one hour's exercise at lunch time. When not at work he was locked up in his cell. Again, the staff left him alone.

He had expected a life sentence and his barrister had advised him that he would only serve about five years, but he did not rely on this. He knew that the average time served by lifers was about ten years. He did add though, that about six months into his sentence he became aware of great variations in the amount of time being served and from then on became very unsure as to how long he would be detained. He said his initial reaction to the sentence was that he should break off ties with the outside world and would have to readjust to his new world in prison. In this respect he regarded letters and visits as a 'wind up', and he deliberately shut out any thoughts of what was happening outside prison. However, he in fact did not sever all ties with the world outside, and said that maintaining contact with what was happening beyond the prison gave him a reason to carry on.

He was soon moved to a maximum security prison where he spent about six months and was accommodated on a wing for long-term prisoners. He appreciated the relative freedom that was given to him on the wing and the association that he enjoyed with other prisoners. He made one particular friend there. He worked in the sewing machine shop, sewing overalls, and then as a cleaner. He became part of a group of four inmates who cooked their own food and spent a lot of time with each other, but unfortunately there was a disturbance in the prison and he, along with many others, was transferred to another establishment. His next main move was to a Category B prison where he stayed for about five months. He seemed to have been quite happy but he knew that he would only spend a short time there.

He was then moved to a Category B prison which catered only for lifers and he was impressed with the facilities available. There was a range of education classes for him to attend and hobbies to pursue, and he felt he could take advantage of these because he knew he would be there for a sufficiently long time. In the event he stayed there for three and three-quarter years. He was on first-name terms with members of staff and the atmosphere was very relaxed and informal. It appears that whilst he was there, a mistake was made in the process of reviewing his case, and this naturally made him extremely frustrated. He had various jobs there, apart from attending education classes; he worked in a typewriter shop as a cleaner, and as the visits orderly.

He was then moved to a semi-open prison for two years, where he did nothing really to better himself. There were very few educational facilities, though he did an electrical wiring course and he started a radio and television course which was interrupted by a transfer to another prison. He also worked on the gardens and as a storeman. It was at the semi-open prison that he was informed of his provisional release date. He described his reaction to this as one of shaking and spinning. He was then transferred to an open prison where he stayed for just over six months. There he took part in the job familiarisation scheme and worked in a home for mentally-handicapped people, which he thoroughly enjoyed. He particularly appreciated the opportunity to help people who were much less fortunate than himself, to resolve their problems and difficulties. He also liked the fact that he was treated as one of the staff at the home and not just as a lifer. Throughout the time at the open prison he was accommodated in a dormitory and he deplored the lack of privacy there. After he was moved to a prison hostel he initially found it quite hard to obtain employment, although eventually managed to do so. He felt that his period of living in a hostel was unnecessary having been in an open prison, because he was still very aware of being subjected to the prison regime.

He accepted that he had committed a serious offence and thereby done something very wrong, though he thought that possibly he ought to have been convicted of manslaughter rather than murder. Nonetheless, he said he had deserved what he had got and accepted the sentence as about right. The label 'murderer' caused him embarrassment and pain because he felt it was not an accurate description of him. He did not like the idea that other people might be afraid of him or treat him as someone special because of being perceived as 'a murderer'. Overall, he felt that his prison experience had made him a more thoughtful, mature individual, and that he could cope well with difficult situations. He also thought that his time in prison had given him the opportunity to understand himself with a greater degree of insight and that he had developed more self-confidence.

Case No. 49

This lifer said he wanted to believe the governor of the prison where he had been detained on remand who indicated that he would serve about five years, for lifers (understandably) grasp at straws. Indeed, he said that one of the reasons why he had pleaded guilty was that he hoped for a shorter period of detention. At the time it was imposed, the life sentence just 'did not register' with him. He was taken to a top security prison where he spent the first 13 months of his sentence. For a week or two he was in a single room in the hospital wing, under observation, and was then moved to a cell in one of the ordinary wings. Some of the staff spoke to him, but he had little contact either with them or with other prisoners. It was about six months before he really began to realise what his sentence meant. He worked in the canteen, which he regarded as a very good job. Association was permitted in the evenings. He tried not to think much about the future and to take life day by day and made an effort to keep his mind occupied.

At the end of the 13 months he was moved to a Category B prison where he worked as a chef in the officers' mess. This was a 'prime job' because it gave him a considerable amount of freedom in the prison and the occasional opportunity to go outside the institution. He received his first experience of life on a long-term wing and commented on the violence and theft that existed on it. But he only spent nine months at that prison and then moved to another Category B prison, but which catered only for life-sentence prisoners and he spent five and a half years there. Regrettably, he regarded this time as one which was wasted. He described the regime at the prison as one of 'total appeasement'. Staff, he said, simply gave prisoners what they wanted in order to keep them quiet. There was much freedom within the prison and ample opportunity for educational and recreational pursuits. He was quite happy to be on first-name terms with staff and inmates and he undertook two correspondence courses there. He spent three and a half years working in the electronics workshop and about 15 months in the canteen.

He was then transferred to a semi-open prison where he stayed for nearly two years. He described this as a 'terrible prison' because there was a lot of noise and petty thieving, and little opportunity for privacy. It was whilst there that he became very fed up with his sentence and realised that he had no real influence over the amount of time that he would spend in detention. He felt that the number of years to be spent in prison was determined at the very start of the sentence and that this could only be exacerbated by bad behaviour.

He then spent three and a half years in an open prison where, as before, he tended to keep himself to himself. The staff were generally very 'invisible' and life there was 'like being in a mine field', by which he meant that there was a great deal of illegal alcohol and other drugs in the prison. He felt that the long-term prisoners were given very little support by the authorities and were left to fend for themselves. He thought it was wrong that they should have to be integrated with short-term offenders who have relatively little to lose if they breached prison discipline. For the first six months there he was accommodated in a dormitory where there was a total lack of privacy, but then he was given his own room. He took a correspondence course in management and also studied for two years at a nearby technical college. He was critical of the amount of time that prisoners had to wait to get answers to their parole applications and he had no faith in the system. He said the pressure was such that after a while he simply did not care what happened to him and became very outspoken. He felt that some prisoners were dealt with much more harshly than others.

He was then moved to a prison hostel for the last nine months of his detention, and had been there for about four months when I spoke to him. He clearly disliked being at the hostel. Firstly, it resembled his time at the open prison in terms of the pettiness of the rules and regulations, and secondly, he felt it was unnecessary. He criticised the system for providing lifers with no training or assistance in coping with the prejudice which potential employers and other members of the public would inevitably show towards them.

He too felt that visits and letters were very important to maintain the family unit and to keep in touch with those people who meant a lot to him. He also said that visits were a good means of releasing tension. He accepted that he was rightly convicted of murder but thought that he ought to have served less time in detention, though it was impossible to put a precise figure on how long he should have been deprived of his liberty. He felt that the prison system needed to show a much greater sense of urgency and of caring about what happens to prisoners when they are released.

Case No. 52

This young man was only 17-years-old when ordered to be detained during Her Majesty's pleasure. He said he did not really understand the sentence. He knew that he was going to prison but had no idea for how long this was to last. Indeed, it took about four or five years before he had any indication as to when he might be released. He had expected to be acquitted and not surprisingly he was shocked and dazed when sentence was passed upon him. From the court he was taken back to the local prison, where he had been kept on remand and spent the first two days in the hospital wing. He was then moved to an ordinary wing for about five months. He was put into a single cell and spent the mornings and afternoons making cardboard boxes. When not at work he was locked up in his cell. Staff tried to talk to prisoners but because the environment was generally quite disciplined prisoners tended to try to remain aloof.

He was then transferred to another local prison for about four months, which he described as a particularly evil prison. It was miserable and dirty and the staff were very strict and some of them tried bullying tactics. He spent the mornings and afternoons screwing nuts into strips of plastic, and he made friends with just a couple of inmates. He never looked towards the future; he simply tried to take each day as it came. He said at that stage he was still very numbed by the sentence. He described himself as 'just a robot'. Staff suggested to him how long they thought he would do, but he never took this seriously.

He was then moved to a young persons' prison for about three and a quarter years. There he did various educational and vocational classes. He thought this was worthwhile because he expected to be there for some time. He worked in the braille unit and put a lot of his energies into this. He also worked as a plumber and in the metalwork shop. There was a good deal of freedom within the confines of the prison and prisoners were free to associate with each other. He got on well with other young prisoners and tended to mix with those who had similar sporting interests to himself. The staff were described as disciplined, but quite reasonable. Most of them addressed prisoners very formally, though one or two used first-name terms.

From there he was moved to a Category B adult prison where he stayed for just under four years. This he described as better than his previous prison, by which he seemed to mean that less discipline was imposed by staff. (Presumably this was because prisoners were adults and not young offenders). Again, there was plenty of freedom within the prison. He did various education and vocational classes though he criticised the lack of money that is given to prisoners who undertake such courses. Most of the prisoners he associated with were fellow lifers, though some were doing as little as three or four years. At this stage he thought he would serve at least ten years in detention and made a conscious decision not to think about the future until he was given a provisional release date.

He was then transferred to another Category B prison for about two years, where there were few privileges and he said he never really felt comfortable. There was less opportunity for association and less physical freedom within the prison.

From there he was sent to a semi-open prison where he spent just under two years, and he seemed to find this a better prison. It was modern and there was much greater physical freedom. He said he was pressured into doing a welding course. His jobs included making electric fires and cleaning and working as a gym orderly. There were lots of short-term prisoners there but he tended to ignore them. The staff there were 'slippery' and he was very aware of being constantly observed. He was then moved to an open prison for two and a half years. Predictably he did not like being accommodated in a dormitory because of the lack of privacy. He was much happier when given his own room where he felt that he was not really in prison because within that room he could organise his own life. He worked on the gardens and as a cleaner. The staff were very mixed, there were some good and some bad. Some could be quite human and friendly, others were overbearing and he felt they were trying to incite prisoners, to test them out to see how far they could control their tempers. He mixed primarily with long-term prisoners because he thought it was impossible to trust those serving short sentences. He felt they tended to 'tell tales' to members of staff. He had no problems on his trips out of prison, and it had taken only about ten minutes to get used to life outside. In this sense it was 'a bit of a let down'. He had been out of prison on a college course, but had not been able to complete it. Home leaves were much appreciated, but they only lasted for four days and he thought that they should be longer.

When I spoke to him he was in a prison hostel where he was serving the last nine months of his detention. He described the last three months as being the longest part of the sentence and the most difficult. He was keen to get on with his own life and to organise things for himself. He regarded the stipulation that he had to be back at the hostel by a certain time each evening as a nuisance, yet he felt that he had benefitted from being able to get back into the routine of doing an ordinary job. Naturally, he was concerned about the reaction that potential employers might show towards him. Visits and letters had been very important, and he said he only really relaxed when in the company of his visitors and he appreciated the feeling of being cared for. He had been bitter at the start of his sentence but that had passed. What mattered to him was that his family had supported him and shown faith and trust in him. He felt that prison staff were not really qualified or trained to do a caring job and psychologists in particular ought to be given a greater degree of responsibility and authority within the system.

Case No. 54

This man said he had expected to be convicted of manslaughter and the police had told him that he would get between five and seven years' imprisonment. He had regarded that as about right in view of the nature of his offence. Receiving a life sentence thus came as quite a shock to him and he was 'knocked for six for weeks on end'. He had had no idea how long he would spend in detention. He had feared there was a possibility that he would spend the rest of his natural life in prison. From the court he was taken back to the local prison where he had been kept on remand and he spent the first night in the hospital wing. He was then moved to the main wing in the prison and spent almost three months there. Initially, he shared a cell with another man serving a very short sentence and he found this very stressful. He worked in the mailbag shop, but there was no association for the prisoners. Meals were taken in the cell. Most of the staff were quite good, though they tended not to make any great attempt to engage prisoners in conversation.

He was then transferred to a maximum security prison where he spent about three and a half years. He was located on a long-term wing and initially he was very frightened. When he first arrived at the prison and went into the reception area he said he was processed 'like a chicken'. He was struck by the mass of white tiles, the electric gates and security cameras. On the other hand, the staff were very different in that they had time to get to know prisoners. They actually made prisoners feel human. He noticed the cards outside each prison cell and he realised that many other prisoners were much worse off than he was for they were likely to serve longer sentences. He described the atmosphere in the wing as very tense at times. He had a variety of jobs there: working as a cleaner, on the incinerator, as an electrician and as a plumber. There was a disturbance at the prison after which the regime became much more strict and, initially at least, prisoners spent much more time locked up in their cells.

From there he was moved to a semi-open prison where he was kept for about two and three quarter years, and he saw this as a very good step. He described his time there as 'OK, but hard'. He felt that after his experience in the maximum security prison he was rather paranoid, listening for keys and suspecting that staff were talking about him. At the same time though, he was pleased with the better conditions in the semi-open prison – for example, there was a toilet and wash-hand basin in each cell, whereas in the maximum security prison there was just a bucket in the corner. He also had much more freedom to move about the prison and to make decisions for himself, and this was something that he found difficult.

The staff were very good and friendly and many were on first-name terms with the prisoners. He worked on the gardens and he was able to see the outside world for the first time in a long while. He felt that a great weight had been lifted from his shoulders. He also worked as a reception orderly and in the kitchen, and he did a vocational training course in welding. Generally, he mixed very well with other prisoners.

He was then transferred to an open prison where he spent about 15 months, and he described that as 'unbelievable', for he could not hear chains rattling and doors banging. In the first 11 months he slept in a dormitory, where tempers became frayed very easily and he was struck by the snoring of other prisoners in the ward and the general amount of noise. He worked on the gardens and as a tractor driver. Naturally there was much physical freedom within the prison, but this time he had no problems in coping with it. He had spent various days out of the prison on shopping trips and attending a local college, and on home visits. He had been surprised at the rise in prices of goods in the shops and noticed how the fashions had changed, and it seemed that there was a greater volume of traffic which appeared to him to be travelling much more quickly than he had remembered. He described the staff at the prison as being first class – they were approachable, helpful and they treated prisoners as human beings and did not look down on them.

However, he was moved out of the prison because he was suspected of being involved in a breach of prison discipline and he was transferred to a Category B closed prison. He spent only a few days there sharing a cell with two other prisoners and was then moved to a local prison for about four months. At that time he had a strong sense of going backwards. He was told that he should work in the mailbag shops, sewing mailbags by hand, but he refused to do this because he felt it was too degrading. He was then given a job as a welder but the person with whom he was supposed to work refused to work with him because he was a lifer, so he used to spend most of the time in the gym.

After those four months he was moved to a semi-open prison for about seven months. In fact, he said it was supposed to be a semi-open prison but it was operated more as a Category B security prison and he hated his time there. There was little work for him to do and he was anxiously awaiting the result of his third parole application which, it seems, was delayed. At the end of the seven months he was transferred to another open prison, and had been there for about a month when I spoke to him and had five more months to spend there. He would then serve a further six months at a prison hostel. This second open prison was much less helpful in preparing lifers for release than the previous one had been. There were fewer opportunities to go out of the institution so as to acclimatise to the world outside and he felt that he had been given very little advice from members of staff there on the sort of problems that he would have to encounter.

He said that it took him about two years really to come to terms with and understand the full meaning of his sentence. Like many long-term prisoners, he had grasped at straws in the early stages of the sentence by, for example, trying to appeal against conviction and/or sentence. He had always tried to think about the future and to be positive in his attitude, though he had not been able to make any firm release plans until he had been given a provisional release date. He had had visits and corresponded regularly with members of his family and his friends, and he felt this was particularly important because it enabled him to keep in touch with the world outside and it gave him a sense of worth as a person.

He was sure that prisoners could not influence the amount of time they spent inside prison by their good conduct because of the dominance of the tariff. He was very conscious of what he regarded as injustices within the penal system, that is, that some prisoners appeared to have committed much more serious offences and did not behave themselves in prison, and yet they seemed to be given shorter periods of detention. He also commented that in his view the trust which the prison authorities appeared to expect to be shown by prisoners should be reciprocated by members of staff. He felt this was the only way in which a constructive relationship could be established between them. By the time of his release he will have spent about ten years in prison, but he said he felt no bitterness, though his experience of imprisonment had made him very cautious. He felt he could anticipate and prevent danger, and that he was able to walk away from potential trouble-spots.

Case No. 56

This lifer said that he felt totally numb at the time that the life sentence was passed upon him and that this continued for three or four days. He spent the first four or five months in a closed prison, initially in a single cell, but then he shared with two other prisoners. During that time he read, slept and cried. For two or three months he was not able to mix with other people other than for 30 to 45 minutes a day. Some of the staff would talk to him and he found this quite useful.

He then spent three weeks in a local prison before being moved to a top security establishment, where he was kept for about two and a half years. There he was struck by the amount of violence on the part of both staff and inmates. He did a full-time course in engineering, and also worked as a cleaner. Again, he did not mix much with other inmates, although those he talked to were not necessarily lifers or long-term prisoners. In many ways he found it easier to talk to someone who had been outside prison more recently. He was told by prison staff that he would serve eight years in detention at most and he had wanted to believe them because that would give him a sense of hope. He always tried to think about the future and he had taken the engineering course because he thought that would facilitate his prospects of employment on release. However, as the result of one of his subsequent reviews at the prison he felt sure that he would serve more than eight years in detention.

From there he was transferred to a Category B prison which catered only for lifers and spent about four years there. He described this as a very good time in that prisoners had more choice in their work and hobbies. There was a good education programme there of which he took advantage. He was initially very wary of the use of first names by staff but he got used to this, though he felt some of them were only superficially friendly. He also worked in the engineering shop and in the typewriter assembly shop. He was then moved to a semi-open prison for about three years where he said the regime was often rather petty, which he attributed to the presence of a large number of immature young prisoners. He worked in the sewing-machine shop repairing the machines, and also took woodwork classes in the evenings.

He had been in an open prison for about four months when we talked, and he saw this as the time when the authorities gave prisoners a chance to rebuild themselves. The lack of a fence and the visibility of the outside world came as a bit of a shock, and he said some prisoners were rather paranoid, feeling that they would not be able to communicate with people outside. He thought that the job familiarisation scheme that the prison operated was a major help in that it gave prisoners the opportunity to readjust to a normal life outside the institution. He also thought the staff were very helpful and supportive. Like many others, he complained that being accommodated in dormitories was very difficult because of the lack of privacy and cleanliness. On the other hand, the new accommodation which the prison was offering was a great improvement. He still tended not to mix very much with other lifers but preferred to talk to short-termers so that he could find out what was happening in the world outside. He described a shopping trip that he had been on as a bit of a shock, not at the increase in prices but simply because of the overall appearance of things, and he was struck by the change in fashions.

He was due to spend the last six months of his sentence in a hostel and he felt that this was a necessary stage so that he could have a chance to save some money and continue the process of gradual release. He said he had only really been able to think in detail about his future after he had been given a provisional release date. For him too, visits and letters had been important as a means of keeping in touch with life outside the prison. He was also helped by the caring and supportive attitude which his family and friends showed towards him, though he admitted that visits could sometimes be a 'bit of a wind-up'.

He found it impossible to determine whether he ought to have been convicted of murder or manslaughter. His 11 years in detention were more than enough, and he suggested that six to eight years would have been more appropriate. He felt that his own feelings and sense of self-recrimination had punished him more than the prison system. Rather unusually, he felt he was able to influence his sentence by good behaviour. He had been led to believe that this was the case by prison staff and he had accepted what they had said.

Case No. 59

The trial judge had recommended that this young man should be detained for at least 20 years. A conviction for murder, and thus a life sentence, had been expected but not the minimum recommendation which came as 'a real shock'. Nonetheless, he thought he would not serve 20 years in prison, though he appreciated that he would be detained for longer than average. He had always felt that the Home Office determined, at a very early stage, the likely length of detention and so he never felt he had any real control over his sentence. He spent the first couple of days of his sentence in the hospital wing which he described as 'bad' because he was segregated in a room by himself and was not able to talk to other prisoners. He was then moved to a young prisoners' wing and was put into a single cell, and there were only about five lifers on the wing. Most of the prisoners there were serving very short sentences and this he regarded as a 'big wind-up'. Initially, he was given considerable status as a lifer although that gradually wore off. He was designated as a Category A prisoner, which he did not like because it meant that he was locked up in his cell for long periods and was not given any work to do. At that stage, he very much 'acted the part' of being a hardened criminal serving a long sentence. He chose not to associate with other young prisoners and talked only to other lifers. He was then moved to an adult wing in prison where staff treated prisoners differently in that they were much more courteous. He mixed with all sorts of prisoners, provided they did not talk about release. He declined to do the work that was allocated to him and since there was no other work available he spent a lot of the time in his cell.

He was then transferred to another maximum security prison for about six months. He had been led to believe by another prisoner that life there was hard. It was a long way from his home town and he deliberately refused to work so that he would be moved to another institution.

His wish was granted and he was transferred to another top security prison where he remained for about six years. He was still only 19 years old at the time and he felt rather frightened at first. He saw that some prisoners there were serving three or four life sentences and regarded the prison as a 'penal dustbin'. He said there was a considerable degree of violence amongst prisoners in the wing and the violence was necessary to show that they would not be 'pushed about'. Prisoners indulged in illicit drinking parties and staff did not intervene. He worked in the carpenters shop for about seven months and then applied for eight different jobs and was refused on each occasion. He gave vent to his anger and frustration by smashing up some prison property and was sent to the punishment block. Afterwards he worked on the garden party which was what he had originally wanted to do. He also did a painting and decorating course and then put the skills he had acquired into practice. He had never felt that there was any point in doing courses which would give him academic qualifications because that would not assist him in getting a job when he was released.

It was after he had served three or four years of his sentence that he began to realise the real meaning of life imprisonment. He appreciated that he would have to spend a long time in detention and therefore set about finding ways of helping to relax and serve his time. The six years he spent in this particular prison were too long and he was very glad to be moved to a Category B prison where he spent about 15 months. This was a much better prison; there was no violence, and the sports and education facilities were good. He mixed with all sorts of other prisoners including short-termers. He began a two-year art and design course and paid a considerable proportion of the fees himself, but was only able to complete two and a half months before being transferred to another institution. His dismay and annoyance at this was tempered though by the fact that he was moved to a semi-open prison, which he knew was a move in the right direction.

He spent a total of about three years at the semi-open prison where the atmosphere was even more relaxed. The fact, for example, that there were no locks on many of the doors was something which he initially found rather difficult to appreciate, but he gradually settled down to his new environment. One aggravating feature of the prison was that many of the other prisoners spent a lot of time talking about getting parole and being released from prison. He also felt that many of the staff were rather childish in their attitude towards inmates. He worked as a cleaner, as a fork-lift driver, and on the prison gardens.

He was then transferred to an open prison where he had been for almost two years when I spoke to him and was due to go to a prison hostel in the very near future. He said he had found his time in the open prison 'a big wind-up' because many of the other prisoners were serving short sentences and they constantly moaned about their problems, and many of them 'told tales' to the staff. Consequently, he said, lifers were under a great deal of pressure in open prisons for they had much more to lose than other prisoners. Like many others, he was very critical of having to sleep in a dormitory, although he had gradually got used to it. Nonetheless, he had particularly appreciated the shopping trips and opportunities to get out of the prison and to get back into an ordinary environment. He had anticipated the increase in prices, but was struck by the fact that people outside seemed rather grim-faced.

He thought that prison tried to make people behave by order, telling them what to do and how to do it, and this was something that had to be fought against for there was a danger that prisoners would lose their personalities. It was important to try to preserve a sense of self-identity.

Case No. 61

This man expected to be convicted of manslaughter rather than murder, and the police had indicated to him that he would get a sentence of seven years imprisonment. He had thought the life sentence meant that he would literally serve the rest of his natural life in prison. He spent the first night after sentence in the hospital wing in his local prison but was then moved to an ordinary wing for about two months. Occasionally, he worked in the tailors shop, and he tried not to think about the sentence. No-one had given him any indication of what was likely to happen to him.

He was then transferred to a top security prison for about three and a half years. The atmosphere there was quite relaxed and he was able to mix with other prisoners and to pursue various hobbies and recreational activities. The staff were quite friendly. Many were on first-name terms with prisoners and tried to help them with any personal problems and difficulties. Unfortunately, however, there were major disturbances in the prison as a result of which the atmosphere became much more tense and the opportunities to associate with other prisoners were restricted. He had a number of jobs there, as a bricklayer and then operating a lathe in the light engineering shop. He also spent some of his time as a cleaner. He said he had not really understood the full meaning of the sentence until he had served about three years, and even then he had no clear idea about how long he would have to serve. Consequently, he consciously tried to shut out any thoughts about the future. He also did not like being associated with other prisoners whom he regarded as serious offenders.

He was then moved to a dispersal prison for about two years, where the atmosphere was relaxed. There were reasonable sporting and recreational facilities and the staff were quite informal in their attitude towards prisoners. He undertook a welding course, which he thought might help his chances of gaining employment when released. He also worked in the kitchens and in the laundry. He was told by the governor that his case did not warrant dispersal conditions and so he was moved to a non-dispersal Category B prison for a further period of two years or so. He appreciated that this was a good move for him. There was considerable opportunity to associate with other prisoners and staff were quite friendly. His main work there was as a carpenter.

He then spent two years in a semi-open establishment where he was able to walk around the prison and there was a much greater sense of space and freedom. Staff were generally very supportive and helpful, particularly when he suffered a personal bereavement. He was then transferred to an open prison and had been there for about six weeks when I spoke to him. He had found it very strange having to sleep in a dormitory but he was gradually getting used to it. Having a single cell for such a long time had afforded him a much greater degree of privacy than he was permitted at the open prison. There was a yet greater sense of freedom and space, but having to mix with short-term prisoners was rather difficult because of their constant talk of parole and personal problems.

He was due to go out of prison on his first shopping trip the day after I spoke to him and he was slightly concerned about encountering traffic but was otherwise very much looking forward to it. He was to serve the last six months of his detention in a prison hostel, which he thought was a good step for him to take because it would give him the opportunity to gradually acclimatise to a more normal life-style.

He still felt that he did not deserve to be regarded as a murderer, and that he should have been convicted of manslaughter and given a ten year sentence. That would have meant that he would have been released in probably less than six and a half years. He said that in many ways he felt his real sentence would start when he was released on licence because of the constant danger that he might be recalled to a closed prison. Nevertheless, he felt that imprisonment had helped him mature and to exercise a greater degree of self-discipline. Like many others, he had never been able to think about his future until he was given a release date. He was also very aware of what he perceived to be injustices within the system. In other words, the sentences which people were required to serve seemed to bear little resemblance to the gravity of their offences.

9 Some Thoughts and Suggestions of Managers and Staff

The third source from which data was collected was a sample of staff who had first-hand experience of looking after life-sentence prisoners. The information which is provided here represents the views and comments expressed by a broad range of individuals, from basic grade uniform officers to senior governors, and including probation officers and prison psychologists and psychiatrists.

MAIN CENTRES

The particular wing which I visited in Prison 'A' accommodated just under 300 prisoners, approximately 10 per cent of whom were serving determinate sentences of five years or more, and the remainder were life sentence prisoners. The majority of the lifers in the wing were in the early phase of their sentences, so that the prison really was their main centre. A small number, though, were further into their sentences and were regarded as 'second-stagers'.

Both the personal backgrounds of the lifers and the nature of the offences of which they had been convicted varied considerably. Since most had only very recently been sentenced by the court when they arrived in the wing, no attempt was made to get them to talk about the crimes or to admit their culpability. At the same time, staff said that the lifers usually offered an 'explanation' or 'account' of what had happened, but these tended to be regarded as of doubtful reliability.

Not surprisingly, many prisoners initially appeared to be suffering from some form of shock, but this eased and the vast majority settled down to the routine of prison life. On average they spent three or four years in this prison and staff remarked that towards the end of that time, quite a few lifers were able to look ahead, albeit rather tentatively. One of the principal influences behind this was thought to be the reviews which were undertaken at about the three-year stage. These were carried out for the purpose of compiling the F75 reports

271

on which career plans were based. Staff felt that the discussion of the matters contained in career plans with lifers – the tariff, areas of concern, and perceived treatment needs – and their proposed progress through the prison system, provided the impetus which fostered thoughts of the future and ultimate release.

Rather than confront prisoners with a requirement that they must discuss the offence and how they proposed to solve personal problems, staff preferred to make it known that they were ready, willing and available if the individual wanted to speak to someone. In addition, one of the governors said that prisoners were advised that reports were prepared at specific intervals about their progress during detention and that this could only be achieved by the establishment of a relationship between them and at least one member of staff. Moreover, the more that staff could glean about a lifer, the more likely it was that the reports would constitute an accurate and comprehensive account of his progress.

It was very rare for lifers to present any control or security problems for staff, including those who were clearly going to be deprived of their liberty for many years to come and the very few who were unlikely to be released at all. One of the general characteristics of lifers was said to be their considerable patience, and many were felt to display great calmness in dealing with tense and stressful situations. A good illustration of this was their tolerance of the inevitable delay that was encountered whenever important decisions affecting them had to be made. This problem of delay was severely criticised by staff at all the establishments I visited. Not only did it cause tremendous tension for the individual prisoner, but it also made it very difficult for staff to maintain good working relationships with their charges. A governor at Prison 'A' said that he had come across cases where the results of the F75 review had not been known until five years after the date of sentence, so that some lifers had been half way through their detention before their career plans were available.

The views of staff at Prison 'A' as to the utility of career plans were typical. They provide a convenient and succinct account of the main features and considerations in each case: they offer a useful 'potted version' of the matters which staff need to know about each lifer. But it was universally accepted that they should not be regarded as 'tablets of stone'. Rather they should be constantly reviewed and updated throughout the sentence and staff should be encouraged to read all the reports in the file and to form their own opinions in the light of what they had learned. A further comment made at Prison 'A' which was echoed in all the other establishments was the need for better and more appropriate training of uniform staff in particular. These are the people who have day-to-day contact with lifers and they have to try to build constructive relationships with them. It was strongly argued that this requires training in various aspects of the behavioural sciences, and their skills in report-writing should be enhanced so that more benefit can be reaped from their regular contact with lifers.

In Prison 'B' there were approximately 130 prisoners serving life sentences, the total population being about 315. Roughly 90 of the lifers were just beginning their sentences; the rest were 'second-stagers'. They generally spent roughly four years at the prison before being transferred elsewhere. Staff here agreed that the personal details of lifers and the gravity of their offences varied enormously.

It was also confirmed that many of those in the very early phases of their sentence experience variable degrees of shock, but this gradually passes during the ensuing months. In any event, by the end of their first year there, the majority have settled down and come to terms with an indeterminate sentence. The major characteristic of those who do not settle was thought to be that they were pursuing appeals against conviction and/or sentence, and they only settled when all possible appeals had been exhausted.

Of those convicted of murder, the majority were said to deny full responsibility, though many admitted being guilty of manslaughter and most accepted that they had killed. The approach of staff was to encourage the lifer to realise and face up to what had happened and to understand the court's sentence. That a prisoner might deny that he deserved to be convicted of murder was not regarded as significant. Staff were much more concerned that he should adopt a positive attitude to his imprisonment.

Interestingly, in apparent contradiction of what was said at Prison 'A', most lifers were felt to be incapable of looking very far ahead, whether they were 'first-' or 'second-stagers'. It was suggested that the earliest point at which they might be able to think about release was when they receive the date of their first LRC review, but even then their position is very uncertain and, understandably, they do not want to build up false hopes. Instead, they tend to notionally divide their sentence into small chunks of time, which they can envisage more meaningfully. This might then lead them to embark upon a particular educational or vocational training course.

As expected, staff indicated that 'second-stagers' were more likely to have career plans than the others. Although plans were useful for the reasons given by their colleagues in Prison 'A', governors at Prison 'B' expressed the reservation that the contents of the plans frequently did not seem to become known to uniform officers – a comment that was repeated by their counterparts in less secure institutions. This was very much in line with the reaction I received from uniform staff, many of whom appeared to have little or no knowledge of career plans.

CATEGORY B ESTABLISHMENTS

Prison 'C' was a dispersal prison, with a total population of 425 inmates, roughly 60 of whom were serving life sentences. The great majority of lifers were 'second-stagers', though for a few the prison was effectively their 'main centre'. Most of them were transferred to a non-dispersal Category B prison and only a small number went directly to semi-open conditions.

Thoughts about the future were said to be very unlikely. The prisoners were usually in the middle stages of their detention and are simply 'marking time'. Motivating them to acquire the desired sense of purpose and direction was thus extremelly difficult and achieved only to a limited degree. A more realistic objective was to 'keep them happy' and thereby avoid any security or control problems. At the same time, staff emphasised that prisoners should be given an honest appraisal of what they could expect and what was proposed as their path through detention. They should not be given false hopes merely to keep them quiet and contented because, as was reiterated at other institutions, difficulties would inevitably arise when the falseness became apparent to them and their hopes were dashed.

Whilst discussing this issue, staff were also aware of the potential problems that might arise when prisoners are transferred to semi-open prisons. As the result of such a transfer, some loss of 'perks and privileges' is almost certain. The fear is that the benefit of taking a step nearer to release may be nullified by a more uncomfortable life-style and what lifers regard as a bloody-minded attitude on the part of the penal system. Similar comments were made at other establishments, although some staff thought that the point was being exaggerated.

There was said to be a considerable variation in the lifers' awareness of the meaning and implications of their predicaments. Some appeared to be quite well informed of the issues contained in their career plan, whereas others seemed to be largely ignorant of the likely length of their detention, the concerns which staff had about them and what treatment or supervision was felt to be appropriate for them. Similarly, some had talked to staff at length about their offence, while others had said virtually nothing about it.

Overall, career plans were again seen as a valuable asset to staff, though the need for constant updating and a flexible approach towards them was stressed. Obviously, at the time they are drafted, it is impossible to foresee what developments or complications might arise in the future. Plans must be reviewed in the light of these developments – as, for example, when a prisoner is sent back from a Category C to a Category B establishment.

As well as confirming the need to ensure that the contents of career plans are communicated to uniform staff, one of the governors at Prison 'C' talked of the general need for staff in the prisons and in P2 and P4 Divisions to work closely with each other. Obviously, those in regular and direct contact with lifers must be aware of decisions made in the Prison Department in London if the proposed management policy is to be implemented, as intended, and if accurate information is to be passed on to the prisoners themselves.

Prison 'D' was a non-dispersal establishment which catered for 90 or so lifers, most of whom were accommodated in one wing. Usually, they would spend four to six years there and would then be transferred to semi-open conditions. The majority came to the prison either from a main centre or from a dispersal prison, but one governor suspected that an increasing number were being sent back from Category C and D establishments.

By the time they get to Prison 'D', most lifers have been given the date of their LRC review and they are able to have some thoughts about their future. Naturally, these thoughts were often rather vague, and it was not uncommon to find that they did not fully appreciate the problems that are likely to face them on release. Some lifers appeared to experience a form of 'mid-sentence depression', especially if their contact with people outside prison broke down. Fortunately, this depression generally disappeared towards the end of their time there.

The majority of lifers could talk about their offence quite openly, but a few still found it difficult to come to terms with the enormity of what had happened. There were also distinct variations in their attitude towards staff and their relationships with them. In some cases they got on well and seemed to be able to have confidence in what staff said and the advice they gave. Others, however, especially those with a record of earlier convictions and who might be regarded as 'professional criminals', preferred to maintain the traditional 'us and them' approach and deliberately kept their contact with staff to a minimum. Obviously, it was extremely difficult in these instances for staff to establish constructive working relationships.

Relatively few uniform officers indicated that they were familiar with career plans – some were aware of their existence, but no more. Those who were familiar with them feared there was a danger that disclosure of their contents to lifers could cause management problems – on discovering the details of their tariff they would become depressed and difficult to motivate. They might even become disruptive and present control difficulties. It was suggested by one or two staff that the tariff seems to be gradually increasing and this was unsettling where lifers felt they were being unfairly detained for longer than their predecessors. Explanations emphasising the need to meet the requirements of retribution and deterrence, and the significance of the risk factor, rarely had any appeasing effects. One of the governors criticised what he regarded as the narrow assumption on which career plans seem to be based, namely, that lifers will necessarily follow a steady path towards a gradually more liberal environment. He felt that insufficient guidance was given about those who do not progress as might be hoped or who are sent back to more secure conditions.

The comment was made that the establishment and maintenance of a good relationship between staff and prisoners is a very time-consuming process. That such relationships can be forged, given the right circumstances, is encouraging, but the implications for staff resources were very clear. At Prison 'D' there had been a recent experiment in which some officers voluntarily ran what might normally be called a 'summer school'. For a week they gave up their own time and participated very closely with a group of lifers on a wide variety of activities and, as a result, the relationship between them had distinctly improved.

At Prison 'E' the controversial question of the segregation of lifers was raised. This was quite predictable for the vast majority of the 140 or so prisoners there were lifers, and the remainder were serving long, determinate sentences. Staff stressed the desire to help prisoners to prepare themselves for release and the need for them to be given as much individual freedom as possible within the confines of the prison. Although a Category B establishment, it was intimated that Prison 'E' seeks to adopt a Category C regime within its walls. Thus, the prisoner can be more responsible for what he does and thereby provide a more reliable indication of the progress he is making. Furthermore, some staff argued that having experienced a more relaxed, 'human' regime, lifers could then be transferred directly to open conditions, without any noticeable problems of adjustment.

Traditionally, a large proportion of the lifers there are what are often referred to as 'domestic murderers', men with no previous convictions who have committed a 'one-off' offence as the result of difficult circumstances, and they are seen as essentially 'non-criminal' and as posing no threat to the public. Two issues were raised regarding segregation. Firstly, some uniform officers argued that 'domestic' offenders should not be integrated with 'professional criminals' because the latter were likely to 'contaminate' unsophisticated prisoners and thus prejudice their prospects of an early and successful release. The governor, on the other hand, was extremely confident that such fears did not materialise, for any prisoner who was regarded as having such an unsettling and disruptive effect was transferred from the prison forthwith.

The other aspect of segregation concerned the broader question whether there should be (more) prisons which accommodate only life sentence prisoners. Staff at Prison 'E' saw them as desirable because the indeterminacy of their sentence puts lifers in a unique position. They have needs and problems which are not experienced by determinate sentence prisoners. Lifers are invariably a very stable group who support and empathise with each other, and they should be accommodated in establishments where they are free from the potentially disruptive influences of certain fixed-term prisoners. As to the danger that subsequent integration with fixed-term prisoners in semi-open and open prisons would be problematic after a relatively cosseted existence, it was suggested that the knowledge that release was nearer at hand would be sufficiently sustaining and would outweigh any unfortunate 'side effects' of the transfer. Life may be a little more uncomfortable, but the most important thing was that the lifer was that much closer to being given his freedom.

Uniform officers especially offered ideas for improving the system of career plans. Some were a little unclear about how much of the detailed contents should be disclosed to prisoners. It was suggested that the plan should be attached to the Confidential Memorandum (which contains a potted but complete history of the case), in the file. More importantly, perhaps, was the idea that the staff who had regular contact with lifers should be much more involved in the drafting of the plans. Uniform officers at Prison 'E' argued that those in P2 Division who are responsible for the plans may be very experienced governors, but they do not possess as much detailed knowledge of the prisoners and are thus less well-qualified to undertake the task.

As to the question of delay in receiving the results of parole applications, the point was made that not only does the individual lifer suffer but so too do other prisoners who share the sense of frustration and the tense atmosphere. Moreover, since staff are usually seen as part of the penal process, their relationships with lifers deteriorate when the system is perceived to be indifferent and not aware of its impact on prisoners.

I visited one youth custody centre, Prison 'F', where there were 36 lifers out of a total population of about 180. In the first few months there, lifers tend to have difficulty in discussing their offence and in facing up to what they have done. But each of them is assigned to a personal case officer and they are gradually able to come to terms with the crime and accept responsibility accordingly. Most of these young lifers have no previous convictions and it was suggested that this may explain why many of them do not appear fully to understand the nature of an indeterminate sentence.

It was interesting to learn that, although at the time of my visit lifers were integrated with other inmates, it was proposed that they and long-term prisoners should be accommodated in one wing. The reasons for this proposal reflected the views expressed by many staff in Prison 'E', that lifers were essentially 'not criminals', and the indeterminacy of the sentence created special needs which set them apart from the others. Furthermore, it was argued that because lifers vary so widely (in their personal circumstances and the gravity of their offence), general policies for their management might not be appropriate. Rather they should be treated as individuals whose personal needs should be addressed, and this clearly called for a large measure of flexibility and variation in their paths through the penal system.

The timing of the transfer of prisoners from a youth custody centre to an adult establishment provided a useful illustration of the danger of adopting too rigid a policy. Transfer to the adult system should, strictly speaking, take place when the individual reaches 22 years of age. But the point was made by some staff that prisoners vary tremendously in their personality and level of maturity, so that some could be better served by moving out of a youth custody centre before they are 22, while others ought to wait until they are older. Amongst the other comments about the existing system it was said that there should be a wide variety of facilities and resources, firstly because of the broad range of prisoners' needs, and secondly because if he stayed there for any great length of time a prisoner might run out of useful things to do.

It was not uncommon to find that lifers at Prison 'F' did not have career plans because they were usually in the initial stages of detention. One uniform officer repeated the concern that the discovery of his tariff at such a relatively early point in the sentence may cause further shock to a young lifer, and thus make it more difficult for him to settle down and use his time constructively. Concern was also shown about the need to introduce lifers to more liberal regimes only very gradually. Some had apparently been transferred from Prison 'F' directly to a hostel, and it was feared that they were invariably ill-equipped to cope with such a sudden increase in freedom and responsibility. It was hoped that mistakes of this nature could be avoided by more careful planning. The loss of 'perks and privileges' which invariably followed a transfer from Prison 'F' to semi-open or open establishments was strongly criticised by all staff. There was no clear benefit to be derived from it, and it was likely to have a very negative effect on the attitude of the prisoners.

Some interesting observations were made by a psychiatrist at the prison about the general impact of detention. He felt that roughly a third of the lifers were 'treatable'. These tended to be people with no previous convictions, who had problems which could be resolved so that they could safely be released after about four years in prison. Detaining people for longer than was absolutely necessary was likely to be counter-productive. Imprisonment usually had an undermining effect on 'normal' inmates (that is, those not suffering from psychological or psychiatric disorders), in that it made them suppress their emotions. There is no opportunity in prison to show or understand such feelings and yet young prisoners especially may need to develop this part of their personalities.

Prison 'G' was the only women's prison that I visited. It accommodated only 13 or 14 lifers, the majority of whom had served about four to six years before arriving there. Generally, they could expect to be given their first LRC review date at the prison, and would subequently be transferred to the open prison. (NB: There are no semi-open establishments for women.)

Some lifers clearly did suffer periods of depression during the middle years of their detention, but with the aid of a good relationship with their case officers they could be motivated to recognise that they had a future and to make some sort of plans for their eventual release. Uniform staff were generally unaware of career plans, although they often found that the Confidential Memorandum was a valuable and convenient means of acquiring a succinct understanding of the case. One of the governors felt that whilst career plans were a helpful method of identifying points of concern about unfamiliar cases, they lacked any guidance as to how staff should deal with those concerns. This was, perhaps, yet another call for more appropriate training of staff, especially in psychology and other behavioural sciences.

SEMI-OPEN PRISONS

There were approximately 60 lifers, representing about a tenth of the total population, at Prison 'H'. The majority had been transferred from a Category B prison, and would almost certainly be moved to an open establishment.

Staff were very conscious that this is the stage at which the emphasis is on testing prisoners to see how they respond when given the opportunity to be responsible for their own conduct. But since the environment in prison can never reflect that which exists outside, the process of testing cannot be regarded as infallible. This led to the proposal by some staff that predictions about the safety of releasing prisoners could be made more confidently if they spent a larger proportion of their sentence in semi-open (and open) conditions – that is, they should be moved out of the closed system more quickly.

Lifers in Prison 'H' were not segregated from other prisoners. Staff accepted that integration did cause problems and pressures for some lifers and, although these problems were unrealistic in that they would not exist in the same form outside prison, they were seen as a useful means of monitoring prisoners' reactions. Staff could get some impression of lifers' levels of tolerance and their powers of self-control, and these were regarded as significant indicators about suitability for release.

It was rather surprising to learn that some lifers seemed to look upon their LRC review date as the time when they would be released. They failed to appreciate that they would be detained for at least three years after the LRC review.

Only those who had been sentenced more recently had career plans. Where plans were available, staff said that they always had to be seen in the light of new developments, and even though lifers were well into their sentence by this time, matters sometimes arose which had not previously been identified. Thus, career plans may have to be revised, sometimes quite radically. It was also suggested that staff should not be reluctant to disclose information to lifers about matters that were contained in their career plans. Keeping prisoners in the dark is obviously not conducive to the establishment of a relationship in which staff and inmates are able to place some trust and confidence in each other. If an atmosphere is to be fostered in which the system and lifers work together towards the same goals, a policy of disclosure rather than secrecy must be adopted.

The comments made by the psychiatrist in Prison 'F' about the adverse effects of imprisonment were underlined by a probation officer in Prison 'H'. A prisoner's emotional development is likely to be frustrated because his emotional response to the offence and his sentence are effectively suppressed. He is left only with the memory of the death of his victim and has no opportunity to grieve.

Prison 'I' accommodated about 40 lifers, 120 long-term prisoners (serving at least five years), and about 300 with sentences of two to five years. Typically, many convicted murderers accepted that they had wrongfully killed someone, but usually felt that manslaughter would have been a more just verdict. The great majority recognised that they must serve a long period of detention, though some appear to underestimate exactly how long this will be.

One of the governors acknowledged that the indeterminacy of the sentence differentiates them from fixed-term prisoners, but he insisted that lifers should not be treated as unique. The problem of indeterminacy will probably be most evident in the first two to five years of detention, but once they understand the nature of the sentence and the fact that they will be released (albeit at some point in the future), the problem will largely disappear. Thus, they should be integrated with other prisoners, to show that the differences between them are not that great, and to avoid difficulties that might be encountered in resettling into the community as a result of looking upon themselves as 'special'.

Since the prime objective of semi-open prisons is to assess to what degree a prisoner would pose a threat to the safety of the public, staff are not concerned with whether he deserves to be released. Lifers are encouraged to look ahead and to think about how they might deal with the problems that will face them. It was argued by one governor that the loss of 'perks and privileges' consequent upon transfer to a Category C institution should not be the subject of reform. They were necessary, he said, in closed prisons where the regime is much more restrictive, but in semi-open conditions there is a much greater level of freedom and autonomy for prisoners so that 'creature comforts' are not needed.

Although useful up to a point, it was stressed that career plans should not be viewed as comprehensive accounts of each case. Staff should not simply rely on the contents of the plans, but should read all the reports that had been prepared on lifers and form their own opinions accordingly. Moreover, it was confirmed that not infrequently new areas of concern became apparent even in the latter stages of detention, so that plans might have to be updated, and sometimes quite fundamentally redrafted.

OPEN PRISONS

An officer at Prison 'J' agreed that lifers were a very 'mixed bunch', but felt that three broad groups could be identified. The younger ones had usually been sent to prison before they had properly matured and the majority of them had not fully matured even by the time they reached the open prison. They tended to underestimate the difficulties they would encounter on release, and staff usually did not find it easy to motivate them. The middle-aged group, mainly 35- to 45-years-old when released, were much more likely to use their time in detention purposefully, completing educational and/or vocational training courses in an effort to improve their chances of obtaining employment. Most of this group were keen to resume and reconstruct their lives outside prison as soon as possible, and they were frequently critical of and impatient with the penal system. In particular, open prison tended to be seen as unnecessary. Older lifers usually found it difficult to get on with much younger prisoners, often complaining of a lack of respect and consideration. Getting them to plan for the future was not always very easy, and it was invariably difficult to get them to make a serious effort to solve their personal problems (such as alcohol, or coping with stress). These lifers might benefit from some sort of special retirement course which would accommodate their needs more specifically.

The point was made that since prisoners can readily see beyond the boundaries of the institution – for there is no fence as such – open prisons should be located in rural areas. To do otherwise would impose too many pressures and temptations on inmates who need to be gradually introduced to a 'normal life'. The ease with which this is effected varies considerably from lifer to lifer, but they all benefit from shopping trips, home visits, working in the community and, sometimes, attending courses at educational establishments outside prison.

Two observations were made about problems which tend to manifest themselves in open prisons but which could be avoided by more appropriate courses of action being taken earlier in the sentence. Firstly, some lifers appear to have been given false hopes about the likely length of their detention, so that by the time they reach open prison they have become extremely cynical and suspicious of the penal system. Not surprisingly, this tends to undermine their relationship with staff and makes it more difficult to get them to prepare themselves fully for release. Secondly, it was suggested that those who have been transferred from semi-open conditions usually adapt more easily to open prison than those who have been moved directly from a Category B establishment. The latter seem less accustomed to assuming responsibility for themselves, and sometimes expect more things to be done for them.

Flexibility is required by the system, by staff and by prisoners. The individuality of lifers and their needs means that different plans and paths should be mapped out for them. Staff should adopt a common sense attitude when interpreting rules and regulations to prisoners: a strict approach may only exacerbate the situation. Lifers in turn should accept that ideal provision cannot always be made for their specific circumstances, and must make the best of what is available to them.

Career plans were relatively uncommon – only lifers who had been sentenced more recently were likely to have them. But staff at Prison 'J' usually preferred to look at each case very closely and form their own judgement of what a prisoner's needs were and what progress had been made.

One of the governors at Prison 'K' said that a particular concern of staff in open establishments was helping lifers to secure employment on release. The difficulties of achieving this were quite obvious, though fortunately most cases were successful. A uniform officer argued that better use could be made of educational and vocational training courses. In many instances, relevant courses are undertaken some years before the lifer is released, so that the benefit he derived from them is reduced. Efforts should be made to ensure that those courses which he completes in the final stages of detention are related to the work he will be doing when he comes out of prison, even if they simply update or refresh his knowledge and skills.

It was also felt that tariffs are getting longer, occasionally they are being exceeded, and sometimes they appear to be inconsistent. No statistics were provided: the remarks simply reflected a 'gut feeling'. The only justification for detaining a prisoner beyond the tariff date is that he is regarded as a threat to public safety; yet I was told this was not the explanation in every case. The clear implication is that the penal system is not as efficient as it should be, and there is the danger that continued detention beyond the optimum release date will prejudice successful re-establishment in the community. As to the inconsistencies in tariffs, the reservations expressed at Prison 'K' reflected those made at other institutions by both staff and prisoners.

Career plans were again confined to only a few lifers who had been in the prison system for comparatively short periods. Few uniform staff seemed to be aware of their existence and one governor repeated the call for more provision for lifers who did not follow the simple route from closed, to semi-open and thence to open conditions.

Finally, it is worth stressing that certain issues were raised by almost every member of staff I spoke to: if uniform staff are going to be more than mere 'turnkeys', they must be given much more training, in behavioural sciences, so that they can use the time they spend with lifers more constructively and improve the process of assessment. Furthermore, since the establishment of a good working relationship with them is very time-consuming, and each member of staff can only be assigned to a limited number of prisoners, more officers are needed as part of the management team.

Lifers generally are a very stable group; they pose no control or security problems, and are intent on serving their time as quietly as possible. Perhaps inevitably, staff may wish to use their stabilising influence on other groups of prisoners who have shown that they can be disruptive, though this may lead to a more uncomfortable and stressful existence for lifers.

10 Conclusions and Implications

This part of the research has been concerned solely with the management of life sentence prisoners based on a sample of convicted murderers. No attempt has been made here to examine the merits and demerits of alternative sentences. More specifically, attention has been focused on that part of a life-sentence which is spent in detention; no effort has been made to investigate the period when lifers have been released on life licence. The timing of this release is determined firstly by the requirements of retribution and deterrence, that is, the nature and gravity of the offence for which the sentence was imposed, referred to earlier as 'the tariff'. But this is a matter upon which the Home Secretary is advised by the judiciary, and thus lies outside the auspices of the prison system. The other factor which affects release, namely the degree of risk which the lifer is thought to pose to the public in general, is the principal and ultimate concern of prison staff.

The policy of P2 Division is that, assuming a lifer is not regarded as an unacceptable threat to society, he should be released at the tariff date. The maximisation of the chances of successful re-establishment in the community, when released on licence, implies (amongst other things) that personal problems and difficulties which might result in reoffending should be identified and resolved during the period of detention. Whilst in prison, the lifer should be accommodated in as secure conditions as the circumstances of his case require, though at the same time the environment must be such as to permit staff to assess his suitability for release.

The contrast in the policies of P2 and P4 Divisions towards male and female lifers respectively is interesting. It has long been accepted that the prison environment is unhelpful in determining whether it would be safe to release a prisoner and that the process of assessment can never be foolproof. Simple logic suggests that lifers should be given as much autonomy as possible so that staff can examine how responsibly they behave when given the opportunity to take decisions for themselves. The essence of the debate is whether this can be achieved satisfactorily within closed conditions as P4 contend, or whether physical manifestations of security need to be reduced and lifers transferred to Category C establishments, as maintained by P2. It is worth remembering that Kingston Prison at Portsmouth claims to operate a regime equivalent to that in a semi-open prison within what is actually a Category B institution. Certainly, the comments of many lifers indicated that the attitude and skills of the staff significantly affected the extent to which they felt a sense of freedom and 'normality': the boundaries of any prison were always very evident to them, whether they consisted of a brick wall or a wire fence. For the moment no firm conclusion can be reached. It is to be hoped that appropriate staff training is provided in accordance with P4's intentions and that a suitably liberal and relaxed environment will be generated within the relevant female establishments. The implementation of the policies of P2 and P4 should be carefully monitored so that their relative successes can be assessed.

This study clearly indicates that the average length of time spent in detention is steadily increasing and, theoretically at least this is likely to exacerbate management concerns. It was, of course, very encouraging to find that lifers generally do not present problems of control or security. The implication that lifers will have to be detained in a greater number of prisons, because they are being detained for longer periods, seems to have been accepted by the Prison Department. For, during the last 18 months or so (since the fieldwork for this study was completed), 11 further establishments now accommodate lifers. Assuming the desire that lifers should not spend too long in one prison is maintained, there is also an increased likelihood that, at some point in the sentence, they will be transferred to institutions with no diminution in security categorisation and this is likely to create the feeling that they are simply 'marking time'. It will be more difficult for staff to motivate them and to encourage them to adopt a constructive attitude to their imprisonment. Moreover, an increase in the amount of time spent in prison is likely to aggravate lifers' fears of the risk of institutionalisation and the greater difficulties they may face in readjusting to the outside world.

The study has also shown that lifers do not always follow a path of gradual progression through the penal system to conditions of greater freedom and ultimate release. The fact that almost 10 per cent of those in the sample were moved back to a closed prison from a Category D establishment or a hostel emphasises the need for constant reviewing of prisoners' cases and updating their career plans. In addition, less than three-fifths of the sample served time in both semi-open and open conditions. The frequency with which prisons 'by-passed' Category C was particularly significant in view of P2 Division's policy that lifers should be transferred to such institutions as soon as possible so that this suitability for release can be tested. This pattern persisted with those sentenced in 1980. Many of the 11 prisons which have recently begun to accommodate lifers are Category C establishments, and P2 Division claims that a higher proportion of lifers now spend time in such prisons. At the same time, it is only right to acknowledge that the system has demonstrated a degree of flexibility by not insisting that all prisons should spend time in all types of establishments.

This, of course, is important because the research confirms that it is extremely dangerous to attempt anything more than a superficial categorisation of lifers. Two men may have virtually identical backgrounds and personal details, and may have committed strikingly similar offences and yet their reactions to their sentence may be radically different. This underlines the calls made by the Control Review Committee (1984) and the Parliamentary All-Party Penal Affairs Group (1986) for an individual approach which recognises that not all lifers should be subjected to a programme of gradually more liberal environments. The fact that lifers usually settle into prison life quite quickly and that they pose very few control problems, allied to the earlier availability of career plans required by the Handscomb case, suggests that many of them might be moved to less secure conditions more quickly than hitherto. This study confirms Brown's (1979) remarks that lifers invariably serve several years in detention before they are classified as Category C or D prisoners. There is a strong argument that they should be transferred to semi-open and open establishments more quickly so that staff would have more opportunity to test them and consider their suitability for release.

Moreover, a system which detained prisoners in closed establishments for shorter periods would decrease the danger of institutionalisation and lessen the theoretical risk that prisoners would have difficulties in coping with increased freedom in the later stages of the sentence. Yet, the overall picture to emerge from this research is that although they usually needed a few weeks to settle into a new prison environment, lifers are unlikely to experience any major problems in adjusting to less secure conditions. There are variations from prison to prison in the way in which the rules and regulations are interpreted, and new arrivals must discover how the regime operates.

Those who have spent longer as Category A or B prisoners are likely to take a little more time to acclimatise to a more liberal atmosphere, but long-term difficulties are rare.

The reduction of so called 'perks and privileges' which follows a transfer from a Category B to a semi-open or open establishment is clearly a highly sensitive issue. Although one or two members of staff claimed that the impact of such a reduction is outweighed by the knowledge that the prisoner is moving closer to release, the bulk of opinion was that the justification for it was very tenuous and that it undermined the lifer's sense of progress and his motivation. The research therefore supports the criticisms made by the Control Review Committee (1984) where it was argued that increased discomfort in Category C prisons had a damaging effect on the psychological credibility of the system. The apparent explanation is that over the years it was felt appropriate to grant more 'perks and privileges' to those in closed institutions to minimise the chances of control problems, that is to keep prisons relatively 'contented'. Then, as they move towards the latter stages of detention, the need to adopt such tactics diminished, so that life became less comfortable in some respects. Given that one of the fundamental aims of the Revised Strategy is to foster a sense of purpose and direction, to encourage lifers to make positive use of their imprisonment, it would be extreme folly simply to ignore the overwhelming criticisms of the prisoners who resent the present system. The adverse effects which it causes, at a critical stage of the sentence, were freely acknowledged by many prison staff. P2 Division has accepted that there should be no loss of perks and privileges resulting from transfers to semi-open or open conditions, but the recent proposal to achieve this by down-grading those granted to prisoners in closed establishments is surely not the appropriate way forward. It is likely to have a very unsettling effect on Category B prisoners and the risk that they will display some form of control problems will increase.

The alternative course of action – to bring the level of perks and privileges in semi-open and open prisons into line with those in closed institutions – would obviously be better received by prisoners, and it has the support of many staff. It would not reduce the impact or deterrent effect of imprisonment, for the argument is about such matters as whether or not a prisoner should be allowed to have his own bedspread or to keep a budgerigar in his cell. But it would be one way of reducing the scepticism and cynicism which is common amongst prisoners in their attitude towards the system. Many feel that it tends all too frequently to require them to 'jump through the hoops', rather than make a sincere and sustained attempt to rehabilitate them.

Under the current policy it is virtually inevitable that lifers will spend the final months of the detention in a prison hostel on the Pre-Release Employment Scheme. It is true that many lifers in the sample had reservations about the utility of PRES, but prison staff and those in P2 Division clearly regard it as a valuable stage in the sentence. Admittedly, it may provide only a limited opportunity to save some money, and it may be comparatively more useful to those who do not enjoy any support from family and friends. But it undeniably represents the closest approximation which the penal system can provide to a 'normal life-style' and thus offers the best indication of how a prisoner is likely to respond to release. It is understood that P2 Division intends to review the PRES and to consider alternative final stages of detention.

It is the policy of the Prison Department to integrate all lifers – male and female – with other prisoners. Whilst it is accepted that the indeterminacy of the sentence is a special feature of their predicament, it is felt inappropriate physically to segregate them from fixed-term prisoners. This research has shown that a policy of integration has mixed blessings. Many lifers in the sample clearly resented it, especially in so far as it forced them to mix with short-term prisoners, and this resentment should not simply be dismissed on the ground that they perceived themselves as a unique group who deserve some sort of preferential treatment. Their fears about compulsory integration were very understandable, for if they got into trouble they had much more to lose than short-term prisoners. Moreover, the frequency with which lifers complained of the unsettling behaviour of short-termers strongly suggests that the complaints cannot be disregarded. Conversely, it is not at all surprising to find that prison staff might want to use the stabilising influence which lifers can have on disruptive prisoners. At the same time, some of those in the sample talked of the benefits of integration – associating with people who spent only short periods in prison, and whose conversations were much less 'prison-orientated', helped them to keep in touch with the outside world.

It may be argued that the pressures on lifers caused by integration are useful in that staff can then judge how they cope with difficult situations, and this provides a valuable testing process which assists in determining a prisoner's suitability for release. But there is surely a good deal of merit in the comments expressed by a number of lifers in the sample, that one of the most effective ways of dealing with such situations is simply to walk away from the source of the trouble. They felt that, for example, having to share a dormitory with other prisoners, effectively denied them this course of action. P2 Division's current policy is that all lifers should be accommodated in single cells, and this should help to alleviate unnecessary problems resulting from an anti-separation policy.

In one respect, however, a form of separation appears to be practised. Some staff fear that those whose offence is regarded as a 'one off' incident, usually resulting from domestic difficulties and who are very unlikely to reoffend or pose a threat to society, may be 'contaminated' by those who are seen as 'professional' criminals who have previous convictions and who may be expected to continue to commit crimes in the future probably for financial gain. 'Domestic prisoners' who are usually a very stable and co-operative group may be influenced by their more 'sophisticated' counterparts so that they are alienated from staff and authority, and thus adopt a much less constructive approach to their sentences. While such fears arise it seems that prisoners are transferred to other institutions to prevent 'contamination' The long-term implication of this practice is that it may create a two-tier system consisting, at one level, of a series of 'sin-bins' accommodating undesirable, professional criminals who are seen as incapable of genuine rehabilitation, and on the other level, groups of domestic offenders for whom the penal system can have a beneficial effect. Thus, notwithstanding the Prison Department's present policy, the question of integration/separation should not be regarded as having been finally settled.

The group referred to here as 'professional criminals' is not synonymous with the notion of 'difficult prisoners' as discussed in the RAG Report (1987). 'Professional criminals' denotes those prisoners who, whilst they do not present serious control problems, look upon imprisonment simply as the necessary price they have to pay for pursuing a career of crime. They have no intention of establishing any sort of relationship with members of staff or of acquiring skills that will enable them to lead a 'lawful' life when released. The possibility of the concentration of these prisoners in specific institutions once again raises some of the fears of the Radzinowicz Committee (1968) in relation to Category A prisoners which led the Committee to favour the dispersal system. Concentrating in one establishment large numbers of prisoners who believe they have been labelled as beyond help is highly undesirable. Naturally, if the population of professional criminals increases in the future, more prisons must be made available to accommodate them if they are to continue to be dispersed.

Staff clearly find career plans helpful in monitoring lifers' progress through the system, but the research has highlighted a number of points which ought to be addressed. Until recently, it was not uncommon that the plans would only become available after the prisoner was four or perhaps even five years into his sentence, and the Divisional Court in Handscomb's case was rightly critical of this. But the new arrangements projected by P2 Division as a result of Handscomb do not appear to bring about the degree of change that is widely sought. Although in cases where the first LRC date is set for four to six years after the first remand date, plans should be drafted after about 18 months have been served, this is unlikely to apply to convicted murderers who comprise roughly three-quarters of the lifer population. They will probably be at least three years into their sentence before their career plans are drafted. The early years of detention will therefore continue to be characterised by uncertainty and doubt, and there must be concern about how far the system seems to be adapting to shake off the Divisional Court's criticism that it has been irrational and unreasonable. The stress to lifers and the embarrassment to staff, which was criticised by Staples (1981) and Maguire *et al.* (1984), may thus be perpetuated to a considerable extent. Whilst tariff dates should now be known within a few months of the sentence being imposed, the obvious difficulty is in reviewing cases thoroughly but expeditiously so that career plans can be prepared more quickly.

It cannot be emphasised too strongly that career plans should not be treated as 'tablets of stone', but should be constantly reviewed and updated in the light of new developments. Notwithstanding the reservations of some prison staff, it is clearly the policy of the Prison Department that the plans should ultimately be drafted by a senior governor grade member of P2 (or P4) Division. At the same time, it is intended that the author of the plans should look very carefully at the reports that have been prepared by staff at the main centre who are encouraged to make their views known. This, though, raises the underlying issue of the utility of reports prepared by uniform staff and their day-to-day contact with lifers. The research has shown universal agreement about the need for better and more appropriate training of staff, especially uniform officers. They need to develop skills in human psychology and behavioural sciences so that they can properly understand and analyse prisoners' conduct, and express this in writing. Guidance is necessary to enable officers to state their opinions clearly and fully in their reports so that the full benefit of their experience can be reflected in the substance of the plans. Getting to know prisoners and assessing their behaviour are very time-consuming, so that each member of staff should be assigned to only a small number of lifers. The expansion of the lifer population carries obvious implications for the members of staff, who must be suitably trained to work with them.

The research has also demonstrated that there is a need to make uniform staff in particular much more aware of the existence of career plans. Clearly, those who have regular contact with lifers must know what is envisaged by those at higher levels of management and what areas of concern and treatment needs have been identified. Uniform officers have a central role to play in the monitoring of a lifer's progress through his/her sentence, and much of the reviewing and updating of career plans should be as a result of what they have discovered.

The intention of the Prison Department is that a member of staff should explain to each lifer in general terms the points made in their plan, namely, the first LRC date, areas of concern and treatment needs. This appears to be the usual practice, though some staff are uncertain about the amount of detail which should be disclosed to prisoners, and this was reflected in the responses of the lifers who were interviewed for whom career plans existed. Some seemed to have a clear understanding of their tariff and so forth, whereas others were largely ignorant of what was in their plan. Clear instructions should be issued to staff that whilst career plans are confidential in that prisoners are not allowed actually to read them, their contents should be discussed carefully so that prisoners are aware of the 'official view' of their case. Here, there was some evidence in the study that occasionally lifers confuse their release date with the first LRC date. Obviously, much care is required to ensure that lifers have an accurate appreciation of these issues.

Discussion of career plans between lifers and staff is, of course, but an illustration of the broader question of the amount of information which should be disclosed to them. In particular, they are not entitled to know the reasons why parole applications are rejected, though occasionally they are given hints by the staff. This type of official secrecy seems to heighten lifers' sense of alienation from the prison authorities, and it is likely to prejudice the chances of persuading a lifer that he and the system are working hand-in-hand towards the same objective. Staff are seen as personifications of the system, and it is difficult to see why a lifer should put any faith in what he is told by them when he cannot be trusted with the reasons behind vital decisions about his future. Surely the recommendation of the Parliamentary All-Party Penal Affairs Group (1986), that lifers be given an explanation of the Parole Board's decisions, should be implemented. It is also important that in their discussions with prisoners, staff should be absolutely honest and should not create false hopes in their desire to avoid control or security problems. Such falseness will be seen as deception by the prisoner and when it is subsequently discovered – as it inevitably will be – it will have a highly damaging effect on the prisoner/staff relationship and may well disrupt preparations for release. There is an awareness of this danger in both open and closed prisons, but the research clearly demonstrates the need for a more concerted effort to ensure that staff are not tempted to take what might appear to be the easy option.

A crucial factor in the success of the Revised Strategy is the extent to which lifers are motivated to use their sentence constructively so that they can re-establish themselves in the community when released. As Raban *et al.* (1983) claimed, and as this research has confirmed, many lifers either felt very isolated or feared that they might experience such feelings. They were acutely aware that they lived in a world that was very different from life outside prison. They often thought they had little or no control over their future progress through the system and had no reliable information about where they would be in a year or two years time. This confirms the view of the Parliamentary All-Party Penal Affairs Group (1986) that lifers need to have a sense of hope if they are to adopt the desired attitude towards their sentence. The fact that the average length of time spent in prison by lifers is increasing will only exacerbate the situation. Many of those talked to complained that although they had been interviewed on various occasions, staff had only a superficial understanding of their problems and feelings. As Raban *et al.* recognised, lifers felt they had been given insufficient opportunity to express themselves.

Although they have been convicted of very serious offences and many of them admit they have taken the life of another human being, lifers retain a keen sense of justice, of what is right and wrong. Their feelings in this respect should not be dismissed simply because of their convictions. For example, their complaints about inconsistencies in the way in which prisoners are treated whereby some are released much sooner than more deserving cases, were echoed by staff. Their annoyance and frustration at having to wait many months before receiving results of parole applications are entirely understandable, and P2 Division has made efforts to have these delays reduced. There is considerable evidence that lifers have profound doubts and reservations about the sincerity of the penal system's claims that it wants to assist them in the process of rehabilitation.

Clearly, they can begin to look to the time when they will be released, even in the early and middle years of detention. But the chances of them using their time constructively to prepare for release will be markedly increased if they are detained in an environment where staff are properly trained to help them get to grips with their personal problems and deficiencies and appropriate facilities (such as educational and vocational training courses) are available. In this latter respect, there is evidence that existing arrangements are sometimes inadequate and that more care is needed to ensure that relevant courses are available during the final months of detention. Lifers also complained about pettiness and 'bloody-mindedness' in the way in which some staff interpreted prison regulations. Again, these complaints should be taken seriously, for they were supported by some of the governor grades and senior staff who were interviewed. This problem may be tackled by careful selection of staff and by proper training, though ultimately there may be difficulties in providing adequate supervision to ensure that the rules are applied in a sensible and reasonable manner.

To a considerable degree the suggestions which are being made here can only be brought about if they are supported by people outside the penal system. Indeed, the extent to which prison staff can put into practice the spirit and intention of the Revised Strategy significantly depends on the amount of political co-operation and goodwill afforded to them. A further illustration of this is the use that is made of the power to release lifers who make exceptional progress whilst in detention before the expiry of the tariff. If this is in fact exercised so that some lifers – albeit very few – are released on licence earlier than originally anticipated, it may persuade prisoners that it is worthwhile making the effort. But if it is not it will probably be regarded by lifers as yet further evidence of the lack of sincerity of the penal system.

Furthermore, political and administrative considerations notwithstanding, there are good reasons for not necessarily treating the tariff as the dominant factor in determining the length of time for which a lifer should be kept in prison. It is widely accepted, especially amongst staff who have had experience of looking after lifers, that there is an optimum time for releasing them. In other words, a point is reached at which the likelihood of successful re-establishment in the community is at its highest. But if lifers are detained in prison beyond this point – for example because of the demands of the tariff – the prospects for a successful release will be reduced. Difficulties will arise which could have been avoided, and there obviously must be grave reservations about a system which causes this risk to be taken. There were cases in this study in which lifers were not ordered to be released until after what some prison staff felt was the optimum time to do so. Whilst it would be dangerous to rely solely on staff opinion, it must be acknowledged that their daily contact with lifers puts them in an excellent position from which to make recommendations of this nature.

Claims that a life sentence is a misnomer because the great majority of lifers are eventually released from prison, are invariably met with the response that licencees serve part of their sentence 'in the community' – they are subject to recall for the remainder of their natural lives – so that the gravity and description of the penalty is upheld. The essence of the sentence is not so much the element of immediate imprisonment as the indefinite threat of detention. Releasing a prisoner a little sooner than was originally thought appropriate to meet the requirements of retribution and deterrence would not *per se* reduce the status or deterrent effect of a life sentence. Rather, the penal system should be sufficiently flexible to recognise that in some cases it is in the public interest that a lifer should be released on licence before the tariff date. The punishment of any group of offenders is far too complicated an issue to be completely dominated by a single factor.

This research reinforces arguments put by Maguire *et al.* (1984) against attaching too much significance to the tariff and it echoes the calls made by the Parliamentary All-Party Penal Affairs Group (1986) to take steps to boost the morale amongst lifers. Unless weight is clearly seen to be given to the views expressed in their reports, staff are unlikely to fulfill the role envisaged in the Revised Strategy. There will be little incentive for them to develop a relationship with their charges, and issues which are crucial to a lifer's successful release into the community may be overlooked. In turn, lifers' sense of isolation and lack of motivation will continue.

Appendix A

LICENCE

Criminal Justice Act 1967

The Secretary of State hereby authorises the release on licence within fifteen days of the date hereof of
who shall on release and during the period of this licence comply with the following conditions or any other condition which may be substituted or added from time to time.

1. He shall place himself under the supervision of whichever probation officer is nominated for this purpose from time to time.
2. He shall on release report to the Probation officer so nominated, and shall keep in touch with that officer in accordance with that officer's instructions.
3. He shall, if his probation officer so requires, receive visits from that officer where the licence holder is living.
4. He shall reside only where approved by his probation officer.
5. He shall work only where approved by his probation officer and shall inform his probation officer at once if he loses his job.
6. He shall not travel outside Great Britain without the prior permission of his probation officer.

Unless revoked this licence remains in force indefinitely.

Home Office   Assistant Secretary
Queen Anne's Gate
                          Supervising Officer

Notes

Subject to the provisions of sections 60 to 62 of the Criminal Justice Act 1967 –3

(1) the conditions of this licence may be viewed or cancelled or further conditions may be added by the Secretary of State;
(2) the Secretary of State may revoke the licence at any time;
(3) if the licencee is convicted of any offence punishable with imprisonment his licence may be revoked by a court.

Appendix B

CRITERIA FOR SELECTION FOR PAROLE

A. Nature of the offence

The parole dossier will show the offence or offences of which the prisoner was convicted and for which he was awarded his present prison sentence. In addition, there should be a police report describing briefly the circumstances of the offence and there may be a record of remarks made by the judge when passing sentence. It is of primary importance that the committee should have a clear picture of what the prisoner did and, as far as possible, what led him to do it. In cases involving violence or drug trafficking the committee will need to know if the offence is one referred to in Section 32 and Schedule 1 of the Criminal Justice Act 1982. If it is, and if the sentence awarded by the Court for that offence exceeds five years imprisonment, account will be taken of the considerations arising from the Home Secretary's statement of 30 November 1983. In all cases of violence, irrespective of the length of the sentence, the committee will note the degree of violence used and whether it was premeditated and cold-blooded or done impulsively or under the influence of drink or drugs. If it was a gang crime, the part played by the particular person is relevant (for example, whether he himself carried or used weapons).

B. Criminal and other history

The police report will also contain a list of the prisoner's previous convictions and usually a short account of his social history and employment record. Often the dossier will contain a social enquiry report made to the court by a probation officer.

This information provides a background to the prisoner's last offence and will show whether that offence was part of a previous criminal pattern of behaviour or, if not, how the prisoner came to commit the offence. This is highly relevant to the question whether he is likely to re-offend after release and, if so, what sort of crime he is liable to commit.

Obviously many previous convictions indicate (in the absence of other factors) a high probability of re-offending. Other indicators of this are persistent offending since an early age, short intervals at liberty between convictions and a record of employment which is poor in terms of the quality of the jobs and the lengths of continuous employment. If the prisoner has committed violent or sexual offences, his medical history will be important. If he has previously been under the supervision of the probation service, his response to that may be relevant to his likely response to parole supervision.

C. Prison behaviour and response to treatment

The main bulk of the dossier will consist of reports by various prison officials including prison officers and instructors who know the prisoner well, at least one assistant governor or principal officer, medical officers and the prison probation officer (who is a probation officer seconded to the prison). There may also be documents relating to prison transfers, disciplinary offences and trade and academic courses.

These reports etc, should build up a picture of what the prisoner has done, and in what light he has shown himself, since his conviction. The particular importance of this is that it is information which could not have been before the court at the time of the sentence. It may show that the prisoner has continued to behave in the way the court would have expected from their knowledge of his history. If, however, he has shown himself in a new and favourable light, the existence of parole enables this to be taken into account in a practical way.

In general, bad conduct in prison is a factor against parole and good conduct a favourable factor. Not only is prison behaviour some indication of behaviour on parole, but the grant of parole to a badly behaved prisoner would affect the morale of both staff and prisoners; the staff because they would see it as an encouragement to bad behaviour and the prisoners because they would see it as unjust to those who behave well but do not get parole.

But there is more to it than that. Prisoners with long or fairly long sentences have been successfully paroled even though, in the earlier part of their sentences, they have behaved badly. The change from bad to good behaviour may be evidence of a genuine change in attitude which deserves parole. It may, however, be merely an insincere attempt to curry favour with the committee and the Parole Board. Consistent good behaviour also may be either a similar attempt to get parole or just another example of a recidivist prisoner's practice of getting through a prison sentence as quickly and quietly as possible – in both cases without any real intention of avoiding crime on release. Reports by prison officials will often give their expert view of the real significance of a prisoner's behaviour.

D. Medical considerations

A prisoner's offence may be associated with mental disturbance, abnormal sexual tendencies, alcoholism or drug addiction. Here the medical reports will be of crucial importance as regards the chances of the prisoner's re-offending and the possible gravity of further offences. In cases of mental disturbance a report by a psychiatrist should be available. In all types of cases mentioned in this paragraph it is necessary to consider what previous treatment has been given in prison or elsewhere, what treatment after release is possible and desirable, what has been the prisoner's attitude towards treatment available in prison and whether he is likely to persevere with necessary treatment after release – which may be made a condition of parole (but not in the hope of forcing it on an unwilling patient).

Such cases can be very difficult. It is right to take account of the possible influence of the supervising probation officer but important also not to overrate his powers of supervision. For example, he cannot ensure that an alcoholic parolee never visits a pub.

E. Home circumstances and employment prospects on release

The report in the dossier by the prison probation officer will usually contain information about a prisoner's home (or the lack of it) and sometimes about his prospects of employment. There may also be a home circumstances report by a probation officer working in the area to which the prisoner will go on release. If such a report is not available and the committee are inclined to favour parole, they should adjourn their consideration of the case for a report to be prepared. (It is not invariable practice to provide a home circumstances report, partly to avoid raising a prisoner's family's hopes in cases where the chance of parole is remote and partly to minimise abortive work by the probation service.)

The home circumstances and employment prospects can be critical for success on parole. If a prisoner has no settled home, no relatives or friends who will help him to keep clear of crime and no job waiting for him; if he will return to the company of previous criminal associates; or, in the case of a violent or sexual offender, if he will return to the environment and circumstances in which he has already offended; then his prospects of rehabilitation are poorer. Conversely, a good home, a job to go to and the absence of the circumstances and temptations which led him into crime before are factors favourable to parole.

It would not, however, be reasonable to regard such ideal home circumstances as necessary conditions of parole. A homeless prisoner may be suitable if a place in a hostel will be available to him. Often a job cannot be arranged before a prisoner is released. More important is evidence of the prisoner's readiness to co-operate with the probation service in their efforts to settle him in an honest life on release and a realistic attitude to the circumstances he will face.

There is a need for special care where a prisoner has committed a violent or sexual offence against a child in his own household and the same child or other children will be members of the household to which he will go on release. The view of the local authority social services department should be available in such cases.

F. Co-operation with parole supervision

The supervision of a parolee by a probation officer during the parole period is an essential part of the parole scheme. The prison welfare officer's report will normally assess the prospects of the prisoner's co-operating with his supervisor while on parole. It is difficult to be sure about this. A previous failure on probation may make co-operation doubtful but should not rule out parole. The prisoner may have matured or otherwise changed. Unless his present attitude to the probation service is rejecting, it is better to give him the benefit of any doubt.

The purpose of parole
A prisoner on parole continues to serve his sentence to his earliest date of release, but he does so in the community, rather than in prison. He is subject to conditions about where he may live and what he may do and is liable to be recalled to prison to serve the balance of his sentence if he breaches any of these conditions.

He is also subject to supervision from the designated probation service to any extent that the probation service thinks appropriate and can receive counselling and practical help in whatever areas of his life are causing difficulties. This advice and help, with the sanction of recall and revocation of licence, can work towards a change of attitude on the part of the parolee, but there should not be unrealistic expectations of what a period on parole can achieve.

Assessment of suitability for parole
The assessment to be made is whether in the longer term interests of the public the risk that a prisoner will commit offences at any time in the future – including the period after the date on which he would, if serving a determinate sentence, have been released – can be reduced or deferred by earlier release on licence. Whether, in other words, it is better in each individual case to release a prisoner into the community under supervision, subject to conditions, or to retain him in custody and then to release him when his sentence expires without benefit of the supervision and support which release on licence would have made available.

This approach of balancing likely risk against potential benefit should be applied to every case, irrespective of sentence length.

Sentences of more than five years

In his statement of 1975 the then Home Secretary drew a distinction between prisoners guilty of grave crimes and less serious offenders. A further distinction results from the [then] Home Secretary's statement of November 1983, in which he said that in future there would have to be the most compelling reasons before he would agree to parole being granted in the case of prisoners serving sentences of over five years for offences of violence and drug trafficking. In such cases the Home Secretary will only grant parole in circumstances which are genuinely exceptional, or if it appears that a period of a few months under supervision would be likely to reduce the long-term risk to the public.

A sentence to which the preceding paragraph refers is one of more than five years imposed by the Court following conviction for an offence of violence or drug trafficking. The actual offences of violence and drug trafficking are those specified in Schedule 1 of the Criminal Justice Act 1982 ...., and include attempting or conspiring to commit such an offence, and aiding or abetting, counselling, procuring or inciting the commission of such an offence as provided by Section 32 of that Act.

Other grave crimes

Apart from these cases, there are others where the nature of the risk to the public demands caution. In almost every case there is some risk that the parolee will commit another offence during the period when, but for the grant of parole, he would have been in prison. It must be a carefully calculated risk, particular care being taken with the cases of prisoners whose records show that, if they re-offend while on parole their offences may be grave crimes. The public has a right to expect that extending the use of parole does not mean exposing the community to that degree of danger. On the other hand it should be borne in mind that in some cases the grant of parole may diminish the risk that a man will commit further crime even after his parole has expired.

Common sense and general experience will best guide committee members in identifying cases where the danger is grave. The following are no more than fairly obvious examples:

(a) A person convicted of more than one sophisticated crime intended to produce a large reward, committed on different occasions, even if violence has not been used or contemplated.

(b) A person convicted of more than one act of violence (including sexual assault) or arson, committed on different occasions, leading to prolonged suffering, disability or stress for the victims.

(c) A person convicted of only one such act of violence (including sexual assault) or arson if owing to his mental condition there is a substantial risk of repetition.

(d) A person concerned, usually as a member of a gang, in a sophisticated crime intended to produce a large reward and accompanied by the use, or readiness to use, lethal weapons, even where the sentence is no more than five years.

Offenders not falling into any of the above categories are less likely to present a grave threat to the public. The infinite variety of cases defies simple classification and members of committees, like members of the Parole Board, must make their own judgements in unusual or borderline cases.

In those serious cases falling outside the Home Secretary's statement of 30 November 1983, the previous policy will continue to apply. The graver the criminal record (and hence the graver the risk to the public of granting Parole) the stronger need to be the reasons for granting it early in the parolable period; but, as the then Home Secretary said in his statement of 4 August 1975, it should not be ruled out altogether. Conversely, if there is just – but only just – a good enough case for granting parole to a prisoner with a grave record, only a fairly short period of parole should be granted. This seems right both as a matter of equity and because the danger to the public will be reduced if the period is short.

The Home Secretary's statement of 30 November 1983

On 30 November 1983 the Home Secretary made the following statement in the House of Commons in reply to a Question for Written Answer:

'On 4 August 1975, the Rt Hon. Member for Glasgow, Hillhead, as Home Secretary, made a statement about the ways in which he proposed to exercise the discretion given him in the Criminal Justice Act 1967 with regard to the release of prisoners on parole. That statement was made after consulting the parole Board and agreeing with them new guidelines for parole selection.

Since then the numbers of prisoners released on parole licence have steadily increased, and in 1982 of all prisoners released from sentences which qualified them for parole consideration 66.3 per cent had been granted parole. I do not propose to exercise my discretion in ways which will significantly affect this trend since it accords with my broad strategy for dealing with crime and offenders.

I must, however, take account of the general public concern about the increase in violent crime and the growing criticism of the gap between the length of sentence passed and the length of sentence actually served in certain cases. I have therefore decided to use my discretion to ensure that prisoners serving sentences of over five years for offences of violence or drug trafficking will be granted parole only when release under supervision for a few months before the end of the sentence is likely to reduce the long-term risk to the public, or in circumstances which are genuinely exceptional. The offences concerned are those where the Secretary of State may not order the early

Appendix B

release of prisoners under Section 32 of the Criminal Justice Act 1982 and are set out in Schedule 1 of that Act. In 1982 about 240 prisoners sentenced for these offences were recommended for parole before their final review: in future, there will have to be the most compelling reasons before I would agree to parole being granted in such cases.

I have consulted the Parole Board about how this objective might best be achieved in a way that ensures that the crucial role of the Board in the parole scheme is maintained. The Parole Board expressed a wish to continue to see all of the cases that are currently scrutinised by the Board following the initial review by the Local Review Committees, in order to give full consideration to the circumstances of each individual prisoner. Accordingly, I have agreed that the present practice should continue on the understanding that the reviews will take account of the policy contained in this statement. Under the statute the acceptance or rejection of a Parole Board recommendation is, of course, a matter for me.

I am asking the Parole Board to implement this new policy with immediate effect. This statement will be issued to Local Review Committees for their guidance. The Board intends to publish the text in its next Annual Report as an addition to the detailed 'Criteria for Selection for Parole', in which there will also be some minor consequential amendments.

Life Sentence Prisoners

The release of life sentence prisoners is at the discretion of the Home Secretary, subject to a favourable recommendation by the Parole Board and to consultation with the Lord Chief Justice and, if he is available, the trial judge. Taking account again of the public concern about violent crime, in future I intend to exercise my discretion so that murderers of police or prison officers, terrorist murderers, sexual or sadistic murderers of children and murderers by firearm in the course of robbery can normally expect to serve at least 20 years in custody; and there will be cases where the gravity of the offence requires a still longer period. Other murderers, outside these categories, may merit no less punishment to mark the seriousness of the offence.

At present I look to the judiciary for advice on the time to be served to satisfy the requirements of retribution and deterrence and to the Parole Board for advice on risk. I shall continue to do so.

The Joint Parole Board/Home Office Committee was established in 1973 to give initial consideration, usually after a life sentence prisoner has been detained for about three years in custody, to the date for the first formal consideration of the case by the Parole Board machinery. The Lord Chief Justice has agreed with me that this is the appropriate time to obtain an initial judicial view on the requirements of retribution and deterrence. In future, therefore, I will decide the date of the first reference of a case to a Local Review Committee following the initial consultation with the judiciary. The Joint Committee has therefore been disbanded.

The first Local Review Committee review will normally take place three years before the expiry of the period necessary to meet the requirements of retribution and deterrence. This would give sufficient time for preparation for release if the Parole Board recommended it, having considered risk. The judiciary will also be consulted when release is an actual possibility to meet fully the requirements of Section 61 of the Criminal Justice Act 1967.

These new procedures will separate consideration of the requirements of retribution and deterrence from consideration of risk to the public, which always has been, and will continue to be, the pre-eminent factor determining release. They will enable the prison and other staff responsible for considering and reporting on life sentencing cases, the Local Review Committees and the Parole Board to concentrate on risk. The judiciary will properly advise on retribution and deterrence. But the ultimate discretion whether to release will remain with me.

Life sentence prisoners who already have a provisional date of release are unaffected by these new arrangements. Those who have reached the stage of being held in an open prison are similarly unaffected, because the four prisoners whose release in the relatively near future would not have accorded with my view of the gravity of their offences have already been returned to closed prisons. Life sentence prisoners whose cases the Joint Committee had asked to consider again will, at the time fixed for that consideration, have a date fixed for their first Local Review Committee review after consultation with the judiciary as I have outlined above. Those who have a date for review by the Local Review Committee already fixed will be reviewed as arranged, but the judiciary will be consulted on retribution and deterrence before the case is referred to the Parole Board.

Appendix B

When a date for a first, or subsequent, formal review is set for several years ahead, the Home Office will review the case on the basis of reports of the kind now prepared for formal reviews, at regular, and in any event not longer than three year, intervals. Moreover, Governors will be told to report at once any exceptional development requiring action. These producers will ensure that I can consider any special circumstances or exceptional progress which might justify changing the review date. But except where a prisoner has committed an offence for which he has received a further custodial sentence, the first formal review date will not be put back. In any event, Ministers will review every case when a life sentence prisoner has been detained for ten years'.

Bibliography

D. J. Birch, 'The Foresight Saga: The Biggest Mistake of All?' [1988] *Criminal Law Review*, 4–18.

Central Statistical Office, *Annual Abstract of Statistics*, No. 122 (London: HMSO, 1986).

S. Cohen and L. Taylor, *Psychological Survival: The Experience of Long Term Imprisonment* (Harmondsworth: Penguin, 1981).

J. B. Coker and J. P. Martin, *Licensed To Live* (Oxford: Basil Blackwell, 1985).

Criminal Law Revision Committee, *Working Paper on Offences Against The Person* (London: HMSO, 1976).

Criminal Law Revision Committee, *Fourteenth Report on Offences Against The Person*, Cmnd 7844 (London: HMSO, 1980).

M. Fitzgerald and J. Sim, *British Prisons* (Oxford: Basil Blackwell, 1982).

E. Gibson and S. Klein, *Murder* (London: HMSO, 1961).

E. Gibson and S. Klein, *Murder 1957 to 1968*, Home Office Research Study No. 3 (London: HMSO, 1971).

E. Gibson, *Homicide in England and Wales. 1967–1971*, Home Office Research Study No. 31 (London: HMSO, 1975).

Robert Goff, 'The Mental Element in the Crime of Murder', Vol. 104, *Law Quarterly Review*, 30–59, 1988.

H. L. A. Hart and A. M. Honore, *Causation in the Law* (Oxford: Oxford University Press, 1959).

Christopher Hollis, *The Homicide Act* (London: Victor Gollancz, 1964).

Home Office, *Criminal Statistics. England and Wales 1986*, Cmnd 233 (London: HMSO).

Home Office, *Managing the Long Term Prison System*, The Report of the Control Review Committee (London: HMSO, 1984).

Home Office, *Report of the Inquiry into Prison Escapes and Security*, Cmnd 3175 (London: HMSO, 1966).

Home Office, *Review of Parole in England and Wales* (London: HMSO, 1981).

Home Office, *Special Units For Long-Term Prisoners: Regimes, Management and Research*, A Report by the Research and Advisory Group on the Long-Term Prison System (London: HMSO, 1987).

House of Commons Debates. Vol. 49, Written Answers to Questions, 30 November 1983. Col. 514.

House of Commons Debates. Vol. 120, Written Answers to Questions, 23 July 1987. Cols. 346–8.

John McVicar, *McVicar By Himself* (London: Hutchinson, 1979).

M. Maguire, F. Pinter and C. Collis, 'Dangerousness and the Tariff' *British Journal of Criminology*, Vol. 24(3) 1984, 250–68.

M. Maguire, 'Lifers, Tariff and Dangerousness', *Prison Service Journal*, April 1987, 13–18.

S. Mitchell (ed), *Archbold. Criminal Pleading Evidence and Practice* (40th edn) (London: Sweet & Maxwell, 1979).

T. Morris and L. Blom-Cooper, *A Calendar of Murder* (London: Michael Joseph, 1964).

T. Morris and L. Blom-Cooper, *Murder in England and Wales Since 1957* (London: Observer, 1979).

V. O'Leary and D. Glaser, 'The Assessment of Risk in Parole Decision Making', in D. J. West (ed.), *The Future of Parole: Commentaries on Systems in Britain and USA* (London: Duckworth, 1972).

J. H. Orr, 'Medical Aspects of the Treatment and Management of Prisoners Serving Sentences of Life Imprisonment', *Prison Medical Journal*, Spring 1981, 2–6.

Parliamentary All-Party Penal Affairs Group, *Life Sentence Prisoners* (Chichester: Barry Rose, 1986).

Prison Department, Circular Instruction No. 2/1986, *Life Sentence Prisoners*.

Prison Department, Circular Instruction. No. 2/1989, *Life Sentence Prisoners*.

Tony Raban, Barrie Crook, Jane Wright and Jo Thompson, *Work With Life Sentence Prisoners at Nottingham Prison* (October 1983).

Report of the Advisory Council on the Penal System, *The Regime for Long-Term Prisoners in Conditions of Maximum Security* (London: HMSO, 1968).

Report of the parole Board 1986. (London: HMSO, 1987).

Report of the Royal Commission on Capital Punishment, 1949–53, Cmnd 8932 (London: HMSO, 1953).

Report of the Work of the Prison Department, 1985/86. Cm. 11. (London: HMSO).

R. Sapsford, 'Life Sentence Prisoners: Psychological Changes During Sentence', *British Journal of Criminology*, Vol. 18, 1978, 128–45.

R. Sapsford, *Life Sentence Prisoners* (Milton Keynes: Open University Press, 1983).

D. Smith (ed.), *Life Sentence Prisoners*, Home Office Research Study No. 51, 1979 (London: HMSO).

John Staples, 'The Management of Life Sentence Prisoners', *Prison Service Journal*, April 1987, 4–7.

Gordon B. Trasler, *The Use of Documentation in Making the Parole Decision* (1978), unpublished lecture, Department of Psychology, University of Southampton.

Stanley Meng Heong Yeo, 'Sentencing Murderers: A New South Wales Innovation', *Criminal Law Review*, 1987, 23–7.

Index

Lightning Source UK Ltd.
Milton Keynes UK
UKOW03f0456170517

301289UK00001B/21/P